Understanding Political Persuasion

Linguistic and Rhetorical Analysis

Douglas Mark Ponton
University of Catania, Italy

Series in Language and Linguistics

VERNON PRESS

www.vernonpress.com

In the Americas:
Vernon Press
1000 N West Street,
Suite 1200, Wilmington,
Delaware 19801
United States

In the rest of the world:
Vernon Press
C/Sancti Espiritu 17,
Malaga, 29006
Spain

Series in Language and Linguistics

Library of Congress Control Number: 2019950952

ISBN: 978-1-62273-932-5

Also available:

978-1-62273-856-4 [Hardback]; 978-1-62273-877-9 [PDF, E-Book]

Cover design by Vernon Press using elements designed by Freepik.

Table of contents

List of Tables

-

List of Figures

Foreword

There are many books on political discourse analysis already, so why add one more to the ever-growing pile of books on the topic? Some of the works frequently cited in this book, by authorities such as Halliday, Fairclough, Wodak, Chilton, Van Dijk, Martin, Van Leeuwen and so on, would appear to cover the whole territory, leaving nothing more to say on the subject. From a certain point of view, this is true, and yet a niche remains, however small. My book has two claims to occupy the niche. Firstly, as worthy as the authors just mentioned are, they each pursue their own research agendas and personal approaches. All plough their furrows, presenting ever deeper, more complex systems that place significant demands on the reader and would-be analyst; think, for instance, of the difference in complexity between the early and some of the later works of Norman Fairclough. It is a question of how far a reader and would-be analyst of political discourse can glean practical tools, from such works, that will enable them to begin actually working with texts.

Secondly, I hope there is merit in a work which synthesises some of the insights of these scholars, and shows how their approaches can be practically applied by the would-be political discourse analyst. The beginning analyst can, at times, experience a sense of bewilderment in front of the mass of theoretical and technical writing in linguistics, in the search for some practical, usable tools. In this book, I try to cover a variety of such tools, demonstrating their usefulness in application to the analysis of a number of political speeches, from different historical periods and diverse social contexts.

The question that has occupied much of my own research has been that of persuasion in political rhetoric, and I have tried, in the following pages, to set out a model of the processes involved that begins with a traditional, Aristotelian perspective, summed up in the familiar concepts of ethos, pathos and logos. Integrated with this simple picture is the area of evaluative language, which I explore using Martin and White's Appraisal Framework (Martin & White, 2005), and notions of argumentation deriving from Toulmin's work (Toulmin, 1958). Later chapters of the book explore the contribution to persuasion of multimodal features such as film, voice quality, colour and music, as well as cognitive devices such as metaphor and analogy. A final answer to the question of how politicians persuade us to do what they want us to (beginning with the obvious step of voting for them!) remains elusive, but I hope that the work will stimulate interest in the analysis of political rhetoric and empower the would-be analyst, as well as delineating some possible pathways towards an integrated model of political discourse analysis.

The book covers a wide range of possible techniques and approaches to political discourse analysis, which I shall now summarise. The first chapter looks at corpus linguistics in a study of deontic modality, comparing persuasive political rhetoric from different historical periods, the eighteenth century and the modern. The second explores the contribution to persuasive rhetoric of rhetorical figures such as alliteration, litotes and metaphor, in Edmund Burke's speech on the necessity for conciliation with the American colonies. Such features, for centuries, constituted the essence of what rhetoric was felt to be, and yet they are largely ignored in many contemporary accounts of political discourse. Chapter three looks at the interplay of parliamentary voices in evidence during Disraeli's speech on the ratification of the Suez canal purchase, showing how his argumentative strategy engages with opposing voices on the question. The fourth chapter features Winston Churchill and shows how political argumentation, in the modern period, can interest not simply listeners in the immediate context but can reach out through mass media to influence the hearts and minds of a much wider audience. Chapter five deals with two acknowledged masters of modern political rhetoric, Martin Luther King and Malcolm X, rival leaders of the black community during the Civil Rights Movement. It shows how their argumentative patterns create in- and out-groups among their listeners, construing a notion of implicit enemy that can be identified not with their white oppressors, but rather with the other leader and his supporters. Chapter six sees Sinn Fein leader Gerry Adams addressing the IRA, attempting to persuade them to abandon violent social resistance in favour of a political path. In chapter seven, the focus is on multimodal resources as two Republican videos are analysed, one by Ronald Reagan and one by G. W. Bush. Finally, verbal and visual metaphor feature in the analysis of UKIP's Nigel Farage and his representations of Europe.

In terms of linguistic features used in the analysis, then, the various studies include: Corpus linguistics (Deontic Modality, chapter one), Rhetorical features (Burke), Engagement (Disraeli), Representation of Social Actors (Churchill), Appraisal Framework and Argumentation (Malcolm X and Martin Luther King), Information Structure (Adams), Multimodality (Reagan and Bush) and Visual and Verbal Metaphor (Farage). The attempt is made to integrate these various features with a model of argumentation in political discourse that is presented in progressive stages throughout the work, gradually becoming more complex towards the later chapters. It is not necessary (nor, perhaps, would it be possible) for the analyst to use all of these approaches at the same time; rather, s/he will most probably be drawn to select an appropriate analytical approach according to specific features of the text or texts in question. I shall have more to say about this at the appropriate time.

My hope, then, is that would-be students of political rhetoric, of whatever level and from a variety of fields within the Humanities, will be able to pick up this book and find tools and techniques that will assist them in actual work on texts. Naturally, it is also that they will be inspired to follow up the suggestions for further reading which they will find in the bibliography.

Chapter 1

Introduction

The question of how political speakers attempt to persuade their listeners has informed much of modern political discourse analysis.[1] However, it is worth beginning this book, which attempts to follow in the footsteps of some of these works, with older accounts of these processes which have, effectively, stood the test of time. In particular, the notions of Aristotle and the context of the ancient Greek polis are worth evoking, however briefly, as a reminder of the essential power of the spoken word.

As Nöth puts it: "To persuade and to convince the public were the pragmatic goals which orators wanted to achieve by means of rhetorical techniques" (Nöth, 1995, p. 339). The many diverse schools of rhetoric and sophistry which flourished in the ancient world are witness to the important place of oratory in public life. It was recognised that the ability to use words to sway an assembly was the politician's chief weapon, and the characteristic form of political debate, in much Greco-Roman oratory, was the *genus deliberativum*, which required a pro/con debate, on the basis of which decisions were taken. It was imperative, then, for any politician to master what Aristotle called the forms of persuasion, and Thucydides makes it plain that Pericles, alongside his military abilities, was also a master of oratory.

With modern parliamentary democracy, oratory has gradually become less important, since political decision-making tends to occur on party lines, and even brilliant rhetorical displays are unlikely to alter the MPs' voting choices. In some of the older parliamentary contexts studied in this book, however, for example in Burke's time, the coercive mechanism of the party whip was in an embryonic state, and his speech takes place in a context that is closer to Athenian realities than to those of our own time. Burke would certainly have hoped to convert some listeners to his cause.

It is also worth pointing out that, though one feature of pro-con debate is undoubtedly the discussion of various possible responses to a real-world situation, the pragmatic purpose of much persuasive rhetoric is not to obtain

---

[1] See the works of some of the authors that will be referred to frequently in this book, for example, such as Fairclough (2000; 2003), Chilton and Schäffner (1997; 2002), Chilton (2004), (Halmari & Virtanen, 2005), Charteris-Black (2005).

a specific result but to influence 'the hearts and minds' of hearers, creating a diffuse consensus for the speaker's preferred ideology or belief system. Bermejo-Luque provides the following useful discussion of these issues:

> One of the most salient features of argumentation, in contrast with other kinds of communication, is that when we argue we not only try to make others aware of what our beliefs are, but we also try to induce these beliefs in others. The way we try to induce beliefs by arguing is by showing them to be correct, that is, by appealing to reasons that would allegedly justify them. Thus we can say that argumentation aims at persuasion by means of justification, and as a result an adequate comprehension of the activity of arguing requires not only an explanation of the way argumentative discourses are able to justify beliefs and claims, but also of their power to produce beliefs in others by offering justifications for them. (Bermejo-Luque, 2011, p. 73)

This perspective will be worth remembering when we ponder the status of political rhetoric in the modern world. Although there may be less emphasis on using rhetoric to gain support for the specific measure under discussion, it clearly has a role to play in spreading beliefs that, though they may not affect the immediate vote, may make their contribution to an ongoing, mediated, nationwide or even global debate at semi-conscious levels of political ideology. These processes may, clearly, produce concrete results for the political party at the next electoral consultation.

Some considerations of the difference between spoken and written discourse are necessary preliminaries: it should be remembered that political speeches, of the kind under consideration in this book, share features of both oral and written communication. They are not spontaneous utterances, but are mostly written to be spoken, and this will involve a certain inevitable analytical difficulty. Halliday and Matthiessen's account of information structure (2004, pp. 87-94), for example, presents the theory with reference to *spoken* language only. What is to be considered as newsworthy (Fries 1994, p. 230) is marked by prominence, with the relevant syllable carrying 'information focus' (Halliday & Matthiessen 2004, p. 89). There would be no problem, were it not for the obvious fact that recordings are not available of speeches before a certain historical date, and even in the modern era, it may be impossible to obtain a recording of a particular speech. In the small collection of speeches studied in this book, recordings are, to my knowledge, only available for those by Martin Luther King and Malcolm X, while doubts remain as to the authenticity of recordings of Churchill's wartime addresses.[2]

The speeches have therefore been studied as *written* artefacts, a necessary compromise, and one that has at least the merit of underscoring effects that persist beyond the immediate historical context, but that will inevitably fail to capture the subtle peaks and troughs of the spoken word, which signal such features in spoken discourse.

The Aristotelian perspective: ethos, pathos and logos

Aristotle describes three main dimensions to persuasion; *ethos*, or the respect engendered by the speaker's character; *pathos*, the appeal to the emotions, and *logos*, the rational argument advanced (Charteris-Black 2005, p. 9). The importance of these three factors is, arguably, as great today as in ancient Greece. On ethos, Aristotle writes:

> There are three things which inspire confidence in the orator's own character - the three, namely, that induce us to believe a thing apart from any proof of it: good sense, good moral character, and goodwill [..] anyone who is thought to have all three of these good qualities will inspire trust in his audience (Aristotle, 1954, p. 91)

This explains the necessity for politicians to preserve an untarnished image, though such factors are highly culture-specific. Bill Clinton's extra-marital adventures may not have provoked many scandals in countries less affected by Puritanism, for example; while, in a British context, the financial misdemeanours of leading Italian figures would be sufficient to end a political career. The persuasive force of any particular message will clearly be augmented if the speaker has a positive ethos, as was the case for Gerry Adams among a Republican audience, or Malcolm X with the black community in Harlem.

Aristotle (1954, p. 25) wrote that "persuasion may come through the hearers, when the speech stirs their emotions", and this factor has consistently played an important part in the history of rhetoric through the ages. Humour, for example, was used by Ronald Reagan in the 1984 presidential head-to-head with Walter Mondale. Asked if he was not getting too old to deal with the pressures of the Cold War, he responded:

---

[2] It has been suggested that some at least were read by an actor imitating Churchill.

I want you to know that I will not make age an issue of this campaign. I am not going to exploit for political purposes my opponent's youth and inexperience[3]

Politicians also frequently try to touch a pathetic chord, moving their audience to experience sorrow or grief. In the wake of the September 11 terrorist attacks, for example, G.W. Bush said:

For those who lost loved ones it has been a year of sorrow, of empty places, of newborn children who will never know their fathers here on earth[4]

Notice here, in passing, the use of the rhetorical figure known as the three-part list (in classical rhetorical studies, *tricolon* or *hendiatris*). This device is common in persuasive discourse and can be used to create a sense of climax or a satisfying sense of completion; here, it does both.

As important as the first two factors were felt to be, Aristotle regarded *logos*, or reason, as the orator's chief persuasive resource. The argumentative force of a speech mostly consists of the reasons that support the orator's favoured solutions, making it persuasive to listeners. For this reason, in the centuries that followed, schools of rhetoric flourished, developing and refining Aristotle's own analysis of the micro-processes involved. The influence of Greek and later Roman, rhetoric on the discursive practices of politicians is still amply felt today.

Aristotle's categories, then, offer approaches to text analysis that have not been supplanted altogether by more modern methodologies, and the notions of ethos, pathos and logos are central to the concept of persuasive political discourse advanced throughout this book.

Some more basic concepts: evaluation, engagement and alignment

This section introduces some key terms that the reader will be reminded of at various points in this book; *evaluation, engagement* and *alignment*. Each represents a component of most, if not all, persuasive political discourse. Evaluation refers to the positive or negative statements advanced by speakers, thereby revealing a system of 'values', which may be aesthetic or axiological, according to the topic: politicians praise some policies, people or aspects of a

---

[3] "Top 10 Memorable Debate Moments". See web references.
[4] Bush: Speech to the United Nations: see Modern Corpus, Appendix, Chapter 1.

situation whilst they denigrate others. Engagement describes the way the speaker represents other views than his own, while Alignment refers to the attempt to persuade the audience to adopt the speaker's own views.

Evaluative language has a central role to play in much more persuasive political rhetoric (see Fairclough 2003: 173). As an example of this, consider the following extract from a speech by Tony Blair, in which the proposal is reinforced by the negative connotations of the word 'fanatics':

The <u>fanatics</u> have to be confronted and defeated

In terms of recent western culture, a 'fanatic' may be someone driven by an ideology to commit anti-social atrocities. Representing a person or group of people with this term is a way of stimulating a range of responses that are in line with the speaker's overall purposes - here, Blair wished to stimulate support for the belligerent policies he advocated. In this book, I use the Appraisal Framework of Martin and White (2005) to classify such references, and in the case of 'fanatics', their classification would be -J: propriety, standing for 'negative Judgement: propriety'.

Hunston and Thompson (2003, p. 142) offer the following description of the Appraisal Framework:

The enormously varied lexical choices are seen as construing a small range of general categories of reaction. The main category or sub-system is AFFECT, which deals with the expression of emotion (happiness, fear, etc.) Related to this are two more specialised sub-systems: JUDGEMENT, dealing with moral assessments of behaviour (honesty, kindness, etc.), and APPRECIATION, dealing with aesthetic assessments (subtlety, beauty, etc.)

Emotion/Affect is viewed as the basis of all our evaluations, and Martin and White (2005, pp. 46-49) outline six variables according to which AF classifies resources from the Affect system:

- Are the feelings popularly construed by the culture as positive or negative?

- Are the feelings a surge of emotion or a kind of predisposition or ongoing mental state?

- Are the feelings directed at some specific external agency, or a general ongoing mood?

- How are the feelings graded: low, median, high?;

- Do the feelings involve intention (rather than reaction) with respect to a stimulus that is irrealis rather than realis?

- Our typology of affect groups emotions into three major sets having to do with un/happiness, in/security and dis/satisfaction.

To take an example from another speech by Tony Blair, commenting on the death of Dr. David Kelly, who committed suicide in 2003, in the aftermath of the Hutton enquiry:

All of us felt, and feel still, <u>desperately sorry</u> for Mrs Kelly and her family[5]

The emotional attitude construed here, sympathy with the suffering, is likely to be positively construed by the culture (variable 1), and the feelings are represented as widely felt, and constant. The feelings are more a 'surge of emotion' than a 'predisposition' (variable 2), and are directed at the 'external agency' represented by the Kelly family (variable 3). The feelings are high intensity (variable 4), because of the use of the high-intensity adverb 'desperately'; they are *realis* (variable 5), and would be coded as: - Affect: unhappiness, misery (variable 6). Blair represents himself, and the rather vague group encapsulated in the phrase 'all of us' (all Labour politicians? The government? The cabinet? The British people?), as good fellows, since they are capable of sympathising with a suffering family. Naturally, from a critical perspective, it is also possible to suggest that the political/pragmatic force of such an utterance relates to exculpation, to removing the suspicion of responsibility for Dr Kelly's fate from Blair himself.

'Tokens' of Affect

References to a speaker's emotional response can be via explicit emotive lexis:

I am <u>proud</u> of all who have fought on my orders[6] (+ Aff: satisfaction)

However, we can also find Affect 'invoked', where the emotion is implicit in a stretch of text with no apparent reference to the emotional sphere (Martin and White 2005: 62). In Churchill's address to the London crowd on VE day, for example, he says:

---

[5] Blair 29/03/2004, (Segell, 2005, p. 244).
[6] "Bush's Speech at the Pentagon". See web references.

So we came back after long months from the jaws of death, out of the
mouth of hell, while all the world wondered[7]

There is no explicit reference to the emotions here, yet the probable
rhetorical aim is to move the hearers to a profound sense of *relief,* mingled
with *pride* at having achieved so much. Such references are termed 'tokens',
and would be signalled, in this case, as t (token) + Aff: security/satisfaction.

The interpretation of tokens is more useful if they are not seen as isolated
fragments of meaning but rather viewed as threads in a verbal/textual tapestry;
as part of an overall rhetorical design that may include allusions, jokes, body
language, gesture, and so on. If we adopt this wider perspective, which would be
further enhanced by considerations of speaker delivery–intonation, pitch, tonic
prominence, and so on–it will be possible to appreciate the kind of prosodic
effects described by Martin and White (2005, pp. 17-25), who focus on lexico-
semantic patterns that recur throughout a text, with each realization deriving
significance from the previous instantiation, and colouring the one that follows.

In the following extract from Churchill's speech, for instance, the speaker's
use of Affect is marked by underscoring for explicit Affect, and italicization
for tokens:

Table 1.1. Evaluation in Churchill's address to VE crowds.

1. *My dear friends, this is your hour.*	t, happiness: cheer
2. This is not victory of a party or of any class.	
3. *It's a victory of the great British nation as a whole.*	t, satisfaction: pride
4. *We were the first, in this ancient island, to draw the sword against tyranny.*	t, satisfaction: pride
5. After a while we were left *all alone against the most tremendous military power that has been seen.*	t, disinclination: fear
6. We were all alone for a whole year.	
7. *There we stood, alone.*	t, satisfaction: pride
8. Did anyone want <u>to give in?</u> [The crowd shouted 'No.']	disinclination: fear
9. Were we <u>down-hearted</u>? ['No!']	unhappiness: misery
10. *The lights went out and the bombs came down.*	t, disinclination: fear
11. *But every man, woman and child in the country had no thought of quitting the struggle.*	t, satisfaction: pride
12. *London can take it.*	t, satisfaction: pride

[7] Churchill 08/051945. In (James, 1980, p. 862).

13. *So we came back after long months from the jaws of death, out of the mouth of hell, while all the world wondered.*	t, satisfaction: pride
14. When shall the reputation and faith of this generation of English men and women fail?	
15. *I say that in the long years to come not only will the people of this island but of the world, wherever the bird of freedom chirps in human hearts, look back to what we've done and they will say 'do not despair, do not yield to violence and tyranny, march straightforward and die if need be-unconquered.'*	t, satisfaction: pride

Miller (2004, p. 286) discusses the importance of the 'semantic location' of an instance of evaluative language, referring to its place in an overall pattern of speaker evaluation. Here we notice how allusions to the joyous nature of the occasion, the framing of events in terms of national unity, and the reference to just wars fought against tyranny (lines 1 - 4), lead into the portrayal of the nation as a David versus Goliath, with repetitious representation of the nation's solitude in this predicament (5,6,7). Up to this point emotive reference has been through tokens, which will be readily grasped by the crowd, whose guiding sentiment on the specific occasion was almost certainly the desire to celebrate. The notion of making a solitary stand against this powerful foe is a further inducement to patriotic pride in the crowd (5-7). At this point, the speaker accesses emotions more directly via the rhetorical questions he uses (8-9). Their response is in explicitly emotive terms ('we did not want to give in, we were not down-hearted'). Emotion has been let out via these explicit references; it now continues to bubble beneath the surface of the speech, colouring the references that follow (see Martin 2003, p. 173).

Judgement

The semantic field covered by Judgement propositions deals with speakers' assessment of human behaviour, which can be positive or negative. Martin suggests the following sub-categories:

Table 1.2. A framework for analysing Judgement in English (based on Martin & White, 2005, p. 53).

SOCIAL ESTEEM 'venial'	POSITIVE (admire)	NEGATIVE (criticise)
Normality (fate) 'is he or she special?'	Lucky, fortunate, charmed	Unfortunate, pitiful, tragic
Capacity 'is he or she capable?'	Powerful, vigorous, robust	Mild, weak, wimpy

Tenacity (resolve) 'is he or she reliable, dependable?'	Plucky, brave, heroic	Rash, cowardly, despondent
SOCIAL SANCTION 'mortal'		
Veracity (truth) 'is he or she honest?'	Truthful, honest, credible	Dishonest, deceitful
Propriety (ethics) 'is he or she beyond reproach?'	Good, moral, ethical	Bad, immoral, evil

A basic distinction is between evaluations relating to 'social esteem' and 'social sanction', which grade judgements according to the perceived gravity of the behaviour in question; the former relate to such matters as ability as, for example, when we speak of an 'able translator'; the latter to the weightier field of moral considerations. There is a potential for references of this latter type to demarcate boundaries between the in-group to which the speaker belongs, and in which he includes members of the audience who agree with him; and the out-group, who self-categorise as such precisely because they will never be won over.

During the Iraq war in 2003, there was ample evidence of such processes in the discourse of western leaders such as G.W. Bush and, in the following case, Tony Blair:

Table 1.3. Blair, evaluation.

| But this new world faces a new threat: of disorder and chaos born either of <u>brutal</u> (i) states like Iraq, armed with *weapons of mass destruction (ii)*; or of extreme terrorist *(iii)* groups. Both hate our way of life, our *freedom, our democracy* (iv)[8] | i. - J: propriety;
ii. t - J: propriety;
iii.- J: propriety;
iv. t + J: propriety |

The in-group/out-group delineation is carried on here through the associations of the evaluative patterns, and the use of the inclusive pronoun 'our'. Listeners are tacitly invited to identify with the in-group–freedom-loving western democracies–whose 'new world' is under threat from rogue states and terrorists. As long ago as 1986, Ronald Reagan referred to the notion that 'one man's terrorist is another man's freedom fighter',[9] and this fragment

---

[8] "Focus on Iraq". See web references.
[9] "Ronald Reagan: Radio Address to the Nation on Terrorism". See web references.

illustrates how evaluation can work, along the boundaries of group identification, to stimulate processes of belonging and community.

Appreciation

Evaluations of objects or naturally occurring phenomena are dealt with under the system of Appreciation. Martin and White (2005, p. 56) outline five basic categories, again with positive and negative polarities, organised as follows:

> Reaction: impact ('did it grab me?')
> Reaction: quality ('did I like it?')
> Composition: balance ('did it hang together?')
> Composition: complexity ('was it hard to follow?')
> Valuation: ('was it worthwhile?')

In the following example, from Churchill, we can appreciate how evaluations of things can slip over into judgements on the human social actors involved in the representation:

> that <u>hideous</u> apparatus of aggression which gashed Holland into ruin and slavery in a few days (Churchill 19/05/1940)

This is apparently an instance of Appreciation, as Churchill evaluates Germany's 'apparatus of aggression', which includes tanks, bombs, warplanes, and so on. The coding, therefore, could be: - Appreciation: quality. However, what is 'hideous' about the German army, from the point of view of speaker and listener, depends on the 'aggression' with which it is used against Britain, which shifts interpretation towards a coding of t,- Judgement: propriety, against the Nazis.

Graduation

Lexis can be graded according to its perceived level of intensity, via a process of selection from a range of options; low, median, or high, as when a picture can be described as 'fair', 'nice', 'okay' (low); 'good', 'pleasant', 'nice' (median); 'superb', 'brilliant', 'marvellous' (high). Martin and Rose (2003, p. 38) say that there seem to be more resources in English for 'turning up' the 'volume' than for turning it down.

Engagement

The Appraisal Framework's work on engagement is inspired by Bakhtin/Vološinov's work in this field (White, 2003, p. 259). Texts, from his perspective, are not isolated, but are instead engaged in processes of interaction with other texts, in what he called 'ideological colloquy of a large scale' (Bakhtin, 1994, p. 139). Texts respond to other texts; they anticipate possible objections, answer points made by other speakers, dispute conclusions or propositions, and so on.

Engagement theory systematises the ways in which interaction between texts is constructed linguistically, making a broad distinction between two types of resource, dialogical expansion and contraction. A *contractive* pattern, 'closing down' dialogical space, is seen in the following:

Removing Saddam will be a blessing to the Iraqi people[10]

White (2003, p. 263), following Bakhtin, terms such propositions, 'monoglossic or undialogized', and uses the term 'bare assertion'. The speaker uses this pattern because he considers the proposition to be factual for the audience. Such statements are generally used, as White (2003, p. 263) puts it, where there is an assumption of 'ontological, epistemic and axiological commonality between textual voice and audience'. Bare assertions can also be seen as attempts to establish the truth status for propositions which are, in reality, of only partial validity (Vasta, 2005, p. 154). Since they make no attempt to engage with alternative positions, they are maximally dialogically contractive.

On the other hand, speakers can construct discourses that represent other positions, that seem open to alternative views than the speaker's own; such resources are known as dialogically *expansive*. Blair frequently used these resources to construct a persona that seemed open to dialogue:

1. I totally understand the concerns of people about precipitate military action[11]

2. I know this course of action has produced deep divisions of opinion in our country[12]

3. There will be some who dismiss all this. Intelligence is not always right[13]

---

[10] "Focus on Iraq". See web references.
[11] "Full Text of Tony Blair's TUC Address". See web references.
[12] "Focus on Iraq". See web references.
[13] "Full Text of Tony Blair's Statement to Parliament on Iraq. *The Guardian*. Guardian News and Media, 24 Sept. 2002". See web references.

Such resources will frequently be found in contexts where the speaker is accessing the views of those who disagree with them, whom they hope to persuade. In 1), for example, Blair aims to persuade such people that their 'concerns' are unfounded; in 2) he hopes to bring round those of different opinion on this course of action; in 3) his own view is clearly that, in this case, intelligence *is* right, and so on.

The interested reader is referred to White (White, 2003), and Martin and White (Martin & White, 2005) for a detailed treatment of these resources; in the current work more details of individual resources will be provided as this becomes necessary.

Alignment: an example

The term alignment refers to the way a speaker attempts to bring his audience 'into line' with his own views. I have selected a portion of another speech by Blair on the Iraqi crisis,[14] in which he compared the current international situation with that of the 1930s, and claimed that Saddam is as much a threat to world peace today as Hitler was then:

Table 1.4. Blair speech on Iraq.

TEXT	ATTITUDE	ENGAGEMENT
1. *The real problem is that, underneath, people dispute that <u>Iraq is a threat</u> (i); dispute the link between terrorism and WMD; dispute the whole basis of our assertion that the two together constitute <u>a fundamental assault on our way of life</u>. (ii)*	t - J capacity i) - AFF: disinclination, fear ii) - J propriety	COUNTER
2. There are <u>glib and sometimes foolish</u> comparisons with the 1930s.	- J capacity	Monogloss
3. No-one here is an <u>appeaser</u>.	- J propriety	DENY
4. But the only relevant point of analogy is that with history, we know what happened.		Monogloss
5. We can look back and say: there's the time; that was the moment; for example, when Czechoslovakia was swallowed up by the Nazis - *that's when we should have acted.*	t - J propriety (irrealis)	Monogloss

---

[14] "Full Text: Tony Blair's Speech. The Guardian. Guardian News and Media, 18 Mar. 2003". See web references.

6. But it <u>wasn't clear</u> at the time.	- APP complexity	DENY
7. In fact, at the time, *many people thought such a fear fanciful.*	t - J capacity	Monogloss
8. Worse, <u>put forward in bad faith</u> by warmongers.	- J propriety (irrealis)	Monogloss
9. Listen to this editorial - from a paper <u>I'm pleased</u>(i) to say *with a different position today*(ii)- but written in late 1938 after Munich when by now, *you would have thought the world was tumultuous in its desire to act. (iii)*	i) + AFF: happiness, cheer ii) t + J capacity iii) t - J propriety (irrealis)	ENDORSE
10. "Be <u>glad</u> in your hearts.	+ AFF: happiness, cheer	
11. Give thanks to your God.		
12. People of Britain, <u>your children are safe.</u>	+ AFF: security	
13. *Your husbands and your sons will not march to war.*	t + AFF: happiness, cheer	COUNTER
14. *Peace is a victory for all mankind.*	t + AFF: happiness, cheer	
15. And now let us go back to our own affairs.		
16. We have had enough of *those menaces, conjured up from the continent to confuse us."*	t - AFF: disinclination, fear	

The basic position around which consensus is being sought is that *the world should act now to deal with the threat of Saddam.* The quotation from the newspaper, in line 9, has the aim of countering the view that we should not act against Saddam. It is an instance of ENDORSE, as Blair's citation is from an editor whose paper has 'changed its position', the inference being that it has moved closer to the speaker's position. Blair thus attempts to enlist the views of 'the press' in his cause.

The engagement column shows that Blair's overall stance is contractive. He makes assertions about the 1930s which can fairly be called 'common ground', since they derive from a widely accepted reading of history. He uses the contractive resource of COUNTER to engage with the views he wishes to refute, those of listeners (the 'people who dispute', in line 1), who refuse to share his view of the Saddam threat.

Negative Judgements, meanwhile, interest both the groups that are opposing action now and those who did so in the 1930s. Appeasers (3), the newspaper editor (9), and 'the world' in general (9) are all negatively judged. Blair turns an inert proposition 'we should have acted then' into an active one - 'we should act now'. The positive affect (happiness, cheer) of the peace-hungry British people after Munich, also backs Blair's position. Just as the hopes of pacifists in the 1930s were baseless, so today, Blair suggests, the longer we fail to act, the worse will the eventual conflict be.

The argument rests on how pertinent the analogy with the 30s is felt to be. Some observers might feel that Blair's own analogy deserves the negative evaluations he metes out to others, i.e. 'glib' and 'foolish' (2). The Churchill Society, however, find it convincing, and suggest on their website that Churchill would have acted in the same way:

> The President of the USA and our Prime Minister have had heaped upon them over the last three months, hostility of an intensity equal to that endured by Churchill during the years he warned about the threat of Hitler. It is as difficult for them as it was for Churchill, to bring home to people the terror that tyrants like Hussein would inflict if allowed to remain in power[15]

If Blair could justify his argument that the threat to world peace posed by Saddam is indeed analogous to that of Hitler in the 1930s, it would be reasonable to expect Britain to unite around his policy on Iraq. By aligning anti-war voices in the present with these mistaken takes on world affairs in the past, Blair counters the views of current pacifists and other opponents of war in general. By so doing, he thereby risks excluding them from his desired consensus, but three considerations are relevant here. Firstly, as Blair himself recognised, some people are 'against all wars' - such people will always exclude themselves from any military option, however justifiable.[16] Secondly, Blair's exclusion of such people is enacted in a context–the comparison with the 1930s–that will show, to all but the most extreme of idealists, just how misguided it can be to apply the principle of non-violence to international politics. Finally, Blair's institutional position as Prime Minister necessitates, in an address of this kind, an attempt to 'rise above political parties', and 'speak for all citizens' (Sauer, 1997, p. 42). The speech must be seen as an attempt to construct national solidarity and, in fact, the rhetorical attempt to convince the unconvinced of the necessity for war was to continue long after the

---

[15] "The Iraq War. The Churchill Society." See web references.

[16] Blair has no respect for pacifists, who he ranks alongside 'anti-Americans' and contrasts with 'sensible people' in the following extract from a later speech: 'Sure, some were anti-American; *some against all wars*. But there was a core of *sensible people* who faced with this decision would have gone the other way, for sensible reasons. "Full Text: Tony Blair's Speech. The Guardian. Guardian News and Media, 05 Mar. 2004". See web references.

conclusion of hostilities.[17] Blair's use of pronoun reference is 'inclusive' (Wilson, 1990, p. 48). He speaks of 'our way of life' (1), and does not attempt to de-legitimise those who disagree with him, representing them with the neutral term 'people' (1). Such people may exclude themselves from the consensus sought by Blair, but they are not represented as outsiders to the political system of which he is the elected leader.

This book takes it for granted that the attempt to achieve alignment is a component of most, if not all, persuasive political rhetoric. In other words, that speakers use their rhetorical and other gifts in an effort to bring their listeners around to their way of thinking. As already pointed out, in the immediate context of today's parliamentary democracies, there are practical limitations to the power of rhetoric. However, given that parliamentary debates represent performances that, thanks to the efforts of mass media, reach the wider audience of potential voters for or against the different speakers, there is no reason to feel that the essential characteristics of persuasive political rhetoric have altered that much over the centuries. The positive ethos of a speaker, his ability to play on the emotions, and the force of his arguments, will still reap tangible rewards at the next election.

There is nothing definitive, it must be stressed, about the instance of analysis just provided. It is an illustration of the application of the Appraisal tools to the construction of rhetorical alignment, but there is no suggestion that this is the only, or the best way to approach political discourse. The rest of the book presents other methods for exploring such questions, and in the end, the choice of which to use will be a personal one.

---

[17] In a speech, over a year after the invasion, Blair was engaged in retrospectively trying to 'convince the unconvinced' that the war had been justified. The opening words indicate his awareness of the potential domestic political cost of the action: 'No decision I have ever made in politics has been as divisive as the decision to go to war in Iraq. It remains deeply divisive today'. "Full Text: Tony Blair's Speech. The Guardian. Guardian News and Media, 05 Mar. 2004". See web references.

Chapter 2

From 'is' to 'ought': deontic modality in persuasive political rhetoric

That political rhetoric has a persuasive character is a truism, and its study dates at least to the days of Aristotle. In classical Greece, ability to speak convincingly on a topic was regarded as the key to political power, and the Aristotelian notions of Ethos, Pathos and Logos have informed most theories of political discourse down to the present day. This chapter, and most of this book, takes the last of these—*Logos*, the word, the logical argument in a text or speech—as the focus of study. It looks at the grammatical resource of deontic modal verbs, an important feature of persuasive political rhetoric, and introduces some key terms and concepts in political discourse analysis, as well as a basic model for the analysis of argumentation.

It is important, at the outset, to acknowledge more general social changes that have taken place since the days of the Athenian polis, that influence the kind of argumentation found in modern political contexts. We can imagine that *genus deliberativum*, in the relatively tiny Greek state, was characterised by a process of public decision-making, followed by real-world action. There would have been a debate, followed by voting, on issues such as an attack by a neighbouring state, for example, some speakers would advocate making peace, others war, and a decision affecting the whole community would be taken. In a more modern *polis*, this type of political context is aptly expressed in the following citation from the Duke of Wellington's speech on Catholic emancipation, in 1829:

> My lords, this is the state of society to which I have wished to draw your attention, and for which it is necessary that parliament should provide a remedy.

Here is the situation, Wellington argues, then asks the assembled parliamentarians; what are we going to do about it?

While it is possible to find traces of such activity in Wellington's day, it is much harder in a modern parliament, mainly because of party whips: the impression is that a modern parliament, such as that of Britain, has become a mere talking shop, whose purpose is to ratify policies which are decided upon elsewhere, perhaps by important politicians, perhaps even by unelected figures such as civil servants. Bayley (2004, p. 10) indeed, casts doubt over the possibility of speakers ever succeeding in changing voting outcomes which, he suggests, are simply determined along the lines of party loyalties,

However, although a shift has occurred during the intervening centuries, from participatory to representative democracy, rhetorical performances from today's politicians still often retain at least the illusion of *genus deliberativum*, presenting discourse on an issue from a problem/solution perspective, i.e. suggesting on the one hand, 'here is the problem', and on the other 'here is our proposed response'. If such rhetoric is not used to convince fellow MPs to support or reject a specific measure, we may ask ourselves why it is still found at all. The answer usually suggested is that MPs are either canvassing support among their fellow party members, or else trying to make electoral capital among the invisible 'overhearers' among the general public, who follow the debates through mass media, and this multiple audience represents another significant difference between the political contexts of the modern and ancient world.

Political discourse is frequently seen in terms which Searle (1969, p. 175), in another field of enquiry and with different motives, calls arguing from 'is' to 'ought'; from a situation in the real world to proposals relating to it. This distinction corresponds to Halliday's 'propositions' and 'proposals', where the former are concerned with 'asserting and denying', the latter with 'prescribing and proscribing' (Halliday & Matthiessen 2004, p. 147). The division also corresponds to two major categories of modality, 'epistemic' and 'deontic', which Fairclough (2003, p. 164) explains as 'what is true' (epistemic) and 'what is necessary' (deontic). The interplay between the two types of proposition seems most effective when a speaker uses epistemic description in order to give maximum support to a deontic proposal, as in the following elegant phrase by William Ewart Gladstone:

> We have given Ireland a voice: we must all listen for a moment to what she says

The first clause in this celebrated quotation is epistemic; the deontic proposal in the second seems a logical sequel, with which it would be unreasonable to quarrel. There is a technical term used in argumentation, also used in this book: it is 'expressed opinion', and refers to the particular position for which a speaker is arguing (Van Eemeren & Grootendorst, 1984). Here, Gladstone's expressed opinion is that the House of Commons needs to pay attention to the views of the Irish people.

From a grammatical point of view, the proposals in political speeches feature what Halliday and Matthiessen (2004, p. 147) call 'degrees' or 'scales of obligation and inclination' between the two absolute poles represented by positive and negative imperative mood. Such absolutes are rarely found in the discourse of democratic leaders. Tony Blair, for example, was not an absolute monarch, and could not use the imperative form: 'Invade Iraq!', to bring about the real-world effect he sought. Instead, he used propositions couched in terms of modal graduation: 'We should invade Iraq', etc.

This chapter explores the linguistic means by means of which speakers construe their expressed opinions, focusing on modal verbs, with particular emphasis on 'must' and 'should'. These two verbs have been selected from the others for the extensive analysis below, in order to explore nuances in the pragmatics of speaker choices between high and median 'intensity'.

There are no specifically 'deontic' modal verbs since the modal verbs that are used to construe deontic modality can also construe epistemic modality (Greenbaum & Quirk, 1990, p. 63). The modal verbs most typically associated with deontic proposals of this kind are, however, *must, should, ought to, need*, as well as the semi-auxiliary *have to*. These are examined across two corpora of political speeches, each with twelve speeches: a modern corpus consisting of two speeches each by Churchill, Malcolm X, Thatcher, Blair, Gerry Adams and G.W. Bush (38,539 tokens), and a corpus of 19th century British political discourse (42,622 tokens) with speeches by Canning, Wellington, Peel, Macauley, Gladstone and Disraeli. The selected speakers are representative figures of their periods, prominent politicians discussing real-world issues of intrinsic interest. The relatively small size of the corpora means that findings are necessarily limited in terms of uncovering generalised diachronic patterns, for example, but this does allow for a closer, more qualitative style of analysis of the local pragmatics of the individual instances.

The focus is, at least in part, diachronic, and aims to explore continuities and contrasts in discursive practises in the political sphere through time.

Methodology (i)

For each modal verb, a KWIC concordance was prepared for both corpora, following the procedures described in Partington (1998), using Wordsmith tools. These served as the data for an exploration of the semantic patterns connected with the various modal verbs (Biber, Conrad, & Reppen, 2004, p. 26). The results were sifted to isolate those instances that showed the modal used in a deontic proposal. I was looking for examples where the verb construes a 'what is to be done?' pattern, in response to a specific real-world problem. This meant eliminating many hits in which the modal in question serves a different function. The process enabled comparison of the patterns that emerged, both within a single corpus and across the two corpora.

Three terms are used to describe the social actors involved in proposals: *speaker, audience* and *addressed*. Speaker is, self-evidently, the politician uttering the proposal.[1] Audience is less straightforward, since, though it may refer to the actual listeners in parliament, or in the speaker's immediate context, it may also include the amorphous body of overhearers, the 'general public' or specific sectors of this, who will learn of his words through various forms of media. It is necessary to relate the corpus findings to the analytical construct of 'intended audience' (Coulthard, 1994, pp. 4-5), if the pragmatic force of a single entry is to be correctly assessed. Malcolm X's aggressive rhetorical style, for example, would appear to risk alienating white listeners. However, this becomes less important if we consider that only black people were present at many of his meetings.

At this point, it is worth specifying the sense in which I am using the term 'pragmatic'. Here, and elsewhere in this book, I have in mind Austin's notion, fundamental to speech act theory and to the whole field of pragmatics generally, that there is a connection between the realm of words and that of real-world effects; in other words, his notion of *perlocution* (Austin, 1962). The relevant questions here would be: what exactly is this speaker trying to achieve through his/her speech? Who is s/he trying to persuade? What real-world effect might result from it?

Finally, the addressed is the social actor or entity of whom the proposal is predicated. The following table should make the analytical framework clear:

Table 2.1. Expressed opinions: corpus examples.

	Text	Expressed Opinion	Speaker	Addressed	Audience
1	Some people seem to forget that we have a Navy. We **must** remind them.	We must assert our naval presence	Churchill	The navy	The nation

---

[1] There are, however, a few cases in which the speaker uttering the proposal is not the source of it, as when Malcolm X says: 'the late President Kennedy and his brother, Attorney General Robert Kennedy, had warned these editors that they must give at least some token gains to the moderate Negro leaders'. This example, which involves the projecting device of Reporting, is pragmatically inert, since the proposal has no direct relevance to the current audience. Where such a construction does have pragmatic significance for the audience, it still makes sense to think of such an effect as originating in the communicative purpose of the Speaker—rather than the source of the Quoted or Reported speech—since s/he was responsible for including that particular message in the speech, and did so for a specific reason.

| 2 | Of course, the nation as a whole **must** support the discovery of basic scientific knowledge through Government finance | We must use taxpayers' money to finance scientific research | Thatcher | The nation as a whole | The Royal Society |
| 3 | After four hundred years of slave labor, we have some back pay coming, a bill owed to us that must be collected | Black people should take action for their civil rights | Malcolm X | American blacks generally | Nation of Islam rally |

Here are three expressed opinions, construed through the use of the modal 'must', collected from the modern corpus. In the first, the 'addressed' seems to be the Navy chiefs, who could be making a greater contribution to the war effort. Churchill seems to be urging them to perform some outstanding military feat, but there are problems with this straightforward interpretation. For example, he gives no details of the feat that he wishes them to perform, so that it is not easy to see how they could comply with his wishes, even if they were persuaded by his argument. It seems more plausible to see the comment as an appeal to Britain's tradition of naval supremacy, the pragmatic aim being to raise domestic morale among Churchill's audience of overhearers, by reminding them of Britain's established tradition of naval domination.

All three instances illustrate my remarks, above, about the difficulty of finding pro-con, Athenian argumentation in modern political rhetoric. Thatcher, for example, argues that it is necessary to spend public money on scientific research, but there will be no concluding vote here - her remarks are to the Royal Society rather than to parliament. Thus, the pragmatic effect of her speech might be to convince the Royal Society of the government's continuing financial support. Or, she may be making a wider, electoral pitch, aligning the Conservative party with the cause of science. In the case of Malcolm X, with his metaphor reminiscent of Martin Luther King's famous 'cheque' metaphor (see chapter five), no specific action is advocated. The reference to the years of slavery and the back pay seem, rather, designed to create a state of agitation in the audience, a willingness to 'do something'–and the importance of this something is underlined by the high intensity modal choice–but it is not clear what the speaker is actually proposing.

It is also of interest to classify the findings using Halliday's (2004) terminology of clause type (Material Process, Mental Process, etc.). This provides some sense of the kind of real-world effect the speaker is seeking. For example, in the interpretation I have just offered above, Thatcher is not seeking the pragmatic outcome of British taxpayer's handing over more money for the cause of science (Behavioural Process); rather, she is seeking a positive mental attitude, of 'support' for the idea that public money should fund scientific research (Mental Process).

Methodology (ii): eliminated references

Where the modal is used to express epistemic modality, the reference was removed:

> The whole fury and might of the enemy must very soon be turned on us (Mod. C: 2)

This is clearly an epistemic proposition, that could just as well have been construed with the future modal 'will'. 'Must' is also fairly frequent as a discourse marker, and examples such as the following were removed:

> I must tell the House that the Falkland Islands and their dependencies remain a British territory. (Mod. T; 2)

Also removed were proposals that, perhaps because they refer to a historical episode, relate to other social contexts than that in which speaker and current audience are involved. For example:

> The founding members resolved that the peace of the world must never again be destroyed by the will and wickedness of any man. (Mod. B: 1)

The social actors involved in this proposal are not the current audience, or speaker, but rather the founding members of the UN.

'Must' or 'should': strong/median obligation

'Must' is defined by the Oxford English Dictionary as: "expressing necessity: am (is, are) obliged or required to; have (has) to; it is necessary that (I, you, he, etc.) should".[2] The use of this high obligation modal is an indicator of the importance of the proposition or proposal, from the speaker's perspective. The same dictionary, meanwhile, defines 'should' as: '(used) in statements relating to the necessity, propriety, etc. of something contemplated as future' (ibid). This definition makes no comparison with the semantics of must, but I follow Halliday (2004, p. 622), who gives *should* as expressive of subjective obligation of median level. While both modals clearly indicate the speaker's

---

[2] "Welcome to the Definitive Record of the English Language". See web references.

preference for one course of action over another, 'must' indicates the absolute necessity of a particular step, 'should' its desirability. In terms of the distinction between epistemic and deontic modality, it is worth noting here that 'must' seems to denote the former, i.e. that something is necessary simply because it is required by the situation. 'Should' may also relate to 'necessity', but in addition has a slightly different nuance, expressed in the above definition in the word 'propriety'. Mention of propriety invokes the existence of ethical codes, religious systems, political ideologies, etc., according to which any action can be evaluated, justified, or argued for. This chapter suggests that, if we wish to explore the expressed opinions in any sample of political rhetoric, the verbs expressive of deontic modality represent a useful starting point. Below I discuss the issues that may be involved in the selection of one modal rather than another.

The references from the modern corpus can be divided into two roughly equal groups, according to whether the addressed is speaker + audience, or some other social actor. This is generally determined by the use of the inclusive grammatical terms 'we', 'us', 'our' or an inclusive formula such as 'the nation as a whole' or 'the world'. The table below shows findings for 'must' in the modern corpus where the addressed is 'inclusive we':

Table 2.2. KWIC for 'must' (inclusive 'we') in modern corpus (C= Curchill, Bl= Blair, B = Bush, T = Thatcher, X = Malcolm X).

Concordance					Speaker/Addressed	
1	be in whole-heartedly. That	**must**	include, provided the	Bl	Incl. 'we'
2	coming, a bill owed to us that	**must**	be collected. If the	X	Incl. 'we'
3	ammunition they need. We	**must**	have, and have quickly,	Ch	Incl. 'we'
4	have been set before us. We	**must**	choose between a world	B	Incl. 'we'
5	If the battle is to be won, we	**must**	provide our men with	Ch	Incl. 'we'
6	while dangers gather. We	**must**	stand up for our security	B	Incl. 'we'
7	by security measures. We	**must**	accept that there is a	Bl	Incl. 'we'
8	the place to start. Seventh, we	**must**	reach out to the Muslim	Bl	Incl. 'we'
9	will run them very hard. We	**must**	not forget that from the	Ch	Incl. 'we'
10	study of climatic change. We	**must**	ensure that what we do	Th	Incl. 'we'
11	of the Royal Air Force. We	**must**	not allow ourselves to be	Ch	Incl. 'we'
12	world directly depends. We	**must**	expect that as soon as	Ch	Incl. 'we'
13	gamble. And this is a risk we	**must**	not take. Delegates to	B	Incl. 'we'

14	forget that we have a Navy. We	**must**	remind them. For the	Ch	Incl. 'we'
15	as it were, bite on. Now, we	**must**	remember that even five	Ch	Incl. 'we'
16	course, the nation as a whole	**must**	support the discovery of	Th	The nation
17	gain the credit for their work	**must**	be harnessed. It is a	Th	The nation
18	defies us again, the world	**must**	move deliberately,	B	The world
19	there all by yourself again. We	**must**	understand the politics	X	Incl. 'we'
20	of our community and we	**must**	know what politics is	X	Incl. 'we'
21	is supposed to produce. We	**must**	know what part politics	X	Incl. 'we'

There seems to be a clear, pragmatic difference between a proposal that *'we should do something'* and one in which the addressed is a third party. In the former case, at least in a rhetorical sense, to decide to do the thing is to do it, since it depends on 'us' only; in the latter, however, the social actor indicated may not want to do it, and rhetorical formulations of his/her obligation may, therefore, have a different pragmatic purpose than that of bringing about the desired action.

The use of 'we' to construe solidarity between speaker and audience has already been the subject of extensive study (Mühlhäusler & Harré 1990; Wilson 1990; Hyland 2007, etc.) and therefore this aspect of the question may be considered as firmly established. Such lines of enquiry have frequently taken a critical direction. For example, the following proposition, from G.W.Bush, arguably involves equivocation over the precise referents of the pronoun in question:

> We **must** stand up for our security, and for the permanent rights and the hopes of mankind (6)

Bush is addressing the UN here, so a natural reading of the pronoun reference here sees it as indicating 'all member countries'. The problem, though, is that Iraq and other hostile nations were also, at the time in question, members of the UN. So who is meant by 'we'? As Miller (Miller, 2004) points out, the speech construes a discourse world that, in the final analysis, pits the USA *against* the UN. The pronoun, in this reading, becomes an instance of 'exclusive we', i.e. 'we but not you' (Wilson, 1990, p. 48; Fairclough, 1996, p. 111). Bush's pragmatic intention could then be seen as stiffening the resolve of listening Americans, whose security is potentially threatened by the UN's inaction.

Though I stated, above, that my purpose in this chapter was to study pro-con rhetoric on real-world issues, it is true that the greater part of these references in the modern corpus relates to rather more abstract questions. There are some that do concern Material Processes, e.g.:

> We **must** have, and have quickly, more aeroplanes, more tanks, more shells, more guns (3)

Here Churchill is straightforwardly arguing for an increase in the production of weapons. However, what is striking is the number of references in the above table that relate to Mental Processes:

- To choose (4);

- To accept (7);

- To reach out to (8);

- To (not) forget (9);

- To (not) allow ourselves to be intimidated (11);

- To expect (12);

- To remember (15);

- To support (16);

- To understand (19);

- To know (20,21)

Such references relate to the speaker's role in what may be called the spreading of propaganda, influencing opinion to imbue society at large with the approved ideology of the speaker's particular group. For example, it is important, in Malcolm X's group, that each member knows 'what part politics plays in their lives', for Churchill that the British people do not become 'intimidated'–or demoralised–because of the perceived enormity of the threat facing them, and so on. The more practical effects of such arguments can also be appreciated from this latter case, as a positive, motivated work-force will be better able to produce weapons of war than a demoralised one.

The other significant group of references are aimed at some other social actor/s, whose behaviour or opinions the speaker ostensibly desires to influence in some way:

Table 2.3. KWIC for 'must' (other addressed) in modern corpus.

Concordance				Speaker/Addressed
22	own people, then America	**must**	set aside some separate	X	White USA
23	humanity, White America	**must**	now pay for her sins	X	White USA
24	for Merthyr Tydfil cannot and	**must**	not ignore—and its navy	Th	Hon.Member
25	lines or natural obstacles, and	**must**	realize that mastery can	Ch	Allied armies
26	of the mind is being, and	**must**	be, devoted to the	Ch	Intelligence
27	the general result. The Armies	**must**	cast away the idea of	Ch	The armies
28	and justice. Second, Britain	**must**	be at the centre of	Bl	Britain
29	the High Command, but	**must**	inspire every fighting	Ch	This spirit
30	but that their directions	**must**	be punctually and	Ch	Ministers
31	and shelter. This government	**must**	supply us with the	X	Government
32	this divine destruction, He	**must**	first separate the	X	He (God)
33	brotherhood, God himself	**must**	first destroy this evil	X	God
34	explosive every day. History	**must**	repeat itself! Because of	X	History
35	political parties. But it	**must**	never be overlooked that	X	A 'fact'
36	vigilance and mind-searching	**must**	be devoted to the	Ch	Intelligence
37	assault. And this spirit	**must**	not only animate the	Ch	This spirit
38	and their subordinates	**must**	know that their chiefs	Ch	Subordinates
39	promises of integration. They	**must**	impress the three	X	Candidates
40	target for hours at a time,	**must**	realize that this re-emba	Ch	Anyone

The possible pragmatic effects here appear to depend on whether the relationship between speaker and addressed is antagonistic/adversarial or neutral/friendly. In the former case, it seems improbable that the intended pragmatic effect is that which is represented in the proposal. Consider the following examples, from Malcolm X:

America must set aside some separate territory here in the western hemisphere (22)

White America must now pay for her sins against twenty-two million 'Negroes' (23)

This government must supply us with the machinery and other tools needed to dig into the earth. (31)

In these extracts, the addressed is either 'white America' or 'the government', and a real-world proposal, in each case a Material/Behavioural Process, is advanced. However, there are problems identifying the desired pragmatic effect of the references, since the proposals are expressed in terms of strong modal obligation where, in reality, there is no such obligation, and X's grammatical choice is out of step with the realities of the situation. In terms of the likely response of the 'addressed' in these cases, we can imagine that any representatives of 'White America', or the government who happened to be listening to the speech, would be unimpressed by a sense of obligation. The government is more likely to go on ignoring the negro's[3] plight than to take any such steps, and this is perfectly well-known both to the speaker and his audience. Such proposals play on this knowledge, and their pragmatic effects are therefore to be sought in terms of their emotional effect on the listeners, as they help to kindle a sense of frustration and anger; to construe solidarity against the addressed rather than convince them to do something.

Where the audience is neutral or friendly, it is more probable that audience and addressed will coincide, and it becomes easier to identify the pragmatic aim of the proposal. Churchill, for example, says:

And this spirit must not only animate the High Command, but must inspire every fighting man (29)

The social actors who are to carry out this proposal–the high-ranking army officers and ordinary foot-soldiers–also constitute the audience of Churchill's speech. The intention here, as above, is to influence the mood of the hearers, to create a mental attitude throughout the community of listeners that is conducive to the attainment of the speaker's more practical goals.

Churchill is the speaker who uses the keyword most frequently. As already suggested, the use of the strong obligation modal might be considered an indicator of a strong leadership style. Only a leader, sure of his authority can consistently use this form, and Churchill, during the war, was head of an all-party government of national unity that was only seldom challenged.

---

[3] Malcolm X himself uses this term.

Must: 19th-century corpus

In this corpus, there were many more discourse markers than in the modern corpus. While the modern corpus had one each of the verbs *say, tell, make* (clear), and *repeat*, there was greater variety here, with verbs including *state, comment, pause, touch* (on), *express, own, call, beg* (leave to say), *make* (a demand on your patience), *detain* (you), and *quote*. There were also many examples of epistemic modality. After eliminating these, together with generalisations and other pragmatically inert references, the cases involving expressed opinion were comparatively few:

Table 2.4. KWIC for 'must' in 19th century corpus (G = Gladstone, C = Canning, D = Disraeli, M = Macauley).

Concordance			Speaker/Addressed	
1	of the Union; but that, too	**must**	be unfolded in all its hideous featur	G	-
2	France on that occasion, we	**must**	not defend Portugal on this. I, sir, li	C	We
3	have given Ireland a voice: we	**must**	all listen for a moment to what she	G	We
4	qualities of the people, we	**must**	now endeavour to add to these qu	G	We
5	moment to what she says. We	**must**	all listen-both sides, both Parties I	G	We
6	a year. But, gentlemen, you	**must**	look to the nature of this property.	D	You
7	it is necessary to exclude, we	**must**	admit those whom it may be safe t	M	We

The emphasis in these extracts is on Behavioural Processes; there are references to looking or listening (1,3,5,6), the pragmatic significance of which seems to focus the attention of the House on something the speaker regards as important. Canning, meanwhile, is representing the views of an opponent rather than advancing his own proposal. Five of the references, then, seem oriented towards the immediate, parliamentary context, urging MPs or Lords to attend to detail, stressing the importance of the measure, or representing other political views on a question. There are only two straightforward cases of deontic modality in Situation-Response pattern, the following from Gladstone:

> instead of trusting simply to the native and sterling qualities of the people, we **must** now endeavour to add to these qualities every advantage that can be imparted by the most skilful and effectual training (4)

And the following from Macauley, striking a curiously contemporary note:

That we may exclude those whom it is necessary to exclude, we **must** admit those whom it may be safe to admit

The data sample is too small, as I stated above, to advance anything more than tentative observations on such a comparison. We may suggest that 'must' seems to be more common as a discourse marker in the earlier texts, while for some reason there are fewer instances of must in argumentation. I shall return to this topic below.

Median level modality: should

The modern corpus provided a significantly higher proportion of Situation-Response type for *should* compared to *must*.

Table 2.5. 'Should' in modern corpus.

Concordance					Speaker/Addressed	
1	US confront these issues, we	**should**	be with them; and we		Bl	Incl. we
2	should be with them; and we	**should**	, in return, expect these		Bl	Incl. we
3	of our weakness. America	**should**	not be forced to take this		Bl	America
4	Council itself. With Japan, we	**should**	ensure we remain its		Bl	Incl. we
5	trust and partnership. We	**should**	deepen it at every turn.		Bl	Incl. we
6	the developing world, Britain	**should**	be their champions. For		Bl	Britain
7	be madness. If we are in, we	**should**	be in whole-heartedly.		Bl	Incl. we
8	critical of it in public. But we	**should**	use this alliance to good		Bl	Incl. we
9	not be its rival. Thirdly, we	**should**	engage with the countries		Bl	Incl. we
10	all be part of it. Of course, it	**should**	go through the UN - that		Bl	America
11	as on our own account we	**should**	be helping in their path of		Bl	Incl. we
12	should guide us? First, we	**should**	remain the closest ally of		Bl	Incl. we
13	is always needed. Europe	**should**	partner the US not be its		Bl	Europe
14	six Negro civil rights leaders	**should**	go an Oscar for the "Best		X	Oscar committee
15	liberals who participated	**should**	get an Oscar as the "Best		X	Oscar committee
16	country. This government	**should**	provide everything we		X	This govt.
17	kind. But this government	**should**	provide the transportation		X	This govt.

18	this race of devils. But we	**should**	not be expected to leave	X	Incl. we
19	really want. White America	**should**	be asking herself: "What	X	WhiteUS
20	means that the black man	**should**	control the politics and	X	Blacks
21	nalism only means that we	**should**	own and operate and	X	Incl. we
22	as I told you, means you	**should**	control you own, the	X	Incl. we
23	the society in which you live	**should**	be under your control.	X	Incl. we
24	for Max Perutz's view that we	**should**	be ready to support those	T	Incl. we
25	had I gone on to say that we	**should**	send HMS "Invincible", I	T	Incl. we
26	previous requests that they	**should**	arrange for the men's	T	Argentina
27	really been demonstrated.	**Should**	we be doing more to	T	Incl. we
28	purposes of the United States	**should**	not be doubted. The	B	The US
29	vices unitedly advise that we	**should**	carry on the war, and that	C	Incl. we

Pragmatics and argumentation: Tony Blair's use of should

For *need, have to,* and *should,* the politician most associated with these 'advice-giving' modals is Tony Blair. Only Malcolm X has a comparable result, but Malcolm X was not in a position of political power. When he says '*the government should do this, white America should do that*', and so on, the pragmatic purpose seems to be to stimulate supporters through a display of rhetorical potency, rather than to advocate or resist a specific policy proposal. At this point, then, it will be of interest to explore Blair's use of these modals in extended samples of argumentative rhetoric, to observe the pragmatic nuances involved in their selection. I will also introduce a model for the analysis of political argumentation that will be developed further throughout the rest of the book.

In Blair's 2003 speech to the Foreign Office conference, he makes the following comments:

1 Of course, it should go through the UN - that was our wish and what the US did. But if the will
2 of the UN is breached then the will should be enforced. Jack Straw has today set out for
3 Parliament in more detail our policy objectives on Iraq. So when the US confront these issues,
4 we should be with them; and we should, in return, expect these issues to be confronted with
5 the international community, proportionately, sensibly and in a way that delivers a better
6 prospect of long-term peace, security and justice.

In the following model (table six), a simplification of Toulmin's (Toulmin, 1958) model of argumentation, the Data section represents the real-world circumstances which underlie the argument, the Warrant the speaker's reasons for making his claim, and the Claim section the specific proposal, or expressed opinion s/he is advocating in this case. Other simplifications of this model have been proposed and applied to political discourse; notably that by Kienpointner (Kienpointner, 1996), whose term, 'argument', includes the proposition advanced by the speaker. I find it helpful, instead, to retain Toulmin's term 'data' as this emphasises the connection, in the model, between epistemic content on the one hand, and deontic on the other:

Table 2.6. A simple model of political argumentation, based on Toulmin 1958.

TEXT: Of course, it should go through the UN - that was our wish and what the US did		
Data	**Warrant**	**Claim**
(because)	**(since)**	**(therefore)**
The UN is the approved international forum for deciding on global issues	The question of Iraq was an important global issue	The US should (was correct to) go through the UN

The data section could/should be greatly expanded here, to include a wealth of historical detail that would assist our understanding of this text; in this case, the controversy surrounding America's decision to go ahead with the invasion of Iraq, despite the UN's final lack of support for such action. In the case of the first 'should', in the text quoted in figure one, above, we need to know that the US did indeed 'go through' the UN in October 2002, obtaining security council resolution 1441, which gave Iraq "a final opportunity to comply with its disarmament obligations".[4] Following this resolution, Iraq's compliance with UN weapons inspectors was felt to be inadequate, and the US and British governments, in early 2003, considered seeking a further UN mandate for military action.

That is not the end of the story, however, and other historical knowledge needs to be brought to bear in order to obtain a fuller understanding of the text. In March, the French government announced that it would not support invasion plans without a UN decision, and it became clear that the US and Britain would not be able to obtain a majority vote among the five permanent members of the UN Security Council. The British and American coalition then

---

[4] The text of this resolution is online at: "Resolution 1441". See web references.

decided that they would simply press ahead and invade Iraq anyway, bypassing the UN completely, thus removing from their actions the legitimacy of UN support. This is a succinct summary of an extremely complex international picture, but even these brief details will provide a picture of some of the tricky waters Blair is navigating in this speech. The approach to context in this book is largely guided by the work of Ruth Wodak and others, who developed the Discourse-Historical method (Wodak, 2001), which will be described more fully in due course.

Each modal verb requires separate analysis, since the expressed opinion in each case is different. The first is retrospective, looking back at the course of action followed by the US in 2002:

Of course, it **should** go through the UN - that was our wish and what the US did (1):

Table 2.7. Blair argumentation (i).

Data	Warrant	Claim
(because)	(since)	(therefore)
The UN is the approved international forum for deciding on global issues	The question of Iraq was an important global issue	The US should (was correct to) go through the UN

The evaluative aspect of *propriety*, which as we have seen can be construed through this modal verb, is prominent here, and the pragmatic point seems to be to show the US in a favourable light–they did 'the right thing' by going through the UN on the Iraqi question. Blair is on safe ground here, since the ethical framework on which his argument rests–that the UN should represent a supra-national body with the power to establish a global legal framework–is one that is widely shared among his audience, the consumers of mass media in mainly western countries. His second proposal is more controversial:

But if the will of the UN is breached then the will **should** be enforced (1-2)

Table 2.8. Blair argumentation (ii).

Data	Warrant	Claim
(because)	(since)	(therefore)
UN decisions establish a legal framework for the world	If they are not enforced, the whole mechanism becomes meaningless	It is right to enforce the UN's decision on Iraq by the use of military force

Here, the same audience might well agree with Blair's argument in principle, on condition that *it is the UN which does the enforcing.* Unfortunately, such was not the case: what happened was that two of the five permanent members of the Security Council, fearing that an eventual vote would not go their way, took it upon themselves to 'enforce' the UNs earlier resolution, interpreting it as a mandate for military action which–as the French position demonstrates–was at the very least an arguable proposition. In terms of the underlying ethical framework to which Blair's first use of 'should' appealed, the 'correct' course of action would clearly have been to have a fresh UN debate on Iraq's alleged non-compliance, and put the question of military action to the vote.

Blair's next deontic statement builds on these (arguably, shaky) foundations, the link with the earlier chain of argumentation indicated by the consequential adverb 'so':

So when the US confront these issues, we **should** be with them (3-4)

Table 2.9. Blair argumentation (iii).

Data	Warrant	Claim
(because)	(since)	(therefore)
What the US is doing is right	We want to do the right thing in international politics	We should be with the US on this question

By waging war in Iraq unilaterally, America was to set herself up, in place of the UN, as a sort of global policeman, against the express wishes of three of the five permanent Security Council members (France, Russia, China). In view of other discourse-historical factors such as Britain's 'special relationship' with the US, the cultural and linguistic ties between the two nations, and so on, Britain's not supporting her traditional ally on this question would have been a dramatic gesture, possibly leading to rupture and further isolating America in a global sense. These are the underlying ethical/ideological considerations relevant to Blair's warrant here, and this concludes Blair's general argument, that Britain should support America's actions. His final use of 'should' switches focus to what the USA should do in return for Britain's support:

we **should**, in return, expect these issues to be confronted with the international community, proportionately, sensibly and in a way that delivers a better prospect of long-term peace, security and justice (4-6)

Table 2.10. Blair argumentation (iv).

Data	Warrant	Claim
(because)	(since)	(therefore)
We have shown our public support for the USA	One good turn deserves another	The US should respond by confronting these issues in a sensible way

The implicit addressed here is the USA, rather than inclusive we. However, there is a crucial vagueness in Blair's language–what does he mean by 'proportionately' or 'sensibly', or 'in a way that delivers a better prospect of long-term peace'? Most western listeners might feel that there is only one appropriate international forum for 'confronting' the international community in these ways, and it is the United Nations, whose authority the United States was set on flouting.

An expressed opinion may represent an overall argument developed by a speaker across a whole speech, rather than a single instance of argumentation within one: it is plain that Blair's overall position in this section of his speech is not "Since the UK is backing it on the Iraqi question, the USA should respond by behaving in a reasonable manner", but more simply: "We should support the Americans over Iraq". The reference to what we might expect the US to do in return, in other words, is simply tacked on to Blair's argument as another reason for supporting them, rather than forming the thrust of an argument that addresses the US and demands that they do something in return for our support.

Analysis of this modal verb, then, allows us to appreciate nuances in argumentation, in the speaker's imagined audience/s, and also to focus attention on underlying axiological questions that may shift according to the co-text of any particular reference.

Blair's use of 'must'

The same speech provides the following examples of Blair's use of 'must':

Second, Britain **must** be at the centre of Europe. By 2004, the EU will consist of 25 nations. In time others including Turkey will join. It will be the largest market in the world.

That **must** include, provided the economic conditions are right, membership of the single currency.

Seventh, we **must** reach out to the Muslim world. This is about three things. It is about even-handedness.

Again, the argumentation patterns in these fragments of text can be identified, as follows (table seven):

Table 2.11. Blair's 2003 speech: 'must', argumentation.

	Data	Warrant	Claim
	(because)	(since)	(therefore)
1	The EU will be the largest market in the world	It is to our advantage to be part of such a big market	We must be at the centre of Europe
2	The single currency is the unit of monetary exchange in the EU	We wish to increase our trading benefits with Europe	We must use the single currency
3	The Muslim world is currently a source of danger for us	We wish to reduce international tensions	We must reach out to the Muslim world

It is much more straightforward to identify the pragmatic significance of this group of references. Here epistemic and deontic elements combine in a simple pattern: *because X is the objective situation, Y must be done.* Margaret Thatcher famously coined the phrase 'there is no alternative' (TINA) for such situations (Fairclough, 2001, p. 129). Strategic considerations (what must be done) are more present in such rhetorical formulations than moral (what it is right to do); as we have seen, above, considerations of propriety tend to be construed using the modal *should.* It is noticeable that, when Blair wishes to give further support to such contentions, he has occasional recourse to the modal 'should':

It will be the most integrated political union between nations. It will only grow in power. To separate ourselves from it would be madness. If we are in, we **should** be in whole-heartedly.

There is an appeal here to a widely shared framework in British social ethics, a suggestion that it is right to be 'in for a penny, in for a pound'.

Modern and 19th century modal usage

The tables below show the significantly greater use of these modals in deontic proposals in modern political rhetoric compared with the 19th century:

Table 2.12. Modal use in modern corpus.

Speaker	Must	Have to	Ought to	Need	Should
Adams	-	4	-	6	-
Blair	4	9	-	13	14
Bush	4	-	-	-	1
Churchill	17	2	-	-	1
Malcolm X	13	6	-	1	11
Thatcher	4	1	-	4	4

Table 2.13. Modal use in 19th century corpus.

Speaker	Must	Have to	Ought to	Need	Should
Canning	1	-	2	-	1
Disraeli	1	1	1	-	-
Gladstone	4	1	1	1	3
Macauley	1	1	3	-	-
Peel	-	-	1	-	-
Wellington	-	-	6	-	3

It is noticeable that, while 'ought to' is not found at all in the modern corpus, it does feature in the earlier body of texts, where it seems to share the semantics of 'should' in the modern. The OED definition confirms that, like 'should', 'ought to' relates to the sphere of propriety:

> That which should be done, the obligatory; a statement using 'ought', expressing a moral imperative.[5]

It is beyond the scope of this book to speculate on possible explanations for these phenomena. From a discourse/historical perspective, one might wish to explore the Victorian preoccupation with duty, with social reform, or Kipling's notion of 'the white man's burden'. Space considerations prohibit a discourse-historical treatment of the potentially fascinating comparison of the parliamentary contexts in the modern period and in Victorian times.

---

[5] "Welcome to the Definitive Record of the English Language". See web references.

It does seem, however, that there could be a close correspondence between the pragmatics of 'should' in the modern corpus which, as we have seen, is used to refer to questions of an axiological nature, and 'ought' as used in the 19th century:

> We say, and we say justly, that it is not by numbers, but by property and intelligence that a nation **ought** to be governed (Macauley)

> I know that there are many in your lordships' House, and many in the country, who think - and I admit that formerly I was of the same opinion - that the state **ought to** have some security for the church (Wellington)

In both cases, the speaker is arguing from an underlying ethic; in the first case, the shared sense among Macauley's listeners, in the parliamentary context, that it is *morally right* for the property-owning classes (who are rhetorically aligned, according to the logic of a striking *presupposition* (Fairclough, 1996), with the *intelligent* members of the population), to govern. In the second, the Duke of Wellington is alluding to a commonly held view, to which he himself formerly subscribed, that it was morally right for the Church of England to enjoy the protection of the state against the Roman Catholic church.

Similarly, though instances are fewer, the pragmatics of 'must' are associated, as in the modern corpus, with the notion that 'there is no alternative'. Gladstone, for example, argues that the conditions of modern warfare mean that it is no longer possible, if we want an effective army, to rely on the native fighting qualities of a people. He then adds:

> we **must** now endeavour to add to these qualities every advantage that can be imparted by the most skilful and effectual training.

It is the situation that determines the necessity contained in this proposal, from the speaker's point of view; a very similar situation in which Churchill was to find himself in the following century, in a different war.

Concluding remarks

In this chapter, I have tried to present some of the basic notions that will run through this book. Political discourse is seen to involve argumentation, in which it is necessary to consider not simply the logic, or lack of it, of any particular argument, but above all the discourse-historical context of a speech, which will enable us to appreciate pragmatic features/effects of a speaker's linguistic choices.

Some concluding observations: firstly, a speaker who uses the 'there is no alternative' strategy tends to select ideational features of the situation that confirm his/her proposal: the proposal will, therefore, be convincing according to the degree to which his audience share their view of the situation. Churchill's warnings of the necessity to boost Britain's air defences, for example, fell on deaf ears during most of the 1930s, and did so until the British population and their representatives in parliament woke up to the dangers of the situation.

Secondly, analysis of modals such as *should* and *ought to*, which involve implicit axiological frameworks, can be interesting in terms of what they tell us about the speaker's allusions to shared belief systems. Together with the resource of 'inclusive we', a deontic modal of this type is dialogically active, construing a discourse world of shared attitudes that may serve the speaker's rhetorical aims by providing a moral/ethical backing to his arguments. However, as in the case of Blair's argumentation on the necessity to support the US over Iraq, each instance in which the modal is used may involve slippage from one implicit ethical system to another; analysis of these features may, therefore, help to account for why an argument is felt to be convincing or unconvincing.

Thirdly, the connection between the power possessed by a speaker and his modal choices may repay study. I mentioned above that Churchill enjoyed unanimous, cross-party support in the war years; moreover, he was the representative of what was still one of the world's super-powers, and was present at the Yalta conference in 1945 as an equal partner of Roosevelt and Stalin. This may help account for his preference for the modal 'must'. Tony Blair, by contrast, though deeply interested in shaping international events, was a much less powerful figure in every sense; this may help explain his preference for 'should'. Meanwhile, G.W. Bush, certainly the most powerful of the six modern speakers, is the leader with the lowest figures for explicit deontic modal proposals. Miller (2004, p. 12), in her study of Bush's speech to the U.N., points out his preference for the future certainty modal 'will' over 'must' in formulating deontic proposals. The U.S., she suggests (ibid: 20), sees itself as above the kind of consensus-building to which Blair devotes so much energy, preferring simply to announce what it has decided to do unilaterally, letting other countries side with her if they wish to.

There remains, unanswered, the diachronic question of accounting for differences in the use of these modals between the two historical parliamentary contexts; to explore this would require both a larger corpus and a much larger book.

Appendix: details of corpora

Victorian corpus

Bloy, Marjorie, Dr. The Peel Web. *A Web of English History.* N.p., n.d. Web. 24 Aug. 2016. <http://www.historyhome.co.uk/peel/peelhome.htm>.

Canning 1. Address on the King's Message Respecting Portugal: Dec. 1826

Canning 2. Vindication of government policies: 18 March 1820

Disraeli 1. Conservative Principles: 3 April 1872

Disraeli 2. Explanation to his constituents of his votes in Parliament: 1842

Gladstone 1. Accomplishments of the Administration: 28 October 1871

Gladstone 2. Government of Ireland Bill: June 7, 1886

Macauley 1. The Reform Bill: parliamentary representation: 28 February 1832

Macauley 2. Extracts from a speech: 2 March 1831

Peel 1. Speech on the repeal of the Corn Laws: January 22, 1846

Peel 2. The Bedchamber Crisis: 13 May 1839

Wellington 1. Speech on the repeal of the Corn Laws: 28 May 1846

Wellington 2. Speech on Catholic Emancipation: 2 April 1829

Modern corpus

Adams 1: Speech by Gerry Adams: 21/10/2003

Adams 2: Plea to the IRA to disarm: 05/04/2005

Blair 1: Speech at the Lord Mayor's banquet: 11/11/2002

Blair 1: Foreign office conference: 06/01/2003

Bush 1: Speech to the United Nations: 12/09/2002

Bush 2: At the Pentagon 'Operation infinite justice': 11/09/2002

Churchill 1: Be ye men of valour: 19/05/1940

Churchill 2: Their finest hour: 18/06/1940

Malcolm X 1: The ballot or the bullet 12/04/1964

Malcolm X 2: God's judgement of white America: 04/12/1963

Thatcher 1: The Falklands emergency: 03/04/1982

Thatcher 2: Speech to the Royal Society: 27/09/1988

Web references

Adams, Gerry. CAIN: Events: Peace: Speech by Gerry Adams, Sinn Fein President, Tuesday 21 October 2003. CAIN: Events: Peace: Speech by Gerry Adams, Sinn Fein President, Tuesday 21 October 2003. N.p., n.d. Web. 29 Aug. 2016. <http://cain.ulst.ac.uk/issues/politics/docs/sf/ga211003.htm>.,

BBC NEWS | UK | Northern Ireland | Text of Adams Speech in Full. BBC News. BBC, 06 Apr. 2005. Web. 29 Aug. 2016. <http://news.bbc.co.uk/1/hi/northern_ireland/4417575.stm>.

Blair, Tony. "Full Text of Blair's Speech." The Guardian. Guardian News and Media, 11 Nov. 2002. Web. 24 Aug. 2016. Full Text: Tony Blair's Speech. The

Guardian. Guardian News and Media, 06 Jan. 2003. Web. 24 Aug. 2016. <http://www.theguardian.com/politics/2003/ jan/07/foreignpolicy.speeches>.

George Bush's Speech to the UN General Asembly. The Guardian. Guardian News and Media, 12 Sept. 2002. Web. 24 Aug. 2016. <https://www.theguardian.com/world/2002/sep/12/iraq.usa3>.

Bush's Speech at the Pentagon. The New York Times. N.p., n.d. Web. 24 Aug. 2016. <http://www.nytimes.com/2002/09/11/national/11TEXT-BUSH.html>.

Churchill, Winston, Sir. "Be Ye Men of Valour." The Churchill Centre. N.p., n.d. Web. 24 Aug. 2016. <http://www.winstonchurchill.org/resources/speeches/ 1940-the-finest-hour/be-ye-men-of-valour>.

Churchill, Winston, Sir. "The Churchill Centre." Their Finest Hour. N.p., n.d. Web. 24 Aug. 2016. <http://www.winstonchurchill.org/resources/speeches/ 1940-the-finest-hour/122-their-finest-hour>.

Malcolm X - Speeches God's Judgement of White America (the Chickens Come Home to Roost). Malcolm X - Speeches God's Judgement of White America (the Chickens Come Home to Roost). Malcolm X Org, n.d. Web. 24 Aug. 2016. <http://www.malcolm-x.org/speeches/spc_120463.htm>.

Malcolm X: The Ballot or the Bullet." Malcolm X: The Ballot or the Bullet. Social Justrice Speeches, n.d. Web. 24 Aug. 2016. http://www.edchange.org/multicultural/speeches/malcolm_x_ballot.html

Thatcher, Margaret. HC S: [Falkland Islands]. Margaret Thatcher Foundation. N.p., n.d. Web. 24 Aug. 2016. <http://www.margaretthatcher.org/document/ 104910>.

Thatcher, Margaret. Speech to the Royal Society. Margaret Thatcher Foundation. N.p., n.d. Web. 24 Aug. 2016. <http://www.margaretthatcher.org /document/107346>.

Chapter 3

Rhetoric and argumentation in Edmund Burke's Conciliation with America, March 22nd 1775

Introduction

Rhetorical figures or tropes such as metaphor, analogy, hyperbole, parallelism and so forth, are a characteristic feature of most political discourse. Although they have been extensively studied since the days of Aristotle, and have formed the basis of most approaches to speech-making down the centuries, it is seldom asked whether such devices are simply stylistic features that contribute to the orator's demonstration of *ars bene dicendi* (Conley, 1990, p. 131), or whether they have some intrinsic persuasive force that justifies the effort which speakers invest in their mastery.

On a website devoted to political rhetoric,[1] for example, we find an explicit connection made between notions of aesthetics, on the one hand, and persuasive effect on the other:

> In classical rhetoric, the tropes and schemes fall under the canon of style. These stylistic features are commonly thought to be persuasive because they dress up otherwise mundane language; the idea being that *we are persuaded by the imagery and artistry because we find it entertaining* (my emphasis)

This chapter explores this latter claim. It finds that it is possible to distinguish between different types of rhetorical figure and suggests that, while some indeed may simply constitute entertaining and/or aesthetically pleasing uses of language, others have a more explicitly persuasive function. While the former may contribute to the persuasive effect of a speech, insofar as they increase a capable orator's ethos among his listeners, the latter must be seen in the same terms as other persuasive devices that are known to the

---

[1] "Tropes and Schemes". See web references.

tradition of critical political discourse analysis. Their role in argumentation, in the logos of a particular speech, it will be seen, is not insignificant. In terms of the challenge outlined by Fahnestock (2009), the chapter attempts to unite insights from the traditional field of rhetorical stylistics with the more modern perspectives on political discourse analysis from fields such as general linguistics and critical discourse analysis.[2] Burke's 1775 speech on conciliation with the American colonies has been selected to exemplify these processes for several reasons, mainly because, as Burke was a practitioner of parliamentary oratory in a grand manner, it abounds in these features, which are found more sparingly in contemporary rhetoric. From a political/historical perspective, it also provides a reminder that the issues facing powerful empires are apt to recur at different historical periods.

Context in discourse analysis

> Every text–that is, everything that is said or written–unfolds in some context of use. M.A.K. Halliday (1994, p. xiii)

The phrase 'context of use', originally used by Firth and Malinowski and then adopted by Halliday, refers to the factors it is necessary to take into account if potential within words is to become meaning. Context knowledge is fundamental to human communication, when we need to disambiguate the multi-referent potentials of words: 'a ball', for example, can be a round object used in games, or a dance attended by Cinderella. 'To shoot' can be to fire a rifle, to go for goal in soccer, or to travel at high speed. Without knowledge of context, it is impossible to know which meaning is relevant in any single instance of communication.

Attention to context is, of course, an essential feature of Critical Discourse Analysis (e.g. Weiss and Wodak, 2003), and of Ruth Wodak's Discourse-Historical approach (Reisigl & Wodak, 2001). In the field of pragmatics, Kecskes and Zhang (2009) (see also Kecskes, 2008) have developed a dynamic model of meaning that gives a central place to the knowledge of the social and interactional context. In pragma-dialectics, too (Van Eemeren and Grootendorst 2004), the social dimension of argumentation is present in the concepts of *externalisation*, which captures the propositional and interactional commitments of the speech acts involved, and *socialisation*, which extends the speech act perspective to the level of interaction (Van Eemeren, 2009, p. 118).

---

[2] See, for example, Chilton & Schaffner 1997, Bayley 2004, Chilton, 2004. For critical discourse analysis Van Dijk & Wodak, 2000, Weiss & Wodak, 2007, Van Dijk, 2009.

While some schools of text-oriented linguistics, such as that of Noam Chomsky, tend to ignore social context, linguistic studies with a social orientation, that emphasise the interpersonal dimension of language, have always attributed to it a key role in developing their theories of communication. Halliday (1978: 62), for example, considers context features under the three headings of Field, Tenor, and Mode. 'Field' relates to the subject matter of a particular discourse; 'Tenor' to the speakers' and addressees' identities, social roles, and so on; and 'Mode' to features of the communicative channel such as whether the discourse is spoken or written. Pragmatics, too, which deals with the connection between speech and its perlocutionary consequences, is equally concerned with context information (Verschueren, 2003, p. 75).

Basic knowledge of context is clearly necessary if we are to understand what the speaker is talking about at all, and will help us to appreciate nuances in allusions to features of the real-world context at the time of the speech. For example, consider this extract from a speech by Blair on Iraq:

> Since then the international community has relied on sanctions and the No Fly Zones policed by US and UK pilots to contain Saddam. But the first is not proof against Saddam's deception and the second is limited in its impact (Blair 23/02/2003)

Here, we need to know what is meant by 'the international community', what 'sanctions' and 'no fly zones' are, who Saddam is, and what is meant by the reference to his 'deception'. Having said as much, however, the question will arise - how do we know what features of social context are relevant? And secondly, how much detail needs to be included in such description? Teun Van Dijk's answers to these points are open-ended:

> Context analysis may be as complex and multi-layered as that of text and talk itself (Van Dijk, 1997, p. 4)

> There is of course no a priori limit to the scope and level of what counts as being relevant context (Van Dijk 1997, p. 14)

By context here, Van Dijk is referring to those "characteristics of the social situation or the communicative event that may systematically influence text or talk" (Van Dijk 1997, p. 3). Such extraneous context features such as whether the speaker has blue eyes or green, or if they keep a dog (ibid: 11) can be excluded. Contexts can be imagined in which these features would be central, but in the case of most political discourse, they can safely be omitted. More relevant are factors such as the power relations of the participants, their ages, jobs, the location of the discourse, and so on. Van Dijk lists *gender, age, class, social position, ethnicity* and *profession* as of probable relevance.

A useful approach to the systematisation of features of the context of situation is proposed by Hyatt (Hyatt, 2005), who lists four aspects of context to be considered. His study looks at newspaper language, but his categories are relevant to a study of political rhetoric:

    i.   Immediate socio-political context. This refers to the state of contemporary actuality, what is in the news at the moment;

    ii.   Medium-term socio-political context. This covers influential contexts that survive for a longer period than the individual story but still are too temporary to be considered aspects of the wider context of culture;

    iii.   Contemporary socio-political individuals, organizations and structures;

    iv.   Epoch [...] or what counts as knowledge or truth in a particular era. This might include the various assumptions of order, structures of inclusion and exclusion and generally how a society legitimates itself and achieves its social identity. (Hyatt, 2005, pp. 521-523)

This approach is also found in the 'Discourse-Historical Method' of Ruth Wodak who, in the spirit of Critical Discourse Analysis, attempts to relate events in text/discourse to the historical patterns of social behaviour that lie behind them:

> [the analyst] makes use of her or his background and contextual knowledge and embeds the communicative or interactional structures of a discursive event in a wider frame of social and political relations, processes and circumstances (Wodak & Meyer, 2001, p. 65)

As a tentative answer to the questions raised above, then, we can consider context features as relevant to the extent that they assist in elucidating the pragmatic significance of a particular communicative event. Decisions over the salience or not of any piece of context information will always rest with the analyst, who will generally find that starting from the text is a useful first step.

Edmund Burke and the American colonies;
(discourse)-historical background

A text like Burke's, naturally, makes it necessary for the analyst to accentuate the 'historical' component of the discourse-historical method (Reisigl & Wodak, 2001; Wodak, 2007), and correct application of Wodak's inter-disciplinary method would no doubt require the collaboration of a historian. It is hard, in fact, for the non-historian to approach a text like this and remember that the world's current dominant superpower was once a fractious colony of the mighty British empire, that the debate is taking place in the parliament of the global superpower of the age, and that the issues raised by the speaker therefore have a global resonance.

Edmund Burke, philosopher and political thinker, was an Irish Whig; one of the leading intellectual lights of his day, he was a member of the famous 'literary club' also frequented by Samuel Johnson. Burke has become associated with the origins of 'British Conservatism' in its best and broadest sense, and the speech on America contains many attitudes familiar to political discourse from our own time, on topics such as the role of nation and state, individual rights and responsibilities, the nature of freedom, and so on. Burke had a paradoxical attitude towards the general public; on the one hand, his biographer testifies to his social egalitarianism (Lock, 1998, p. 185), but he has also been identified as among the originators of the 'fear of the masses' that was a feature of British conservatism during the 18th and 19th centuries (Barbalet, 2006).

The movement that was to culminate in the American colonies gaining their independence from the British crown began over a question of taxation. Since the seven years' war with France, which ended in 1763 with the peace of Paris, successive British administrations had aimed to defray the costs of 'protecting' the colonies, where the military conflicts had taken place. These fiscal measures had led to tensions that periodically boiled over into acts of rebellion, the most notorious being the 'Boston Tea Party' in 1774, where a valuable cargo of imported tea was destroyed. In retaliation, Lord North, George III's prime minister, sent more British soldiers to America. The first military action took place at Concord in April, 1774, and it was apparent, from the first engagements, that the colonists would put up a determined fight.

The revolt was viewed differently in Britain according to party loyalties, though the term 'party' here, it must be remembered, needs qualification. Political influence in the 18th century was divided between two main power bodies: on the one hand, the Tories, land-owning nobility loyal to 'king and country'. On the other, the Whigs, the new force that, following the constitutional unrest of the previous century, were looking to make parliament more powerful than the monarch. Among several important pamphlets that were published on the issue were Johnson's 'Taxation no tyranny' (1775), which argued the king's case; on the other side was Tom Paine, the firebrand Whig, who published what was to become the manifesto of the colonists' cause, Common Sense (1776), in which he wrote a line which still recurs in modern American rhetoric:

The cause of America is in a great measure the cause of all mankind[3]

As we have already seen, however, although parliament was divided into two broad groups under the terms 'Whig' and 'Tory', the similarities in terms of social background, intellectual outlook and so on were far greater than their differences.

Rhetorical figures: decorative, focusing and pragmatic

This section explores the contribution of rhetorical figures to the overall persuasive effect of Burke's speech. It must be said, at the outset, that the analysis below only regards a selection of the actual text, consisting of a short introductory section and the closing peroration. This is due to the extreme length of the speech, which must have taken several hours to deliver.[4] The peroration, that part of the speech where an orator tends to concentrate himself for a final attempt to persuade his listeners, is especially rich in rhetorical devices.

A useful distinction, for analytical purposes, can be made, between rhetorical figures of three broad types: decorative, focusing, and pragmatic. The first of these regards devices which presents prose in elegant variation (Fowler, 2009) from normal practice, with the aim of, as Quintilian puts it, 'delighting the hearer'.[5] According to Reisigl (2009), for classical rhetoric this was, indeed, the chief function of many tropes. Some of these figures, if overused, can have the opposite effect, as readers of Orwell's 'Politics and the English Language', considering his strictures on the overuse of litotes, will remember.[6] The second group focus the listeners' attention on the speaker's message, while the final group are those where the persuasive function,

---

[3] "Paine, Thomas". See web references.
[4] For the full text of this long speech see (Fidler & Welsh, 1999, pp. 119-146).
[5] "Butler, Harold Edgeworth. Quintilian, Institutio Oratoria, Book 9". See web references.
[6] "Orwell, George. George Orwell: *Politics and the English Language* and the English language". See web references. Quintilian himself, in the passage just quoted, also warns explicitly about the danger of overusing the decorative figures.

discussed above, is felt to be uppermost (see (Nöth, 1995). Some of the figures belong to more than one possible category. For example, although alliteration, the primary stylistic feature of Old English poetry, is clearly a decorative resource, it can also have a focusing effect. As Robert Harris writes, it: "calls attention to the phrase and fixes it in the reader's mind, and so is useful for emphasis as well as art".[7] Likewise, it is arguable that most, if not all the rhetorical figures included below in the other sections also share something of a decorative function.

Decorative figures

Below (table one) are listed those rhetorical features in which, it is felt, the principal function is that which Jakobson (1999) refers to as the 'poetic':

Table 3.1. Decorative rhetorical figures in Burke's speech.

Resource	Reference	Description[8]
Alliteration	10. everything hastens to **d**ecay and **d**issolution	Repetition of a word-initial consonant
Asyndeton	34. the wealth, the number, ~~(and)~~ the happiness of the human race.	Omission of generally preferred conjunctions
Litotes	31. Magnanimity in politics is **not seldom** the truest wisdom	Elegant variation; here, for *frequently*
Sententia	32. we ought to auspicate all our public proceedings on America with the old warning of the Church, *Sursum corda!*	Makes use of a well-known maxim or proverb

Focusing figures

All rhetoric is persuasive at some level; hence, all of these figures, these "forms of speech artfully varied from common usage" (Quintilian, *Inst. Orat.* IX.i.2)[9] have persuasion as their overall function. Nevertheless, some purpose is served by distinguishing the decorative and the focusing categories from the pragmatic, where the persuasive intent is more manifest. The principal function of the devices in the focusing category is that of drawing the attention of the

---

[7] "Harris, Robert A. A Handbook of Rhetorical Devices. Virtual Salt". See web references.
[8] Definitions of many of these figures can be found at Harris's web-site (see previous note).
[9] "Book 9 - Chapter 1: Quintilian's Institutes of Oratory". See web references.

audience to what the speaker regards as significant. Since one of the essential felicity conditions (Searle, 1969) for any persuasive attempt is that listeners are actually paying attention at the moment the deontic proposal is announced, focusing enables the speaker to make sure that, at the very least, the proposal gets across. However, to claim more for these resources is problematic; it remains to be demonstrated how the simple fact that the audience appreciates what the message is will make them more likely to accept it.

Table 3.2. Focusing rhetorical figures.

Device	Instance	Comment
Amplification	7. Not peace through the medium of war; not peace to be hunted through the labyrinth of intricate and endless negotiations; not peace to arise out of universal discord, fomented from principle, in all parts of the empire; not peace to depend on the juridical determination of perplexing questions, or the precise marking the shadowy boundaries of a complex government.	Amplifies the proposition in 6.(below), specifying very precisely what is intended by 'peace'
Anadiplosis	6. The proposition is peace. Not peace.	Takes up last word of preceding clause
Anaphora	7. not peace to be hunted [..]; not peace to arise [..]; not peace	This repetitive effect frequently - as here - combines with *parallelism*
Bicolon	15. They may have it from Spain, they may have it from Prussia	An expression containing two parallel phrases
Binomial	20. your registers and your bonds, your affidavits and your sufferances, your cockets and your clearances	Two words, generally of the same grammatical category, joined by a conjunction. Burke uses three binomials together here in a kind of tricolon (see below)
Conduplicatio	23. it is the spirit of the English communion that gives all their life and efficacy to them. It is the spirit of the English constitution	Takes up a key word/phrase from preceding clause
Diacope	27. No! surely, no!	Repetition after a one-word interval
Diazeugma	19. you break that sole bond which originally made, and must still preserve, the unity of the empire.	One subject with multiple verbs
Ellipsis	2. Struggling a good while with these thoughts	Omission (after struggling)

Hyperbaton	13. Slavery they can have anywhere	Departs from usual word order
Hypozeugma	21. your Letters of office, and your instructions, and your suspending clauses are the things	Multiple subjects
Parallelism	10. the cement is gone, the cohesion is loosened	Use, in successive clauses, of a similar syntactical pattern
Polysyndeton	21. your Letters of office, and your instructions, and your suspending clauses	Features a conjunction which could be omitted
Tricolon	34. not by destroying, but by promoting the wealth, the number, the happiness of the human race.	A figure with three parts of similar or identical structure.[10] This is also an example of Asyndeton; combining focussing and decoration; and also Climax.

The focusing effect of the figures used here can be better appreciated by examining their co-operation in the deontic proposal for which Burke seeks consensus in this speech; that peaceful methods, rather than the use of force, should inform attempts to settle the differences with the colonies. Since this is his main proposal, there are clearly good reasons for wishing to draw attention to it, and several of these focusing devices are used in combination:

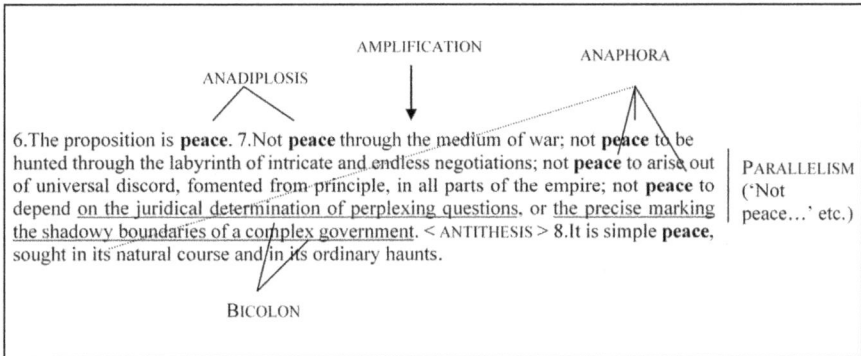

Figure 3.1. Focusing devices in a deontic proposal.

---

[10] This definition, and that for binomials, is from Partington (1998, pp. 126-9). Other definitions are taken from Perelman and Olbrechts-Tyteca (1969) and Harris (see note 8, above).

Burke also uses resources, here, from the Pragmatic category - Antithesis and Metaphor, to which I shall return below, and the decorative resource of Alliteration ('the **p**roposition is **p**eace', etc.). In order to appreciate the focusing function of the rhetorical figures, simply read the passage aloud, and you will notice how *tonic prominence* (Halliday & Matthiessen, 2004, p. 89) inevitably interests the repeated keyword, 'peace'. Also worthy of note is the discrepancy in length between first and last sentences when compared to that in between. The first makes a terse pronouncement, to which attention is drawn by Alliteration. This is then amplified at length, in a series of negative propositions, the grammatical complexity of which seems to symbolise the difficult matters dealt with at the semantic level; grammatical simplicity returns in the antithetical clause, which again symbolises the essential simplicity of the proposed solution.

Pragmatic figures

The term pragmatic, as mentioned above, refers to Speech Act Theory (Austin, 1962; Searle, 1969), which attempts to connect verbal actions with the real-world effects that ideally follow from them. The function of persuasion, meanwhile, is an instance of Austin and Searle's notion of perlocution. These resources mostly concern patterns of evaluation, in attempts to align listeners with speaker values; presupposing responses, and interacting with listeners in various ways that can be labelled, in the terms of Bakhtin and White, 'dialogical' (see Martin & White, 2005):

Table 3.3. Pragmatic rhetorical figures.

Device	Instance	Comment
Allusion	7. through **the labyrinth** of intricate and endless negotiations	Reference to some shared cultural framework
Analogy	26. Do you imagine, then, that it is the Land-Tax Act which raises your revenue? that it is the annual vote in the Committee of Supply, which gives you your army?	A "resemblance of structures" (Perelman & Olbrechts-Tyteca, 1969, p. 372)
Antithesis	23. Dead instruments, passive tools as they are, it is the spirit of the English communion that gives all their life and efficacy to them	Contrasts two ideas by juxtaposing them
Climax	28. which gives you your army and your navy, and infuses into both that liberal obedience without which your army would be a base rabble and your navy nothing but rotten timber.	"arranging words, clauses, or sentences in the order of increasing importance, weight, or emphasis" (Harris)

Epithet, transferred epithet	28. your navy nothing but **rotten** timber (*epithet*); 23. **Dead** instruments, **passive** tools as they are (*transferred epithets*)	Transferred epithet: "an adjective modifying a noun which it does not normally modify, but which makes figurative sense' (Harris)
Eritesis	25. Is it not the same virtue which does everything for us here in England?	A question which enjoins a specific response; the speaker expects this to be 'obvious' (also termed 'rhetorical question')
Expletive	27. No! surely, no!	"lends emphasis to the words immediately proximate to the expletive" (Harris)
Hyperbole	9. [..] no force under heaven will be of power to tear them from their allegiance.	Deliberate exaggeration.
Metaphor	1. To restore order and repose to an empire so great and so distracted as ours	"Compares two different things by speaking of one in terms of the other" (Harris)
Paradox	19. you break that sole bond which originally made, and must still preserve, the unity of the empire.	"uniting words that appear to be mutually exclusive" (Perelman & Olbrechts-Tyteca, 1969, p. 444)
Procatalepsis	29. All this, I know well enough, will sound wild and chimerical to the profane herd of those vulgar and mechanical politicians who have no place among us	Engages with listeners of different views

Metaphor and Analogy have a significant role to play in the argumentative structure of the speech, and I shall consider them in more depth later. Let us first explore the other rhetorical figures listed here.

1) *Allusion.* The connotations of the word 'labyrinth' in its Grecian sense imply an evaluation of the hypothetic 'negotiations' as - *App: complexity.* The figure relies on shared cultural knowledge between speaker and audience. The metaphor of the labyrinth is an appropriate one for 'intricate negotiations': it is significant that, in the myth to which allusion is made, not 'peace', but a monster, lurked in the heart of the maze.

2) *Antithesis.* Mann and Thompson (1987, p. 12) claim that the intended effect of Antithesis is to "increase the reader's regard for the situation presented". In what they call the 'nucleus' resides a proposition for which the speaker has positive regard. In this case, *the spirit of the English communion*–a fundamental term in the argumentative structure–is claimed to be responsible for the efficient functioning of the body politic. This effect is

enhanced by the evaluative language on either side of the comparison: 'dead instruments, passive tools' (- App: Valuation); 'the spirit of the English communion that gives all their life and efficacy to them' (+ App: Valuation).

3) *Climax.* This is a kind of crescendo which makes a specific point in a very forceful way, an effect that builds up across a sequence of text, to end in a dramatic high-point. Comparing Burke's speech with Churchill's 'Finest hour' speech, examined below in chapter four shows some similarities both at syntactic, semantic and pragmatic levels:

> It is the love of the people; it is their attachment to their government, from the sense of the deep stake they have in such a glorious institution, which gives you your army and your navy, and infuses into both that liberal obedience without which your army would be a base rabble and your navy nothing but rotten timber (Burke)

> Let us therefore brace ourselves to our duties, and so bear ourselves that, if the British Empire and its Commonwealth last for a thousand years, men will still say, 'This was their finest hour.' (Churchill)

Syntactically, the climaxes seem to build through a series of hypotactic, preparatory clauses, to peak at the end of the final clause; in the Burke speech, there is the additional focusing resource of Bicolon. In terms of content, there is a certain grandeur in both. Burke's theme is the origin of civic responsibility, Churchill's features patriotic pride in Britain's imperial tradition. Both speakers use evaluative language from the judgement: propriety system, and both conceive the institutions referred to (government, the British Empire and Commonwealth) in terms of *intensified positive judgement: propriety.*

4. *Epithet; transferred epithet.* Epithets frequently function as *evaluators* of the nouns they modify. Consider this example from Burke, which combines evaluative epithets with the decorative device Litotes and the Pragmatic figure of Antithesis:

> 31. Magnanimity in politics is not seldom the truest wisdom; and a great empire and little minds go ill together.

The evaluative patterns here are as follows:

> Magnanimity in politics (+ J: propriety) is not seldom the truest wisdom (+ J: propriety); and a great empire (+ App: valuation) and little minds (- J: capacity) go ill together.

Burke is arguing to an audience, many of whom are personally involved in the running of the 'great empire', that they should not approach the task with 'little minds' but instead show 'magnanimity' and 'true wisdom'. Whether or not they find his arguments convincing, the role played by the evaluative epithets in the attempt to persuade is manifest.

The transferred epithet, because of its application to a noun with which it would not normally collocate, is generally focusing; but in the following example, its significance is also pragmatic:

> 29. All this, I know well enough, will sound wild and chimerical to the profane herd of those vulgar and mechanical politicians who have no place among us: a sort of people who think that nothing exists but what is gross and material, and who, therefore, far from being qualified to be directors of the great movement of empire, are not fit to turn a wheel in the machine.

Here Burke mixes metaphors; the first from the semantic field of 'animals'– *wild, chimerical, herd*; and the second from that of 'machines'–*mechanical, material, directors, turn a wheel in the machine*. The collective noun 'herd' is striking enough because of its metaphorical application to human beings; animals, too, are not generally termed 'profane' (- J: propriety). The transferred epithets here, then, both focus attention on Burke's judgement of these politicians, and deepens it through the metaphorical associations evoked.[11]

5) *Eritesis*. Explanation of this device, which is better known as 'rhetorical question' relates to the Engagement resources of the Appraisal framework, discussed above. By pre-supposing that the response of the audience would be the simple 'yes' or 'no' that the figure takes for granted, the speaker engages with them in a direct way. Use of the device is generally a sign that the speaker is confident that the response will indeed be the expected one, so the proposition advanced can henceforward be taken as 'established' between speaker and audience. In the example in the table, Burke's question aims to prepare the ground for the *analogy* which he wishes to make, between the situation in the American colonies and that in England:

> 25. Is it not the same virtue which does everything for us here in England?

---

[11] The first case of transferred epithet seems happier than the second; since, in the latter case the insult is undercut by the following 'the empire is a machine' metaphor. If the empire is a machine, then 'mechanical' politicians would seem well-qualified to run it.

A positive response here from the audience will prepare the ground for the coming argument, implicit here (well, then, if it is the same virtue that does everything for us here in England, why deny it in the case of the colonies?).

6) *Expletive.* In Burke's speech, the only Expletives co-occur with the rhetorical questions, and represent the speaker providing the 'obvious answer':

> 26. Do you imagine, then, that it is the Land-Tax Act which raises your revenue? That it is the annual vote in the Committee of Supply, which gives you your army? or that it is the Mutiny Bill which inspires it with bravery and discipline?
>
> 27. No! surely, no!

Here, however, Burke seems to concede, via his 'surely', that there are others–perhaps, mindful of the term 'herd', used earlier, there may be *many*– who would disagree with him.

Adams and Churchill also use an Expletive, 'of course'; these, like Burke's 'surely', are instances of what Engagement theory calls concur, the representation of the speaker's confidence that the proposal/proposition will be accepted without demur by his audience. As well as their pragmatic force, in instances of this kind, Expletives clearly also exercise a focusing effect.

7) *Hyperbole.* This is, like Climax, a form of rhetoric that aims to persuade by excess. In the text, Burke represents the result desired by all; i.e., the reinforcement of the loyalty of the colonies to the British crown, and casts their allegiance in terms of intensified positive judgement:

> 9. no force under heaven will be of power to tear them from their allegiance (t + J: propriety, intens.)

This emphasises the desirability of the outcome by presenting it in an exaggerated form.

8) *Paradox.* There is only one, twice uttered paradox in Burke's speech, but it encapsulates the crux of his overall argument:

> 19. you break that sole bond which originally made, and must still preserve, the unity of the empire.

The centrality of this paradox–that granting the colonies their freedom is actually the only way to secure their allegiance–will be better appreciated once we have examined the argumentative structure of the speech.

9) *Procatalepsis.* This resource, too, is familiar from Engagement theory, being generally a form of dialogical contraction involving counter, or deny, in which the view of an opponent is enunciated only to be refuted or rejected in some way. In political rhetoric, it commonly takes the form of the 'Straw Man' technique, in which the speaker represents his opponents' views in a weakened form and then proceeds to refute them.

Argumentation, Metaphor and Analogy

Argumentative structure

Burke's overall argument is that the American colonies can only be 'kept' if, paradoxically, they are given their freedom. This is to see the question in a pragmatic light–how to attain the desirable real-world effect of keeping the American colonies. But Burke's vision of the British Empire raises him above the merely pragmatic, as he outlines an idealistic scenario of nations spontaneously adhering to British rule because they find in it a guarantee of the highest possible moral good, i.e. *freedom.* Implicit in this world view is a sense of comparison, that regards other colonial movements (e.g. those of Spain and Prussia, line 15) as denying this good to the peoples they conquer. His vision of empire requires that the men in charge, his current audience, be men of equally lofty vision, if the empire is not to degenerate into the exploitation of conquered races by 'vulgar and mechanical' politicians, whose only interest is for what is 'gross and material' (29). The ultimate sanction of Burke's vision is the Divine; politicians are urged to 'elevate [their] minds to the greatness of that trust to which the order of Providence has called [them]' (33).

There, is therefore a double focus to the argumentation in this speech (figure two, below). On the one hand, Burke makes a general plea for the importance of freedom as the paradoxical source of the cohesion of the Empire; on the other, he urges parliamentarians to rise to the sublimity of this world view–to reject a materialistic, exploitative vision of the empire, and realise instead the moral responsibilities that they have, as divinely appointed custodians of vital moral realities in different parts of the world.

Table 3.4. Argumentation, Burke speech.

TEXT: As long as you have the wisdom to keep the sovereign authority of this country as the sanctuary of liberty, the sacred temple consecrated to our common faith, wherever the chosen race and sons of England worship freedom, they will turn their faces towards you.		
Data	**Warrant**	**Claim**
(because)	(since)	(therefore)

The American colonists (the chosen race and sons of England) are currently in revolt	Freedom is the essence of 'authority' in this country	We should give the American colonists as much freedom as possible

TEXT: By adverting to the dignity of this high calling, our ancestors have turned a savage wilderness into a glorious empire, and have made the most extensive and the only honorable conquests, not by destroying, but by promoting the wealth, the number, the happiness of the human race.		
Data	**Warrant**	**Claim**
(because)	**(since)**	**(therefore)**
The empire was originally only a savage wilderness; its current glory is the result of past administrators promoting the happiness of conquered races rather than destroying them	Current MPs are responsible for running the empire	We too should rise to the dignity of this noble calling

The following sections explore the roles played by metaphor and analogy in the development of this argument.

Metaphor

Most writers on the subject agree that metaphor is a means of representing one aspect of experience in terms of another,[12] though in order to account for its role in persuasive processes, this basic notion needs some expansion. Charteris-Black's phrase 'persuasive subliminal communication' (2005, p. 570) is an apt description of its effects, while Chilton (2004, p. 52) speaks of its potential to activate inferences "almost spontaneously".

Carlshamre (2004)[13] points out that metaphor is conventionally regarded as the most beautiful of the tropes, and is the only one named by Aristotle in his Rhetoric. In many recent lists of tropes and schemes, metaphor is simply characterised as another trope.[14] It has been viewed, like them, as simply another aesthetically pleasing element, embellishing discourse that otherwise might seem dry or mundane. This traditional view of metaphor has been strongly challenged by Lakoff and Johnson's book *Metaphors We Live By*

---

[12] See, for example Lakoff & Johnson, 1980, pp. 8-9; Lakoff, 1993; Partington, 1998, p. 59; Fairclough, 2001, p. 99; Martin & Rose, 2003, p. 103; Chilton, 2004, pp. 51-2; Cienki, 2004, p. 409.

[13] "Carlshamre, Staffan. Metaphors in Text Semantics". See web references.

[14] Carlshamre dates the emergence of the tropological terminology to a period between Aristotle and Cicero.

(1980). There it is proposed that metaphor should be seen as a fundamental part of our cognitive make-up, one of the key ways in which humans organise their experience, and make sense of the world. Complex or abstract phenomena such as Love or Time, the authors argue, are experienced metaphorically, to such an extent that the processes have become habitual and therefore generally pass unnoticed. They posit the existence of what they call orientational metaphors (Lakoff & Johnson, 1980, p. 14), which condition not just our interpretation of reality but fundamental patterns of cognition. Human consciousness is driven, in their view, by such notions as UP is GOOD, and its corollary DOWN is BAD (ibid: 16). That UP IS GOOD is a basic human cognitive structure is reflected, according to Lakoff and Johnson, by its use in everyday language to indicate a variety of positive values, in various domains of life; for example, the spiritual/moral: *the highest, the moral high ground, uplifted, upright, raised from the dead, to have high moral standards;* the realm of feelings*: on an up, on a high, on top of the world, upbeat, over the moon, walking on air, etc.,* or the social realm*: top of the tree, top-notch, top dog, social climber,* and so on.[15]

Halliday (2001) explores the role of such cognitive mechanisms, in a discussion of the persuasive significance of the term growth, which is used as a positive-sounding metaphor in multiple social contexts. Economic growth, for example, is something which politicians know electors will vote for–despite the vagueness of the term–and in doing so, they are also influenced by the unconscious associations of the orientational metaphor GROWTH IS GOOD. Charteris-Black (2005, p. 5) also accounts for the persuasive power of Metaphor in ways that confirm Lakoff and Johnson's descriptions:

> Metaphor influences our beliefs, attitudes and values because it uses language to activate unconscious emotional associations and it influences the value that we place on ideas and beliefs on a scale of goodness and badness

Advertisers seem to concur with Lakoff and Johnson: a standard phrase like 'more bang for your buck' activates another of these orientational metaphors (MORE IS GOOD), aiming to create a sort of psychic lip-licking in message receivers, against which conscious effort has to be directed if the persuasive attempt is to be resisted.

---

[15] Partington (Partington, 1998, p. 113) finds the metaphors UP-DOWN extremely pervasive in the language of business.

For an example of metaphor employed as a persuasive rhetorical device, consider Burke's first use of metaphor, positioned at the very outset of the speech:

> 1. To restore order and repose to an empire so great and so distracted as ours is, merely in the attempt, an undertaking that would ennoble the flights of the highest genius, and obtain pardon for the efforts of the meanest understanding.

Here there seem to be three distinct metaphors:

1)   The empire is a madman;

2)   A genius is a bird;

3)   Feeble thinkers are criminals.

I shall return to the metaphor comparing the empire to a madman shortly; for the moment let us concentrate on the second; the conventional one that connects human genius with flight, a metaphor that goes back at least to the Greek legend of Icarus and Dedalus. Shortly after this speech was delivered, Burke's friend Dr. Johnson was to use it in a well-known comparison of the poets Pope and Dryden.[16] The explanation of its pragmatic, persuasive effect rests on how far we accept Lakoff and Johnson's theory of orientational metaphors. From their perspective, when we hear a speaker talking about 'the highest flights of genius', our decoding of the metaphor automatically activates processes of psychic selection, determined by our unconscious adherence to orientational metaphors. Burke's proposition, then, would be persuasive because it activates the unconscious emotional associations implicit in the orientational concepts of 'flight' and 'height'. Parenthetically, it must be observed that it is impossible to make claims with any certainty about the actual *effects* of any instance of metaphor, since Burke's audience is long-gone; the only way of determining this would have been to ask each listener about his reaction to the metaphor. This applies, *mutatis mutandis*, to any talk about the effects of rhetorical devices on actual audiences, and is the main reason why discourse analysis must concentrate on persuasion from the point of view of the resources and strategies available to speakers.

---

[16] 'If the flights of Dryden therefore are higher, Pope continues longer on the wing'. "Pope and Dryden From 'Lives Of The Poets' by Samuel Johnson". See web references.

The following table illustrates the metaphors found in Burke's speech, organised in terms of their themes:

Table 3.5. Metaphor.

Line	Theme	Metaphor
1. To restore order and repose to an empire so great and so distracted as ours	The Empire	The Empire is a madman, in need of repose and order
10. the cement is gone, the cohesion is loosened, and everything hastens to decay and dissolution.	The Empire	The Empire is a house
24. the spirit of the English constitution which, infused through the mighty mass, pervades, feeds, unites, invigorates, vivifies every part of the empire, even down to the minutest member.	The Empire	The Empire is a living organism
29. are not fit to turn a wheel in the machine.	The Empire	The Empire is a machine
7. not peace to be hunted	Peace	Peace is a hunted animal
8. simple peace, sought in its natural course	Peace	Peace is a river
8. and in its ordinary haunts	Peace	Peace is a forest animal
17. This is the commodity of price,	Freedom	Freedom is a commodity
18. This is the true Act of Navigation	Freedom	Freedom is a parliamentary act
19. you break that sole bond which originally made	Freedom	Freedom is a bond
1. merely in the attempt, an undertaking that would ennoble the flights of the highest genius	Genius	A genius is a bird
1. and obtain pardon for the efforts of the meanest understanding	The efforts of a mean understanding	Mean thoughts are criminals
2. Struggling a good while with these thoughts, by degrees I felt myself more firm	Thoughts	Thoughts are wrestlers
7. through the labyrinth of intricate and endless negotiations	Negotiations	Negotiations are a maze
9. they will cling and grapple to you	The colonies	The colonies are humans - clinging children (or wrestlers)

11. As long as you have the wisdom to keep the sovereign authority of this country as the <u>sanctuary of liberty, the sacred temple</u> consecrated to our common faith	The sovereign authority of this country	The authority is a sanctuary and a temple
14. It is a weed that grows in every soil	Slavery	Slavery is a weed
29. the profane herd of those vulgar and mechanical politicians	Politicians	Politicians are animals

Metaphors connect different domains of experience. Perelman and Olbrechts-Tyteca (1969, p. 373) call the subject of the metaphor–what we wish to characterise–the Theme, as in the table above. The second domain, which is mapped onto the former, or with which comparison is evoked, they term the Phoros. When, for example, slavery (theme) is characterised as a weed (phoros) (line 14), the question arises: in what respect can slavery be compared to weeds? The creativity of the recipient or hearer is therefore engaged, since they must endeavour to discover the Grounds of the comparison. This last term refers to the precise meaning of any metaphor, intended by the user and perceived by the recipient. The speaker is not, of course, using the metaphor to proclaim that slavery grows in gardens, or is generally green in colour. The force of the comparison is, rather, that slavery, like weeds, is found in many countries; that it tends to spring up despite the best efforts of gardeners (enlightened politicians) and that it has a choking, negative effect on the societies where it is allowed to flourish. A distinction has been made between genuine metaphors such as this one, and so-called 'dead' or 'dormant' metaphors, metaphors which have been used so often that they have passed into the language to the extent that no effort is necessary on the part of the recipient to decode them (the sands of time, the lap of luxury, into thin air, etc.).[17]

Considering the grounds of Burke's metaphors will help us to appreciate further their persuasive function. The empire, for example, is compared to:

---

[17] What Partington (1998, p. 119) calls a 'dead' metaphor–he gives the example of 'cash-flow', comparing money to a liquid, so frequently used that it has become 'genre-specific technical language'–Perelman and Olbrechts-Tyteca (1969, p. 405) term 'dormant'. Their idea is that such metaphors can be 'resuscitated' by, for example, developing the phoros: 'our cash has just flowed out of the door'.

Table 3.6. Metaphors for the empire: phoros and grounds.

Phoros	Grounds
1) A madman	Like a madman, parts of the empire break out into occasional fits of violent activity; they need order and repose rather than forceful repression
2) A house	If you remove the cement and mortar from a house it will collapse; and the same will happen to the empire if the colonists' faith that the government have their highest interests at heart is destroyed
3) A living organism	In the same way that the body is vivified by the life-force, or spirit of a person, so the empire is sustained by the spirit of the English constitution
4) A machine	Just as a machine needs responsible hands to guide it, so do the complex mechanisms of empire

The Grounds for these metaphors of empire are closely connected to aspects of the argumentative structure outlined above; the inferences of each seem to augment the persuasive force of the deontic proposal involved there. For example, with the first, the 'Empire is a madman' metaphor: the natural state of the colonies is order, calm, respect for the law, and so on. Just as a madman, temporarily distracted, needs soft handling and reassurance in order to pacify him, so tranquillity will be restored in the colonies by the same treatment. Alternative, more drastic solutions are warded off. It would be counter-productive to start beating a distracted lunatic with sticks or fists; these measures would only produce more violent convulsions.

The empire metaphors are also associated with evaluative language, which further heightens their persuasive force (Partington, 1998, p. 59; Ponton, 2011). We have already seen, for instance, how the mere attempt to restore order to the empire is associated with intensified positive judgements, with the flights of genius, and with moral nobility.

The two other major topics that Burke treats metaphorically are peace and freedom. The sylvan associations of his metaphors for peace seem particularly appropriate to a discourse on the American colonies, bearing in mind the vast wildernesses of the continent, as it would have appeared to an 18th-century audience:

It is simple peace, sought in its natural course and in its ordinary haunts

Table 3.7. Peace metaphor.

Phoros	Grounds
1) Peace	Like a river, peace is a natural state or phenomenon. Like a wild animal, peace is found everywhere

The seeker after peace, listeners might feel, need only wander through the American forests; peace will suddenly break upon his sight, like a mighty river. The simplicity of peace with America is contrasted to the labyrinthine complexity of peace negotiations, so familiar to the European context.

The metaphors for freedom, on the other hand, are curiously bureaucratic, relating to an *act*, a *commodity*, and a *bond*:

> 18. This [freedom] is the true Act of Navigation, which binds to you the commerce of the colonies, and through them secures to you the wealth of the world.

> 19. Deny them this participation of freedom, and you break that sole bond which originally made, and must still preserve, the unity of the empire.

In characterising freedom as an act, Burke is perhaps highlighting the fact that, like everything in the British Empire, it ultimately depends on the British parliament. The Grounds for the paradoxical metaphor of freedom as a bond would seem to be the following:

Table 3.8. Bond metaphor.

Phoros	Theme	Grounds
A bond	Freedom	In the same way that a bond ties one person to another, so granting another person their freedom–and guaranteeing it–creates a bond of gratitude, from recognition of what they stand to lose

A century or so later, another British statesman, W.E.Gladstone, in the context of Irish Home Rule, was advancing an analogous argument:

> Tightening the tie is frequently the means of making it burst, whilst relaxing the tie is very frequently the way to provide for its durability, and to enable it to stand a stronger strain (Vict. G:2)

Analogy

In order to further establish his point, Burke uses an analogy. This figure of speech is connected, by Perelman and Olbrechts-Tyteca (1969, p. 399), to metaphor, seeing the latter as a condensed form of the former. Analogical comparisons can have three or four terms. The four-term form is: A is to B as C is to D. Consider the following example, from the Washington Monthly online:

Corbyn is to the Labour Party what Bernie Sanders would have been to the Democratic Party, had he won–someone so far left as to be unable to get anything done.[18]

This example explicitly spells out the sense in which the analogy is to be taken, i.e. that Corbyn's political views are too far left for the practical realities of public life.

In the three-term form, the propositions have one term in common: A is to B as C is to B. In one of his speeches in 2003[19] on Iraq, for example, Blair compared Saddam Hussein to Hitler, developing an argument that rested on the following analogy:

Saddam is to world peace what Hitler was to world peace

Analogy works because the terms of the phoros present logical connections which the audience will readily appreciate (i.e. that Sanders' left-wing views make him unfit for governmental responsibility, or that Hitler was a menace to world peace). If they then accept that the situation represented by the theme is a true analogy, then the speaker's argument will be persuasive.

Burke also develops a four-term analogy, whose effectiveness depends on the establishment of the truth-value of a certain assertion; an epistemic rather than a deontic proposition. What is it he asks, in the final analysis, that enables the mighty machine of the empire to function smoothly? The empire works, not because of bureaucratic mechanisms, but because the whole structure is infused by the spirit of freedom. Freedom is the paradoxical 'bond' that alone can 'preserve the unity of empire' (line 19). This, as we saw above, is the warrant for Burke's argument as a whole. Bureaucratic and commercial instruments and objects, by contrast, are all afforded negative evaluation:

(from 21-22) your registers, bonds, affidavits, sufferances, cockets, clearances, letters of office, instructions, and your suspending clauses. These things do not make your government. <u>Dead</u> instruments, <u>passive</u> tools as they are (- App:Valuation)

Burke presents an analogy with the smooth operation of the British body politic, expecting his listeners to concur that the state runs smoothly because of

---

[18] "Quick Takes: More Brexit Fallout". See web references.
[19] "Blair, Tony. Full Text: Tony Blair's Speech. *The Guardian.* Guardian News and Media, 18 Mar. 2003". See web references.

the love of the people; [..] their attachment to their government, from
the sense of the deep stake they have in such a glorious institution (28)

They will, therefore, also accept his assessment of the importance of
freedom in the running of the empire. The analogy relates the following four
terms: freedom, the smooth running of the Empire, the love of the people, and
the smooth running of the English state:

Freedom is to the smooth running of the Empire

WHAT

The love of the people is to the smooth running of the English state

The persuasive force of the terms of the phoros (the comparison with the
English state) is augmented by the evaluative language in which these things
are presented, as well as by the use of Climax:

> 28. It is the <u>love</u> of the people (+ Aff: Affection); it is their <u>attachment</u>
> to their government (+ Aff: Affection), from the sense of the deep
> stake they have in such a glorious institution (+ App: Valuation,
> intens.), which gives you your army and your navy, and infuses into
> both that <u>liberal obedience</u> (+ J: propriety) without which your army
> would be a <u>base rabble</u> (- J: propriety) and your navy nothing but
> <u>rotten timber</u> (- J capacity).

The weak point of this analogy would seem to be, with the benefit of the
long perspective of history, that the state of affairs presented in the phoros is
not as self-evident as Burke might have wished. Burke's vision here, of love for
government and institutions as the primary cohesive force in British society,
strikes a highly idealistic note, at least to the modern ear. In this regard, the
collaboration of a historian would appear to be vital, since they could bring to
bear relevant information from the social context to explain how such an
assertion was likely to have been received by Burke's listeners. The persuasive
force of Burke's argument, ultimately, rests on this.

Concluding remarks

This study has explored the pragmatic functions of various rhetorical devices,
attempting to link them to the question of persuasion. We have seen how
metaphor and analogy have their place in the argumentative structure of
Burke's speech, and how the persuasive force of metaphor is augmented both
by the evaluative force of the individual metaphor, and by its association with
evaluative propositions.

Burke's argument ultimately rests on the analogy discussed above, which occupies a key place in the argumentative structure. The parallel is a coherent one, and points at an essential question regarding the nature of society. What is the essential nature of the social bond? Burke suggests that it is the love that the people feel for the institutions that are able to guarantee them every social good, and in particular their freedom. In the post-modern period, this is still a subject open to debate, but to appreciate its status in Burke's day would necessitate the collaboration of a specialist social historian or political philosopher. Such arguments have been pondered by philosophers since the time of Plato's Republic, with Hobbes's Leviathan (1660) a landmark in British political philosophy, and the Social Contract of Rousseau (1762), another notable contribution, in Burke's own day. Burke's argument, then, will be convincing to the extent that his listeners accept his view of the nature of the social contract.

Without a doubt, Burke's argument here would have been some way over the heads of the 'profane herd' of 'vulgar and mechanical' politicians who made up at least a part of his audience. Such considerations explain the exhortation, in the speech, for listening members to rise above pettiness, and interpret their roles with idealism as well as a sense of responsibility. Only from the kind of lofty perspective from which Burke is speaking about the realities of imperialism is it possible to characterise the relations involved as the free association, for mutual benefit, of different nations.

Although Burke's speech is a fitting representative of the more erudite political culture that, once graced the government of Britain; and, to that extent, can be seen as a voice from the past, there is also something curiously familiar about the discursive construction of a high-flown moral position when combined with a project of empire. It is tempting to compare Burke's stance on empire with more modern voices, which speak of the necessity to bring values like 'democracy', 'freedom', the 'rule of law', and so on, to far-flung places–a discourse which was frequently encountered, for example, in various international forums during debate on the merits of invading Iraq in 2003.

We have seen, then, how traditional rhetorical devices may fit into the model of political argumentation that is being developed in this book and, in particular, that they are not simply to be regarded as decorative resources, but rather that they may play a central role in the advancement of political argumentation.

Appendix

Text	Rhetorical figure
1. To restore order and repose to an empire so great and so distracted as ours is, merely in the attempt, an undertaking that would ennoble the flights of the highest genius, and obtain pardon for the efforts of the meanest understanding.	Parallelism Antithesis Metaphor
2. Struggling a good while with these thoughts, by degrees I felt myself more firm.	Ellipsis Metaphor
3. I derived, at length, some confidence from what in other circumstances usually produces timidity.	Antithesis
4. I grew less anxious, even from the idea of my own insignificance.	
5. For, judging of what you are by what you ought to be, I persuaded myself that you would not reject a reasonable proposition because it had nothing but its reason to recommend it.	Alliteration
6. The proposition is peace.	Alliteration
7. Not peace through the medium of war; not peace to be hunted through the labyrinth of intricate and endless negotiations; not peace to arise out of universal discord, fomented from principle, in all parts of the empire; not peace to depend on the juridical determination of perplexing questions, or the precise marking the shadowy boundaries of a complex government.	Anadiplosis (takes up 'peace', last word of previous phrase) Antithesis (peace through the medium of war) Parallelism in the infinitival phrases beginning 'not peace..' Allusion/metaphor (Peace is a minotaur, and negotiations a maze) Anaphora Amplification
8. It is simple peace, sought in its natural course and in its ordinary haunts.	Parallelism (prepositional phrases) Metaphor
9. Let the colonies always keep the idea of their civil rights associated with your government-they will cling and grapple to you, and no force under heaven will be of power to tear them from their allegiance.	Metaphor Hyperbole
10. But let it be once understood that your government may be one thing and their privileges another, that these two things may exist without any mutual relation - the cement is gone, the cohesion is loosened, and everything hastens to decay and dissolution.	Parallelism in participle phrases Metaphor Alliteration

11. As long as you have the wisdom to keep the sovereign authority of this country as the sanctuary of liberty, the sacred temple consecrated to our common faith, wherever the chosen race and sons of England worship freedom, they will turn their faces towards you.	Metaphor Allusion (Burke appropriates the 'chosen race' from the Jews for the English) Epithets (sovereign authority, sacred temple)
12. The more they multiply, the more friends you will have, the more ardently they love liberty, the more perfect will be their obedience.	Parallelism, anaphora Alliteration Paradox Antithesis
13. Slavery they can have anywhere.	Hyperbaton
14. It is a weed that grows in every soil.	Metaphor
15. They may have it from Spain, they may have it from Prussia.	Parallelism, anaphora
16. But until you become lost to all feeling of your true interest and your natural dignity, freedom they can have from none but you.	Parallelism 'your...' phrases Hyperbaton ('freedom' puts the object in thematic position)
17. This is the commodity of price, of which you have the monopoly.	Parallelism with 18 'This is..' Metaphor
18. This is the true Act of Navigation, which binds to you the commerce of the colonies, and through them secures to you the wealth of the world.	Alliteration Metaphor Diazeugma (binds...secures)
19. Deny them this participation of freedom, and you break that sole bond which originally made, and must still preserve, the unity of the empire.	Metaphor / Paradox Diazeugma (made...preserve)
20. Do not entertain so weak an imagination as that your registers and your bonds, your affidavits and your sufferances, your cockets and your clearances, are what form the great securities of your commerce.	Parallelism, hypozeugma (multiple subjects) Alliteration
21. Do not dream that your Letters of office, and your instructions, and your suspending clauses are the things that hold together the great contexture of this mysterious whole.	Parallelism with 20, Polysyndeton, hypozeugma
22. These things do not make your government.	
23. Dead instruments, passive tools as they are, it is the spirit of the English communion that gives all their life and efficacy to them.	Hyperbaton Antithesis Transferred epithet (dead instruments, passive tools)

24. It is the spirit of the English constitution which, infused through the mighty mass, pervades, feeds, unites, invigorates, vivifies every part of the empire, even down to the minutest member.	Parallelism, anaphora with 23 'It is…' Diazeugma Conduplicatio Metaphor Alliteration
25. Is it not the same virtue which does everything for us here in England?	Eritesis
26. Do you imagine, then, that it is the Land-Tax Act which raises your revenue? that it is the annual vote in the Committee of Supply, which gives you your army? or that it is the Mutiny Bill which inspires it with bravery and discipline?	Analogy Parallelism, anaphora / eritesis
27. No! surely, no!	Expletive
28. It is the love of the people; it is their attachment to their government, from the sense of the deep stake they have in such a glorious institution, which gives you your army and your navy, and infuses into both that liberal obedience without which your army would be a base rabble and your navy nothing but rotten timber.	Parallelism, anaphora in phrases with dummy 'it' Hypozeugma Hyperbole Epithet (rotten timber); Climax, Bicolon
29. All this, I know well enough, will sound wild and chimerical to the profane herd of those vulgar and mechanical politicians who have no place among us: a sort of people who think that nothing exists but what is gross and material, and who, therefore, far from being qualified to be directors of the great movement of empire, are not fit to turn a wheel in the machine.	Antithesis Procatalepsis Metaphor Hyperbole Transferred epithets (*Profane* herd, *mechanical* politicians)
30. But to men truly initiated and rightly taught, these ruling and master principles, which in the opinion of such men as I have mentioned have no substantial existence, are in truth everything, and all in all.	Antithesis
31. Magnanimity in politics is not seldom the truest wisdom; and a great empire and little minds go ill together.	Litotes (not seldom) Antithesis Epithet (Great empire, little minds)
32. If we are conscious of our situation, and glow with zeal to fill our places as becomes our station and ourselves, we ought to auspicate all our public proceedings on America with the old warning of the Church, Sursum corda!	Sententia (applies a maxim)
33. We ought to elevate our minds to the greatness of that trust to which the order of Providence has called us.	Allusion

34. By adverting to the dignity of this high calling, our ancestors have turned a savage wilderness into a glorious empire, and have made the most extensive and the only honorable conquests, not by destroying, but by promoting the *wealth, the number, the happiness of the human race.*	Antithesis Hyperbole Epithet (savage wilderness) Tricolon Asyndeton ('and' omitted at the ending list)
35. Let us get an American revenue as we have got an American empire.	Parallelism
36. English privileges have made it all that it is; English privileges alone will make it all it can be.	Parallelism, anaphora

Chapter 4

Benjamin Disraeli. Vindication of purchase of the Suez Canal shares, 14th Feb. 1876

Introduction

This study presents a consideration of persuasive rhetoric in a specifically *parliamentary* context. It focuses on the interplay in argumentation between the speaker's own argument, and the way it relates to potential challenges represented by alternative views, proposed by other speakers in the same debate. Parliamentary speeches of both modern and Victorian epochs are frequently heteroglossic, in White's sense of the term. In other words, although a speech is a monologue, such monologues are 'intertextually and contratextually interwoven as MPs respond to what has been said previously, not just in the House but elsewhere' (Bayley, 2004, p. 24). The study of Disraeli's speech will focus in part on the devices used by the speaker to reference the views of other participants in the debate, as well as how questions of stance and evaluation influence the persuasive effect of the speech as a whole.

The parliamentary context

Bayley (2004, p. 12) writes of parliament:

> Parliament, as the very etymology of the word suggests, is the site of discussion, of debate; its activity is linguistic activity, and the discourse of parliament results in (or is the final stage of a process which results in) concrete action in the outside world

Chapter One, above, dealt with differences between modern parliaments and their 19th-century counterparts, at the level of the prevailing lexical preferences for construing proposals. Some other significant differences in context must also be briefly discussed. Firstly, although the speech studied here presents the 'Tory' leader closely involved in a verbal tussle with the 'Liberal' leader–and hence would seem to be a 19th-century version of the kind of heated exchanges that characterise Prime Minister's question time in the Commons today–the apparent similarities need qualification. The two-party system that typifies modern British politics was in its infancy in the days of Disraeli and Gladstone. There was, of course, no Labour party, and the dividing line between the two large groups in the Commons was that referred to by Sir Robert Peel in a speech in 1838:

> The question only is–what, in a certain state of public opinion, and in a certain position of society, is the most effectual way of maintaining the legitimate influence and authority of a territorial aristocracy?[1]

The House of Lords, which consisted mainly of landed aristocrats, would have been in considerable cross-party agreement on this point. Secondly, a comparison of historical contexts also reveals the transformation that Britain's international role has undergone in the intervening period, declining from its position of undisputed world leader in the 19th century. Speeches from the former epoch are still characterised by a confidence in Britain's power, reflected in Disraeli's pronouncement in this speech:

> The argument that we are to do nothing–never dare to move, never try to increase our strength and improve our position, because we are afraid of complications is certainly a new view of English policy, and one which I believe the House of Commons will never sanction (27)

Despite these differences, however, parliament had the same legislative function that it enjoys today, and many of the essential procedures associated with this function were also present. Legislation had to be debated, voted on, the measure passed to the House of Lords, and so on. The two houses were, even more than today, sites of rhetorical confrontation and display, where speakers really practised the arts of verbal persuasion. Although Bayley casts doubt over the possibility of today's politicians succeeding in changing voting outcomes, this would seem to be more a feature of modern parliaments. Tighter party organisation, and in particular the greater effectiveness of the whips, means that modern MPs have little effective freedom in this sense, but these mechanisms were largely unknown in the 19th century.

Socio-historical context

We can think of the foregoing description of the parliamentary context as part of the immediate/medium-term socio-political context, remembering Hyatt's checklist of relevant context information, presented above. In this sense, we will also need to know some details about the purchase of the Suez Canal, and

---

[1] "Bloy, Marjorie, Dr. The Peel Web. *A Web of English History.*" See web references.

some of the individuals involved, Hyatt's third feature. The study is also interesting in terms of Hyatt's fourth category:

> iv) Epoch, or what counts as knowledge or truth in a particular era. This might include the various assumptions of order, structures of inclusion and exclusion and generally how a society legitimates itself and achieves its social identity. (Hyatt, 2005, pp. 521-523)

Consideration of a parameter such as 'structures of inclusion and exclusion' draws attention to fundamental differences between the parliamentary context in the nineteenth century and that in the modern period. Lines of social demarcation, in Disraeli's time, had softened somewhat when compared with those of the eighteenth century which, as we have seen, excluded from parliamentary representation most outside the ranks of the landed gentry; but they were still a far cry from our own day. There would have been no women MPs listening to Disraeli, nor would women have voted for him, for example. Part of the epoch factor also relates to the possession of an Empire, which was arguably at its apex during the years of Disraeli's career. Disraeli's speech here is infused with an almost tangible sense of power, of control over global events of the highest importance, which is quite absent from British parliamentary rhetoric today.

Britain's imperial possessions reached their furthest extent in the 19th century. During the first part of Queen Victoria's reign, the empire was in a phase of relative stability; no major gains were made, but the period saw Britain prosper thanks to cheap raw materials from her colonial possessions and the presence of ready markets for her manufactured goods. One such market, India, was of particular strategic importance to the cotton trade, and the opening of the Suez Canal in 1869 made possible the establishment of a secure and rapid route between the two nations. The canal project had been supported by Britain, but was funded mainly by the Egyptian Khedive. During the summer parliamentary recess of 1875, because of the Khedive's financial difficulties, the opportunity arose to purchase his shares, which amounted to almost 50% of the total. In this way, though Britain would not be acquiring a controlling interest in the canal, it would enjoy significant influence. Disraeli, the British Prime Minister at the time decided to act swiftly, without waiting for parliament's return to ratify the scheme. He did, however, have the support of Queen Victoria, and was able to borrow the necessary sum from the Rothschild family. The debate in which this speech occurs was for the subsequent ratification of Disraeli's action.

Argumentation: expressed opinion

The explicit argument advanced by Disraeli is that the purchase of the Suez Canal shares should be ratified by parliament (see Appendix B). Disraeli's first concern is to dispose of various critical points raised by opponents during the earlier part of the debate, which involves the rhetorical device of *procatalepsis*; representing the views of opponents only to show that their arguments are wrong. It will be noticed that Disraeli uses the device of Quoting (Martin & White, 2005, p. 36) to represent the views of Gladstone. It is, unfortunately, not possible to know how accurately he reports what his opponent actually said. As Caldas-Coulthard (1994, pp. 296-7) points out, such representations in argumentation are generally partial at best, and speakers can perpetrate the 'straw man' technique, that is, to present a rhetorical version of an opponent's argument that can easily be knocked over (Damer, 2005, p. 183)[2] Before he advances his own argument in favour of the proposal, there is a sequence of these objections, that Disraeli deals with in turn.

The argumentative structure of this section, then, in terms of the Toulmin model, is as follows:

Table 4.1. Argumentative structure, opening section.

TEXT: I have always, and do now recommend it to the country as a political transaction, and one which I believe is calculated to strengthen the Empire (128)		
Data	**Warrant**	**Claim**
(because)	**(since)**	**(therefore)**
Her Majesty's government has purchased a substantial quantity of Suez Canal shares	This is a sound political transaction that will strengthen the Empire (line 128)	We should ratify the purchase (lines 116-117)

Here it is worthwhile adding another element in Toulmin's model of argumentation, what he calls a 'rebuttal' clause; this can generally be introduced by the conjunctive adverb 'unless', and indicates conditions under which the claim will be invalid. In this case, it would be as follows:

---

[2] Damer (2005, p. 183) comments: A successful attack on this straw-like substitute is not a successful attack on the *actual* position or argument of the opponent. A good argument must effectively address the *strongest* version of a position or argument on the other side of an issue.

UNLESS: you accept some of the arguments put forward by opponents (e.g. in lines 1-102)

The various arguments that Disraeli turns aside to deal with during the first part of this extract, can therefore be seen as constituting *Rebuttal* clauses, whose acceptance, by listeners, would lead to the defeat of his argument. Before examining Disraeli's argument in favour of the proposal, I shall first examine how he attempts to defeat some of these potential rebuttals.

The first objection

The first potential rebuttal occurs in the summary of Gladstone's argument in lines 1 - 13:

1. The right honourable Gentleman takes a position from which

2. it is certainly difficult to dislodge him, because it is perfectly

3. arbitrary.

4. He says - "You have no votes."

5. He views the question abstractedly.

6. He says - "Here is a company, and you have a great many

7. shares in it, but you are not allowed to vote, and therefore it

8. follows you can have no influence."

9. But everybody knows that in the world things are not managed

10. in that way, and that if you have a large amount of capital in

11. any concern, whatever may be the restrictions under which it

12. is invested, the capitalist does exercise influence.

The represented argument is as follows:

Table 4.2. Argumentative structure, Gladstone's first objection.

TEXT: you are not allowed to vote, and therefore it follows you can have no influence (6-8)		
Data	**Warrant**	**Claim**
(because)	(since)	(therefore)
You have a great many shares, but you cannot vote	Shareholders who cannot vote have no influence	You have no influence

Disraeli defeats this argument by attacking the Warrant, appealing to real-world facts that 'everybody knows'; even shareholders who cannot vote, if they have a large enough amount of capital, exercise influence. As will be seen for the second objection, the argument presented and defeated here by Disraeli is not a particularly strong one; thus, we might feel that he has used the straw man technique just described.

Gladstone's second objection: evaluation and stance

Gladstone's views are also involved in the second potential rebuttal, and here I shall begin to look at the roles played by both evaluation and intersubjective stance in the refutation of the argument, using some of the categories described, above, in the discussion of Martin and White's taxonomy of Engagement resources. The relevant passage is lines 14-27:

Table 4.3. Gladstone's second objection.

	Text	Stance	Attitude
14	'Then the right honourable Gentleman says - [Quoting]	ACKNOWLEDGE	i) - J capacity,
15	'You have no real control (i) over the purchase you have		
16	made; and yet that purchase will lead to great	PRONOUNCE	ii) - App
17	complications (ii).'		composition,
18	Sir, I have no doubt that complications will occur. They	MONOGLOSS	complexity
19	always have occurred, and I should like to know the state		
20	of affairs and of society in which complications do not		
21	and will not occur. *We are here to guard the country* (iii)		iii) + J capacity
22	against complications, and to guide it in the event of		
23	complications; [Reporting] and the argument that we are	COUNTER	
24	to do nothing - *never dare to move, never try to increase*	[JUSTIFICATION]	iv) t- Aff
25	*our strength and improve our position* (iv), [because] we		disinclination,
26	are afraid of complications (v) is certainly a new view of		fear
27	English policy, and one which I believe the House of	PRONOUNCE/	v) t - J tenacity,
	Commons will never sanction.'	CONCUR	high

Disraeli's representation of the views expressed by his opponents is construed via the heteroglossic resource of acknowledge and the rhetorical device of Quoting. The argument has the following basic outline:

Table 4.4. Argumentation, Gladstone's second objection.

Data	Warrant	Claim
(because)	(since)	(therefore)
The purchase of the Suez Canal shares will involve us in great complications (16-17)	We are afraid of complications	We should do nothing - (never dare to move, never try to increase our strength and improve our position) (23-25)

If we consider the evaluative force of the terms involved in Disraeli's reconstruction of Gladstone's argument, we can appreciate how the argument, as presented, assists in its own defeat. The warrant supposes Her Majesty's proud imperial government to be 'afraid' (- Affect disinclination, fear) of something so trivial as 'complications'; this negative state of mind evokes a strong negative judgement, as Disraeli shows the government paralysed by fear. It seems improbable that Gladstone would have committed himself to such an untenable position; more likely that Disraeli has constructed, and defeated, another straw man. The switch from Quoting in line 15-17 to Reporting in line 23 could be of significance in this regard. In the former case, Disraeli cites Gladstone's actual words, while in the second, he provides a gloss, which, naturally, may not correspond exactly with the original.

Dialogically, this exchange is rather curious, since we find the speaker conceding the correctness of an opponent's view, somewhat unusual in debating. The notion that complications will result from the purchase is a serious criticism, however, it is such only if the complications represent consequences which would, in the view of the House, outweigh any benefit accruing from the purchase of the shares. Either Gladstone did not sufficiently specify the nature of these complications, or else Disraeli has performed the straw man operation, since he is able to effectively trivialise Gladstone's objection. This exchange is an instance of the palpable sense of imperial power with which the whole speech is infused.

The extract illustrates, once again, the essentially parliamentary orientation of much 19th-century political rhetoric. Instead of expanding on the possible real-world effects covered by the term 'complications', Disraeli focuses on the role of parliament in dealing with whatever those complications might be. The monogloss, with its use of inclusive 'we' (21) explicitly highlights this role, containing an implicit positive judgement on the institution of parliament, emphasising parliament's importance by excluding the rest of 'the country':

We are here to guard the country against complications (t + J capacity)

Far from representing a reason to reject the proposal before the House, then, Gladstone's objections are re-contextualised into a flattering reference to parliament's capability of dealing with potential complications.

The remaining objections: heteroglossia

Questions of dialogical stance in this section of the speech have a recursive quality, with Disraeli, for example, *commenting* on what the Marquess of Hartington *said* about what the Chancellor of the Exchequer *said* about Gladstone's *objection*. Examples of this fourfold heteroglossia are presented in the following table, where '<', followed by the relevant resource, indicates dialogical expansion, and '>' dialogical contraction (White, 2003). Relevant verbs are underlined, and speech marks in the 'Stance' column indicate direct speech (table five):

Table 4.5. Heteroglossia (i).

Line		Stance
30	But the noble Lord (The Marquess of Hartington) who	Disraeli < "acknowledges" Hartington
31	has just addressed us <u>says</u> many points were made by	Hartington < acknowledges Gladstone
32	the right honourable Gentleman which the Chancellor	
33	of the Exchequer did not <u>answer</u>.	Hartington > denies Chancellor

Disraeli now proceeds to go through a list of the points allegedly not answered by the Chancellor. The first collapses as Gladstone intervenes in direct speech to deny that Hartington's original representation of his views was accurate:

> (34) There is no precedent of a British Ministry treating with a private firm; my right honourable Friend did not answer that. [Mr. Gladstone: I did not say so.] The right honourable Gentleman, however, says he made no observation of the kind.

The following references show the typical pattern that Disraeli uses in this section; expansive as he represents the objections of Hartington or Gladstone; contractive as he uses the bare assertion to counter or deny these objections in fairly summary fashion, using the resource of pronounce to further contract the dialogical space:

Table 4.6. Heteroglossia (ii).

Line		Stance
39	Then the noble Lord <u>says</u> my right honourable Friend	Disraeli < "acknowledges" Hartington
40	never <u>answered</u> the charge about speculations in Egyptian	Hartington > denies Chancellor
41	Stock. Well, I have <u>answered</u> that charge.	Disraeli > "counters" Hartington
42	The noble Lord <u>says</u> my right honourable Friend	Disraeli < "acknowledges" Hartington
43	never <u>touched upon</u> the amount of the commission.	Hartington > denies Chancellor
44	I have <u>touched upon</u> it.	Disraeli > "counters" Hartington

This curt, dialogically contractive way of dealing with the objections raised by the opposition perhaps shows that Disraeli believes the House will need no further persuasion. A straightforward pattern is preferred to the more thorough argumentative treatment afforded to other propositions, such as that examined above. The table below summarises the various objections that Disraeli deals with, together with the engagement resource he employs:

Table 4.7. Disraeli's responses.

Line	Stance	Construed by
9	COUNTER/PRONOUNCE	Everybody knows
26-27	COUNTER/PRONOUNCE	One which I believe the House of Commons will never sanction
34-35	(WITHDRAWN BY GLADSTONE)	
41	COUNTER/PRONOUNCE	My right honourable Friend never answered the charge...I *have answered* that charge.
44	COUNTER/PRONOUNCE	Never touched upon the amount of the commission...I *have touched upon it.*

Dismissal of opponents' points tends to abruptness, generally a simple counter or deny, with a considerable emphasis on Disraeli's own authority, via pronounce and use of the first person pronoun 'I'. Where the objection is deemed worthy of more extensive treatment, as in the examples already analysed above, Disraeli offers a more complete version of the opposing argument and attempts to defeat the Warrant, as we saw in the extract dealing with 'complications'. Lines 74-85 contain the final example of this, as he offers the following summary of another argument by Gladstone:

Table 4.8. Argumentation, Gladstone's final objection.

Data	Warrant	Claim
(because)	(since)	(therefore)
We abandoned a strong position for one of a more doubtful character (74-75)	The duty of government is to adopt the strongest positions possible	We were wrong to do this

Here Disraeli attacks, not the Warrant, but the Data; he denies the factuality of his opponent's assertions, offering instead a different version of a *realis* situation. Where Gladstone speaks of a former 'strong position', Disraeli evokes a different picture and, by the contractive resource of endorse, slyly involves opposition politicians in his own assessment:

(86-92) The work [the International Commission] did was greatly assisted by our Predecessors, and by a number of other able and eminent men; but, as I have said, no one who remembers all the circumstances of the case and what has occurred since, can for a moment pretend that our position with regard to the Canal was then satisfactory.

This is a typical parliamentary resource, familiar also in our own day, which consists of blaming the previous government for current problems. However, Disraeli applies it with considerable subtlety here, especially by his use of positive evaluation of the unnamed 'able and eminent men' (+ J: capacity), which makes it harder for these politicians of the opposition to eventually disclaim their own roles in the affair. He insinuates, in fact, that these authorities might have shared his own negative evaluation (- Appreciation, Valuation) of 'our position with regard to the Canal'. Use of the projecting verb 'pretend', with its evaluative semantics (- J: veracity), instead of a neutral choice such as 'think', 'maintain' or 'suggest' is another deft touch. The alternative view–that our position with regard to the canal *was* satisfactory–

can only be maintained, says Disraeli, through an act of verbal deception. The proposition that 'our position with regard to the Canal was satisfactory', then, is effectively countered.

Disraeli finally offers an argument in justification of his contention that the position is stronger than Gladstone believes:

> 103-105. I feel that at this moment our position is much stronger, and for the reason that we are possessors of a great portion of the capital invested in the Canal.

This argument rests on the same warrant as that used to defeat the first objection, discussed above, i.e. that possession of shares in a business provides a capitalist with influence. The supporting notion that this proposition is something that 'everybody knows', is here left implicit.

Disraeli next attacks Gladstone's arguments in a general way; pausing, as it were, for breath after dealing with the first eight objections, he passes the following evaluative comments on the objections as a whole:

> 48-54. These are matters which to a great degree must be matters of opinion; but the most remarkable feature of the <u>long harangue</u> (t - App Reaction, Impact) of the right honourable Gentleman the Member for Greenwich is that it was in a great degree a series of <u>assumptions, abstract reasonings, and arbitrary conclusions</u> (- App Valuation), after which he sat down quite surprised that the Vote should be passed unanimously, and requesting his allies to attack us for not answering that which we have felt <u>not to be substantial</u> (- App Valuation), but to consist of assumptions which we believe experience will prove to be <u>entirely false</u> (t - J veracity).

Having thus summed up his opponents' views and dealt with possible objections to his own position, Disraeli proceeds to outline the expressed opinion for which he is seeking parliamentary approval.

The expressed opinion: we should vindicate the purchase

Disraeli finally enunciates the explicit proposal for which the entire speech has been preparation, announcing it with a high-intensity modal of obligation:

> 116. What we <u>have to</u> do tonight is to agree to the Vote for the purchase of these shares.

His principal argument is contained in the third proposition of a tricolon that has the form of 'Not A, Not B, But C', in which the first two terms deny that consent is being sought on commercial or financial grounds; Disraeli's principal recommendation for the scheme is its political benefit:

> 117-130. I have never recommended, and I do not now recommend this purchase as a financial investment. I do not recommend it either as a commercial speculation although I believe that many of those who have looked upon it with little favour will probably be surprised with the pecuniary results of the purchase. I have always, and do now recommend it to the country as a political transaction, and one which I believe is calculated to strengthen the Empire.

Argumentation here is as follows (table nine):

Table 4.9. Argumentation, Disraeli's expressed opinion.

Data	Warrant	Claim
(because)	(since)	(therefore)
Her Majesty's government has purchased a substantial quantity of Suez Canal shares	Political transactions that strengthen the Empire are desirable	We should ratify the purchase

A possible 'rebuttal' section can be added to this picture, as follows:

> UNLESS you accept some of the opposition's arguments - which, however, have all been refuted

We could also further enrich the picture with another refinement of Toulmin's model, that of 'backing' for the warrant (Toulmin, 1958, p. 95), a component which has the function of strengthening the warrant with additional arguments, for instance:

Table 4.10. Disraeli's argument: Backing.

1. The British public want the Empire to be maintained, strengthened, increased (line 136) 2. The British public think we are obtaining a great hold [...] in Africa, and [...] they believe that it secures us a highway to our Indian Empire and our other dependencies (lines 138-141)

Of interest is the fact that backing for the warrant is construed in terms of what the British public ('the country') *think* of the proposal, what they *believe*, and what they *want*. Disraeli's final justification does not refer to the proposal itself; i.e. that we should ratify the purchase because, for example, it greatly strengthens the Empire. Rather, he uses another argument which rests on an implicit warrant, one that points towards the development of representative parliamentary democracy in Britain, as the following diagram shows:

Table 4.11. Disraeli's expressed opinion: implicit warrant.

Data	Warrant	Claim
(because)	**(since)**	**(therefore)**
The country thinks: 1) we are obtaining a great hold and interest in […] Africa 2) it secures to us a highway to our Indian Empire and our other dependencies 3) the step displays propriety and wisdom	The duty of government is to interpret the will of the country	We should ratify the purchase

What Disraeli means by 'the country' is not quite the same thing as a politician referring to 'the British people' today would mean; nevertheless, that Disraeli's final, conclusive rhetorical shot aligns the perspicacity of the country against the obtuseness of opposition politicians is, we might feel, a modern touch.

Table twelve sums up the dialogical work in Disraeli's enunciation of his expressed opinion:

Table 4.12. Evaluation and Attitude.

Line	Text	Attitude	Stance
128 129 130	I have always, and do now recommend it to the country as a political transaction, and one which I believe is *calculated to strengthen the Empire (i)*	i) t + App Valuation	PRONOUNCE
131 132 133	That is the spirit in which it has been accepted by *the country, which understands it* (ii) though the *two right honourable critics may not (iii)*.	ii)t+ J capacity; iii)t - J capacity	ENDORSE
134 135 136 137	They are really <u>seasick of the 'Silver Streak.'</u>(iv) (The English Channel). They want the Empire *to be maintained, to be strengthened; they will not be alarmed even it be increased (v)*.	iv)Affect: unhappiness; v)t + J capacity vi) + App Valuation;	ACKNOWLEDGE ENDORSE
138 139	Because they think we are obtaining a <u>great hold and interest</u>(vi) in this <u>important portion</u>(vii) of Africa -	vii) + App Valuation;	ENDORSE

140	because they believe that *it secures to us a highway to*	viii) t + App	JUSTIFICATION
141	*our Indian Empire and our other dependencies(viii)*,	Valuation;	
142	the people of England have from the first recognized		
143	the propriety and the wisdom(ix) of the step which	ix) + J propriety	
	we shall sanction tonight.		

A generally contractive dialogical pattern is found here too, as Disraeli foregrounds his own subjective evaluations. The force of the appeal to the country, although it uses the expansive device of, is also contractive, since the speaker uses the references to endorse his own positions.

Concluding remarks

This study has illustrated the usefulness of an approach to argumentation that considers a speaker's use of dialogical stances, alongside the deployment of evaluative language, in an attempt to achieve alignment of his listeners with his own views. Disraeli's dialogical stances, which tend to the contractive pole, are probably influenced by his knowledge that a substantial basis of consensus existed on the question at the outset of the debate. He refers to Gladstone's 'surprise' at the unanimity which was demonstrated in lines 69-70; and, as we have seen, he rebuffs a fair number of objections with a simple assertion. The purchase of the Suez Canal shares was undoubtedly a political coup for Disraeli, offering attractive prospects for Britain that even his opponents could hardly deny. In Disraeli's recognition of the importance of the views of the enfranchised portion of the British public, the discourse briefly goes beyond its typically Victorian orientation to the parliamentary setting, prefiguring the more modern conception of politicians as representative figures, interpreting the 'will of the people', and posturing towards them in an attempt to secure a wider base of consent than afforded by the immediate parliamentary context.

In terms of the model for the analysis of argumentation in political discourse, the chapter has added two more possible features of an argument in its references to Toulmin's categories of Rebuttal and Backing. Naturally, these need not be applied in every case, but may serve in situations in which analysis wishes to highlight these aspects. The same goes for the question of stance, which can safely be omitted from certain studies of argumentation but may be central to others.

Appendix: Disraeli's speech on the Suez Canal, 14/02/1876[3]

1	The right honourable Gentleman takes a position from which
2	it is certainly difficult to dislodge him, because it is perfectly
3	arbitrary.
4	He says - "You have no votes."
5	He views the question abstractedly.
6	He says - "Here is a company, and you have a great many
7	shares in it, but you are not allowed to vote, and therefore it
8	follows you can have no influence."
9	But everybody knows that in the world things are not
10	managed in that way, and that if you have a large amount of
11	capital in any concern, whatever may be the restrictions under
12	which it is invested, the capitalist does exercise influence.
13	Then the right honourable Gentleman says - "You have no real
14	control over the purchase you have made; and yet that
15	purchase will lead to great complications."
16	Sir, I have no doubt that complications will occur.
17	They always have occurred, and I should like to know the state
18	of affairs and of society in which complications do not and
19	will not occur.
20	We are here to guard the country against complications, and
21	to guide it in the event of complications; and the argument
22	that we are to do nothing - never dare to move, never try to
23	increase our strength and improve our position, because we
24	are afraid of complications is certainly a new view of English
25	policy, and one which I believe the House of Commons will
26	never sanction.
27	I think under these two heads all the criticisms of the right
28	honourable Gentleman are contained.
29	But the noble Lord (The Marquess of Hartington) who has just
30	addressed us says many points were made by the right
31	honourable Gentleman which the Chancellor of the
32	Exchequer did not answer.
33	There is no precedent of a British Ministry treating with a
34	private firm; my right honourable Friend did not answer that.
35	[Mr. Gladstone: I did not say so.]
36	The right honourable Gentleman, however, says he made no
37	observation of the kind.
38	Then the noble Lord says my right honourable Friend never
39	answered the charge about speculations in Egyptian Stock.
40	Well, I have answered that charge.
41	The noble Lord says my right honourable Friend never
42	touched upon the amount of the commission.
43	I have touched upon it.

---

[3] "Suez Canal Shares". See web references.

44	He says that we never thoroughly cleared ourselves from the
45	charge of not buying the 15 per cent shares.
46	I am here to vindicate our conduct on that point. In purchasing
47	the shares we did, we purchased what we wanted, we gained the
48	end we wished, and why we should involve the country in
49	another purchase, when we should thereby only have repeated
50	the result we had already achieved I cannot understand.
51	The noble Lord says my right honourable Friend never
52	expressed what expectations we had of receiving the £200,000
53	a-year from the Khedive, but we do not suppose that interest
54	which is at the rate of 5 per cent is quite as secure as it would
55	be if it were at the rate of 3¼ per cent.
56	Then the noble Lord says that my right honourable Friend
57	never met the charge of the right honourable Gentleman that
58	our policy would lead to complications with other nations.
59	We believe, on the contrary, that, instead of leading to
60	complications with other nations, the step which we have
61	taken is one which will avert complications.
62	These are matters which to a great degree must be matters of
63	opinion; but the most remarkable feature of the long harangue
64	of the right honourable Gentleman the Member for
65	Greenwich is that it was in a great degree a series of
66	assumptions, abstract reasonings, and arbitrary conclusions,
67	after which he sat down quite surprised that the Vote should
68	be passed unanimously, and requesting his allies to attack us
69	for not answering that which we have felt not to be
70	substantial, but to consist of assumptions which we believe
71	experience will prove to be entirely false.
72	The right honourable Gentleman charged us, lastly, with not
73	having answered a charge of having abandoned a strong
74	position.
75	The right honourable Gentleman pictured us as having been
76	in a good position before this - a position which he charged us
77	with having abandoned for one of a more doubtful character.
78	Here again, what proof does he bring of the charge he makes?
79	We found ourselves in a position which has been called a
80	strong position, but we could not for a moment think that our
81	position with regard to the Canal was satisfactory.
82	The International Commission sat, as honourable Members
83	know, before the Conservatives acceded to power, and the
84	work it did was greatly assisted by our Predecessors, and by a
85	number of other able and eminent men; but, as I have said, no
86	one who remembers all the circumstances of the case and
87	what has occurred since, can for a moment pretend that our
88	position with regard to the Canal was then satisfactory.
89	At the moment Turkey was in a very different position from
90	that which she occupies at present, as far as authority is
91	concerned.
92	The Khedive himself was in a very good position; and yet
93	those who are familiar with what occurred at that time know

94	the great difficulties which the Government experienced, and
95	the very doubtful manner in which, for a considerable time,
96	affairs looked with regard to the whole business.
97	Therefore I do not agree with the right honourable
98	Gentleman. I feel that at this moment our position is much
99	stronger, and for the reason that we are possessors of a great
100	portion of the capital invested in the Canal.
101	The noble Lord himself has expressed great dissatisfaction,
102	because I have not told him what the conduct of the
103	Government would be with regard to the Canal in a time of
104	war.
105	I must say that on this subject I wish to retain my reserve.
106	I cannot conceive anything more imprudent than a discussion
107	in this House at the present time as to the conduct of England
108	with regard to the Suez Canal in time of war, and I shall
109	therefore decline to enter upon any discussion on the subject.
110	What we have to do tonight is to agree to the Vote for the
111	purchase of these shares.
112	I have never recommended, and I do not now recommend this
113	purchase as a financial investment.
114	If it gave us ten per cent of interest and a security as good as
115	the Consols, I do not think an English Minister would be
116	justified in making such an investment; still less if he is
117	obliged to borrow the money for the occasion.
118	I do not recommend it either as a commercial speculation
119	although I believe that many of those who have looked upon it
120	with little favour will probably be surprised with the pecuniary
121	results of the purchase.
122	I have always, and do now recommend it to the country as a
123	political transaction, and one which I believe is calculated to
124	strengthen the Empire.
125	That is the spirit in which it has been accepted by the country,
126	which understands it though the two right honourable critics
127	may not.
128	They are really seasick of the "Silver Streak." (The English
129	Channel).
130	They want the Empire to be maintained, to be strengthened;
131	they will not be alarmed even it be increased.
132	Because they think we are obtaining a great hold and interest
133	in this important portion of Africa - because they believe that
134	it secures to us a highway to our Indian Empire and our other
135	dependencies, the people of England have from the first
136	recognized the propriety and the wisdom of the step which we
137	shall sanction tonight.

Chapter 5

Winston Churchill's speech:
'their finest hour', June 18ᵗʰ 1940

This chapter explores the insights that can be gained from an approach based on the analysis of the representation of social actors, integrating this with the Appraisal Framework to assess the speaker's use of evaluative language.

With this analysis of one of Churchill's speeches, the book moves towards the modern period. Certain important socio-cultural changes, that affect the speaker's relations with his audience, must be borne in mind here, and for the rest of the book. Many of Churchill's parliamentary speeches were adapted for broadcast to the nation and, while it is clear that one of his rhetorical aims is to inform parliament of unfolding events, and seek consensus for his preferred policies, it is equally certain that he aimed to take advantage of the possibilities offered by the technology of his time, to reach a wider audience. He is arguably the first modern politician in this sense, addressing himself to the task of influencing not just events in parliament, but the mood of a whole nation. Indeed, the speech selected here, one of his most celebrated wartime addresses, could be seen as having as its aim the intangible one of improving the nation's morale, rather than of achieving any specific goal in the parliamentary context.

Churchill avoids direct deontic proposals in this speech; instead, the persuasive effect is realised, to a considerable degree, via patterns of representation of the social actors involved in the conflict. His representation of the Allied forces suggests that they are superior to their German counterparts, despite the force of recent events. To the extent that this is accepted by the listening population, it will have the desired effect on their morale.

Historical background: the Second World War

Churchill is celebrated for his oratory and wrote his own speeches. The speech studied here is one of his best-known, an exhortation to the British people, that terminates with the often-quoted lines:

> Let us therefore brace ourselves to our duties, and so bear ourselves that, if the British Empire and its Commonwealth last for a thousand years, men will still say, 'This was their finest hour.'

With Churchill in mind, Charteris-Black (2005, p. 32) aptly writes that:

> The politician who attached great importance to oratory in the classical sense was also the one who had the greatest opportunity to employ it for that most vital of political objectives: national survival

This speech was given at a particularly dramatic moment in the Second World War, just after the Dunkirk evacuation had turned a desperate military scenario into a kind of triumph, though Churchill was at pains to temper national rejoicing with his admonition that "wars are not won by evacuations" (James, 1980, p. 711).

British and French policy towards Hitler had been dominated, in the 1930s, by appeasement, the political expression of a more general desire to avoid a second military conflagration. Following the First World War, the French placed their trust in the Maginot line, a chain of forts which stretched from Switzerland to their borders with Belgium and Luxembourg. The line finished at the forest of Ardennes and, because of the hilly nature of the terrain, a major German offensive through the forest was considered impossible. The attack was expected near Liege, from where they could penetrate into the flatlands of Flanders. However, in a manoeuvre that demonstrated considerable military verve, the Germans moved their forces through the forest, and began a push to the coast to cut Allied lines, stranding the British Expeditionary Force in Belgium. The Allies were confounded by the rapid new methods the Germans had developed with their armoured columns, and were trapped in and around the town of Dunkirk.

A desperate mission to bring off the surviving troops was launched, involving improvised convoys of fishing boats and other vessels from the British channel ports, which succeeded beyond Churchill's most optimistic expectations. This was largely due to the efforts of the volunteer sailors, the Royal Air Force, and the fact that the German commander had decided to rest his columns, which had suffered heavy losses during the campaign. The success of the Dunkirk operation gave Churchill the chance in this speech to strike a positive note. He mentions, in fact, that he had feared that his task would, instead, have been to announce the loss of the entire force, over 300,000 fighting men (James, 1980, p. 709).

'Us' and 'Them', the representation of social actors

A methodological tool that accounts for the rhetorical significance of patterns of representation of social actors is offered by Theo Van Leeuwen's 1996 study, which focuses on grammatical features such as agency and activation/passivation, and sees the phenomena of inclusion/exclusion as central features of representational strategy. The various categories in his taxonomy will be briefly presented as they are used in the analysis.[1] The study also attempts to incorporate the more complete attitudinal descriptions of the Appraisal Framework into Van Leeuwen's method, where the approach to evaluative language, termed 'appraisement', is less fully developed.

A feature of wartime political rhetoric, probably as old as human conflict itself, is the polarisation that takes place at the discursive level into two great camps, 'us' and 'them'. At the level of propaganda, all good qualities are associated with the former group, all bad with the latter. This phenomenon has been amply explored in discourse analysis (see, e.g. Miles, 1989; Oktar, 2001; Chilton 2004, etc.). In recent global history, instances of outgroups featuring in mediated political discourse have been terrorist organisations such as Al Qaida and ISIS, so-called 'rogue' states such as North Korea or Zimbabwe, while less identifiable targets include 'radical Islam', 'racists', 'sexists', 'anti-Semites', etc. Generally, these groups or individuals belonging to them are targeted with negative propriety evaluations, as in G.W. Bush's speech to the UN on Iraq, cited above, which attacked Saddam's morals with the rhetorical aim of de-legitimising him.

In this speech, needless to say, the in-group is represented by the British and the out-group by the Germans. However, evaluative language in this speech does not regard the moral sphere; Churchill is more concerned with Judgements of *capacity*. Hitler is only mentioned by name three times, and only once in a context of explicit negative Judgement (line 126 refers to Hitler's 'despotic control', a token of - J propriety).[2] The speaker's main attention is concentrated on describing the forces involved in the struggle, foregrounding capacity, in an overall argument that claims the allies are actually more capable than their apparently all-conquering adversaries.

The Appraisal Framework is a useful tool for focusing on the characterisation of in-group and out-group, because of the central role played by evaluative language in such discursive processes. One might expect to find

---

[1] Some of the discourse features identified by Van Leeuwen - activation/passivation, nominalisation, agency - are also used by Fairclough in a checklist of questions for use in Critical Discourse Analysis (Fairclough, 2001, p. 93).

[2] This is not to say that Churchill never, in other speeches, 'demonises' Hitler. He was heard to say, with reference to the invasion of Russia, that 'if Hitler invaded Hell, I would make at least a favourable reference to the Devil in the House of Commons'. In his speech on Russia, in particular, his rhetorical picture of Hitler reaches impressive heights of invective, calling the German leader 'a monster of wickedness, insatiable in his lust for blood and plunder', and 'this bloodthirsty guttersnipe' (James, 1980, pp. 761-2).

Churchill using expressions that praised 'our' social actors, institutions, organisations and so on, while damning their German counterparts; and in fact, many social actors from the Allies are the subject of positive evaluation. We do not find, however, in a kind of rhetorical mirror image, an analogous pattern of negative evaluation of German social actors and institutions. Rather than denigrate the Luftwaffe, their pilots, machines and so on, or high profile political characters such as Goebbels or Goering, Churchill prefers to ignore them. Van Leeuwen (1996, p. 39) calls this rhetorical strategy 'Exclusion', or 'Backgrounding'. An example of Churchill's tendency to exclude enemy social actors is evident in the opening, where he plunges straight into a description of complex military realities:

> I spoke the other day of the colossal military disaster which occurred when the French High Command failed to withdraw the northern Armies from Belgium at the moment when they knew that the French front was decisively broken at Sedan and on the Meuse.

Here, there is no mention of the German army at all. By using the verb 'occur' in connection with the military disaster, Churchill makes it sound like a natural event, rather than the result of a military reversal. The military detail that he adds, in causative relation to the disaster, implies that, had the French High Command not made a strategical error, the disaster would not have 'occurred' at all.[3] Passive agent deletion (Trew, 1979, p. 106) conceals the identity of the aggressor–we are simply told that the French front was 'decisively broken', but not by whom. Had the introduction mentioned the German army, speaking of their 'inflicting a colossal military defeat' on the Allies, for example, the rhetorical effect would have been very different. Evaluation of the German forces in such accounts would, inevitably, have required Churchill to use high-intensity positive capacity judgements, so it is not difficult to appreciate why the British leader, aiming to improve domestic morale, chose to frame his message differently.

Social Actors in Churchill's 'Finest Hour' speech

One of the most striking features of Churchill's speech is its multifarious reference to social actors of many kinds, as can be seen from the complete text analysed (see appendix). Space prohibits an analysis of all references to social actors in the speech, so I shall concentrate on the Allied and German military

---

[3] Some de-legitimisation is at work here vis-à-vis the French High Command, who are shown as responsible for the disaster.

forces on land, sea and in the air. This would seem to be the most salient groups of references, in terms of Churchill's probable rhetorical goals, rather than those to politicians, bureaucrats or members of the general public.

Allied and enemy ground forces

The following table illustrates Churchill's references to allied ground forces:

Table 5.1. Allied ground forces.

	Reference	Social Actor
2	This delay entailed the loss of *fifteen or sixteen French divisions* and threw out of action for the critical period the whole of *the British Expeditionary Force*.	15 or 16 French divisions, The B.E.F.
3	*Our Army* and *120,000 French troops* were indeed rescued by the British Navy from Dunkirk but only with the loss of their cannon, vehicles and modern equipment.	Our Army, 120,000 French troops
5	When we consider the heroic resistance made by *the French Army* against heavy odds in this battle	The French Army
6	However, *General Weygand* had to fight without them.	General Weygand
7	Only *three British divisions* or their equivalent were able to stand in the line with their *French comrades*.	Three British divisions French comrades
36	During the last few days we have successfully brought off the *great majority of the troops* we had on the line of communication in France; and *seven-eighths of the troops we have sent to France since the beginning of the war*-that is to say, about *350,000 out of 400,000 men*-are safely back in this country.	Great majority of the troops 7/8ths of the troops 350,000 out of 400,000 men
39	We have, therefore, in this Island today a *very large and powerful military force*.	Large and powerful military force
41	We have under arms at the present time in this Island *over a million and a quarter men*.	Over a million and a quarter men
46	We have also over here *Dominions armies*	Dominions armies
48	And *these very high-class forces from the Dominions* will now take part in the defence of the Mother Country	Forces from the Dominions

Van Leeuwen describes two macro ways of referring to social actors involving groups; *Aggregation* and *Collectivisation*. The former quantifies groups of participants, treating them as statistics, while the latter uses some lexical term to express a collectivity: *nation, community,* or *committee,* for example (Van Leeuwen, 1996, p. 49). It is axiomatic, for Van Leeuwen, that such terms are rarely if ever ideologically neutral; rather, they reflect some underlying ideology, or serve some rhetorical end, especially when found in a political context.

Churchill's speech offers the following examples of Aggregation in references to ground forces on the Allied side:

> 15 or 16 French divisions, 120,000 French troops, three British divisions, 7/8ths of the troops, 350,000 out of 400,000 men, over a million and a quarter men

And for Collectivisation:

> The British Expeditionary Force, our army, the French army, French comrades, the great majority of the troops, large and powerful military force, Dominions armies, forces from the Dominions

As noted above, these tend to receive positive evaluation:

- *The Royal Air Force*: 'the exploits of our fighter pilots-these splendid men, this brilliant youth' (+ J propriety, + J capacity) (10);

- We have, therefore, in this Island today a *very large and powerful military force*. (+ J capacity) (39);

- *The Canadian contingent*: 'these very high-class forces from the Dominions.' (+ J capacity, intens.) (48);

- *General Smuts*: 'General Smuts of South Africa - that wonderful man.' (+ J capacity); 115

The rhetorical significance of such a representational pattern of 'our' forces will become more apparent if we consider Churchill's representation of those of the out-group:

Table 5.2. Representation of social actors: enemy ground forces.

	Reference	Social Actor
5	When we consider [...] the enormous losses inflicted upon *the enemy* and the evident exhaustion of *the enemy*.	the enemy
37	Others are still [...] fighting with considerable success in their local encounters against *the enemy*.	the enemy

40	those who have already measured their quality against *the Germans*	The Germans
53	the invasion of Great Britain would at this time require the transportation across the sea of *hostile armies* on a very large scale	hostile armies (irrealis)
65	the Navy have never pretended to be able to prevent raids by *bodies of 5,000 or 10,000 men*	bodies of 5,000 or 10,000 men (irrealis)
66	The efficacy of sea power [...] depends upon *the invading force* being of large size	the invading force (irrealis)
69	even *five divisions*, however lightly equipped, would require 200 to 250 ships	five divisions (irrealis)
81	the British Navy was not able to prevent the movement of *a large army* from Germany into Norway across the Skagerrak	a large army (reference to Past)
89	raids by *parachute troops* and attempted descents of *airborne soldiers.*	parachute troops, airborne soldiers (irrealis)
101	the extraordinary and unforeseen power of the *armoured columns*, and by the great preponderance of the *German Army*	armoured columns, German Army

References to the German troops involved in the recent battle are few in number, limited to:

the enemy (37), the Germans (40), armoured columns (101), the German Army (101)

There is no mention of 'Panzer divisions', nor any details given of the strength of enemy forces. Rather, the first clear reference to the German soldiery depicts them as the Pyrrhic victors of a closely-fought battle:

the enormous losses inflicted upon the enemy and the evident exhaustion of the enemy (5)

In short, Churchill could well be reporting, here, on a military victory for the Allies, instead of on a disastrous defeat that, but for a miraculous evacuation, could have spelt the end of Britain's capacity to continue the war. The single instance of a reference to the enemy's military strength comes at a late moment in the speech, in an isolated explanation for the defeat in France; even here, however, while admitting the 'extraordinary power' (101) of the Germans' military machine, there are references to mitigating factors. Had the Allies made more 'fortunate' strategical choices, or 'foreseen' the enemy's strength, the outcome might have been different:

That battle was lost by the <u>unfortunate strategical opening</u>, by the extraordinary and <u>unforeseen</u> power of the armoured columns, and by the great preponderance of the German Army in numbers (101)

Van Leeuwen's category of Exclusion refers to the *non-representation* of social actors; in other words, speakers/writers may decide not to include a social actor in their descriptions; like the other categories, this choice can have significant consequences (Van Leeuwen, 1996, p. 38). Churchill does not identify, in this fragment, the social actors (of which he himself might conceivably have been one) who failed to foresee the power of the armoured columns, eliding the Agent/s involved by the use of an adjective. Similarly, by referring to the opening of the battle as unfortunate he accesses the Judgement: *normality* system, rather than that of *capacity*, thus absolving the Agent/s, who are again unidentifiable, from a degree of blame. The Allies, in this perspective, have simply been unlucky.

Other references to the German forces are in hypothetical (irrealis) invasion scenarios in which Churchill speaks, for example, of an 'invading force of large size' (66), though he reassures his hearers that in such an eventuality: "all the men (would be) drowned in the sea or, at the worst blown to pieces with their equipment while they were trying to land" (69*).* He frequently uses Backgrounding (ibid: 39) for the German forces; this is a softer form of exclusion, where the reader is able to infer who the social actors are likely to be, although they are never mentioned by name. A variety of representational techniques are involved:

- Passive agent deletion, as we saw in the opening section, above: 'the French front <u>was decisively broken</u> at Sedan and on the Meuse' (1), and: 'the battle in France <u>has been lost</u> (4)';

- Nominalisation of Verbal Processes, which makes events seem like natural phenomena. Of this device Fairclough (2003: 179) writes: "Nominalisation is the conversion of processes into Nominals, which has the effect of backgrounding the process itself - its tense and modality are not indicated - and usually not specifying its participants, so that who is doing what to whom is left implicit." For example: 'This <u>loss</u> inevitably took some weeks to repair' (4);

- Verbal Groups which serve the same function - see the discussion of 'occur' above, and also, here: 'The disastrous military events which <u>have happened</u> during the past fortnight' (34).

Instead of admitting that the German forces, by their superiority in terms of men and machines, their innovative tactics and military dynamism, had crushed resistance from an Allied force of almost equal numerical and mechanical strength,[4] references to actual fighting feature allied social actors in positive light. This is apparent if we consider the Attitude readings involved:

- When we consider <u>the heroic resistance</u> (+ J tenacity) made by the French Army against heavy odds in this battle, *the enormous losses inflicted upon the enemy* (t + J capacity, intens.) (5);

- They have suffered severely, but <u>they have fought well</u> (+ J tenacity) (8);

- Others are still fighting with the French, and <u>fighting with considerable success</u> (+ J capacity) in their local encounters against the enemy (37);

- those who have already measured their quality against the Germans and found themselves at <u>no disadvantage</u> (+ J capacity) (40).

Evaluation alternates between the tenacity and capacity systems, emphasising either the courage of the troops or representing the Allied armies as equal to their opponents, despite the military defeat suffered, using capacity or tenacity references. The numerical and technical strength of the allied ground forces are emphasised in these references: despite the fact that the military events represented a series of crushing successes for the enemy ground forces, by these means Churchill hopes to rescue a degree of discursive success from a scenario of military disaster.

The Navy

Churchill's representation of the other services, the Navy and the Air Force uses analogous techniques. References to Britain's naval power include examples of Collectivisation:

---

[4] World War II historian Charles B. MacDonald differs from Churchill by maintaining that the Allies were actually stronger numerically than the Germans: 'The French, Dutch, Belgians, and British together had approximately 4,000,000 men available, in contrast to about 2,000,000 Germans who might be used against them', whilst the two opposing forces were 'approximately equal' in terms of artillery and tanks. MacDonald, Charles B. Thread: Fall of the Low Countries. See web references.

the British Navy, the Navy, a Navy, the Admiralty, the British Fleet

There are also instances of Instrumentalisation (Van Leeuwen, 1996, p. 670), which refers to social actors via reference to the instrument/s they use to carry out the activity they are engaged in. Examples include:

our submarines, our long-distance blockade, and our surface ships

There are also examples of Assimilation, Van Leeuwen's more general term for mechanisms whereby social actors are referred to in terms of the groups they belong to, rather than as individuals. Those belonging to the in-group receive positive evaluation:

large numbers of <u>competent</u> officers, <u>well-trained in tactics</u> and <u>thoroughly up to date</u> (+ J capacity) (79)

Van Leeuwen (1996, p. 59) uses the term Impersonalisation for references using abstract nouns, or nouns referring to non-human objects. An example here would be Churchill's phrase *our great <u>superiority</u> at sea (72)*. These nautical references appear to index Britain's tradition of global maritime dominance. There is also an echo of her illustrious naval history in Churchill's use of the term 'armada' (69) to refer to a potential German invading fleet. Once again, it is revealing to compare this pattern with representation of the German fleet, where no mention is made of any such entity as a 'German Navy'. The German ships, instead, are backgrounded in phrases like: *the transportation across the sea of hostile armies (53)*, and *any large seaborne expedition (75)*, which in any case are *irrealis* as Churchill is only speculating about a possible future invasion of Britain. There is a vague reference to 'other forces' (Assimilation), and a few instances of Instrumentalisation: 'mine-sweepers', and the battleships 'the Scharnhorst and the Gneisenau' (60), which are highlighted as 'the only heavy ships worth speaking of', in contrast with Germany's 'magnificent battle fleet' of World War One. This last reference, in fact, is the only time the term 'fleet' is used in connection with the German naval forces; positively evaluating, in other words, something that the Germans no longer have. The difference in evaluative force between 'magnificent' (+ App Valuation, high intensity), for the former fleet and 'worth speaking of' (+ App Valuation, median intensity) for the current one, further underlines the message that the German fleet has declined considerably since the earlier conflict.

Churchill also refers to the Italian seaborne power, and here he does use the collective term 'Italian navy', and also Nomination, in an ironic representation of Mussolini's naval ambitions:

61. We are also told that the Italian Navy is to come out and gain sea superiority in these waters. If they seriously intend it, I shall only say that we shall be delighted to offer Signor Mussolini a free and safeguarded passage through the Strait of Gibraltar in order that he may play the part to which he aspires.

The Italian forces are construed as hardly existing as a battle fleet by comparison with that of Britain, certainly not capable of mounting a serious challenge to Britain's traditional naval supremacy. The irony is construed via the specific form taken by the Nomination here, where Churchill deliberately gives Mussolini the same appellation as a common individual, denying him the respect of a titular reference. In an instance of Van Leeuwen's category of Overdetermination (ibid: 61), he is also compared to an actor, wishing to 'play a part', and clearly de-legitimised thereby.

The Air forces

The British air force is also represented collectively, in the terms:

the British air force, our Air Force, an Air Force, a very powerful Air Force

These terms are variously pre- and post-modified in evaluative combinations like:

- A <u>very powerful</u> Air Force (+ J capacity, intens.), which has proved itself far <u>superior in quality, both in men and in many types of machine</u> (+ App Valuation, intens.) (93);

- The entire metropolitan fighter <u>strength</u> of the Air Force (+J capacity) (99)

The pragmatic impact of the rhetorical device of repetition was well-known to the Greek rhetoricians, who called it Anaphora. Here, the ordinary semantic associations of the word 'force', a technical term in the military register, seem to emerge, by virtue of Churchill's continued repetition of it in Nominal groups like those just quoted, and in others like 'our entire fighter <u>force</u>', 'our fighter air <u>force</u>', 'a very large bomber <u>force</u>'. The same applies to the word 'strength', as in 'our fighter <u>strength</u>'. The effect is to drive home the notion that Britain possesses a powerful air force. Impersonalisation is also used in this context, as it was in the naval, in the phrase 'air superiority' (96). Positive evaluation also occurs in Churchill's glowing characterisation of 'the few':

our fighter pilots - these splendid men (+ J propriety), this brilliant
youth (+ J capacity) (104).

On the German side, although there is a solitary reference to the German 'Air
Force', there is no use of the term 'Luftwaffe', only one other use of the term
'force', and none of 'strength'. Churchill admits that our Air Force is, regrettably,
not equal to that of 'the most powerful enemy (+ J capacity) within striking
distance of these shores', but this is mitigated by mathematical claims that
speak of the infliction, by the RAF, of 'losses of as much as '*two and two-and-a-
half to one*' (t + J capacity), and even '*three or four to one*' (t + J capacity).

There is a vague Nominalised reference to *Hitler's air weapon*. This reference
is also an Impersonalisation (Abstraction), in which the multitude of social
actors involved are represented by the singular term 'weapon'; Hitler is,
therefore, represented as only having one 'weapon', whereas references to
Allied air powers are, as we have seen, diverse. As with representations of the
Navy, the cumulative rhetorical effect is to represent the Allied air strength as
fundamentally superior to that of the Germans.

Other representational patterns

Exclusion/Inclusion

Van Leeuwen's framework, as already indicated, enables attention to be
focused on patterns of Inclusion and Exclusion. The framing of a discourse
entails selection of which social actors involved in the immediate context
should be foregrounded, which left in the background, and which excluded
altogether. Such choices depend on the pragmatic purpose of the speaker:

> Representations include or exclude social actors to suit their interests
> and purposes in relation to the readers for whom they are intended
> (Van Leeuwen, 1996, p. 38)

Churchill's treatment of the German troops in the opening, examined above,
serves one of his main rhetorical goals, the lifting of home morale. By avoiding
references to 'crushing Panzer divisions', 'devastating attacks by the Luftwaffe',
'Blitzkrieg', 'German heavy artillery', and so on, he seeks to minimise any
negative reactions among his hearers in terms of fear of the foe. In the same
way, the numerous references of diverse types to Allied forces, as examined
above, have the aim of reassuring listeners of the superiority of those forces
and their ability to deal with the situation.

The rhetorical option of Inclusion is not necessarily favourable to the social
actors concerned; rather it emphasises their role as participants in the

processes described, in ways that suit the overall scope of the speaker. The statistical patterns associated with Inclusion/Exclusion in Churchill's speech, in fact, confirm the expectation that allied forces are generally included and those of the Germans excluded, as the table below shows:

Table 5.3. Inclusion/Exclusion Allied and German (Ground) forces.[5]

	Total References	Inclusion (Percentage)	Exclusion
Allies	81	52 (64.19%)	29 (35.81%)
Germans	63	23/63 (36.50%)	40/63 (64.50%)

Collectivisation and Aggregation, then, are also rhetorically significant insofar as they function as resources for Inclusion. The tendency to exclude German forces in representations of their actions creates a diminishing effect, whilst inclusion of the Allied forces magnifies them. Butt et al. (2004, p. 274) discuss this in relation to G.W. Bush's tendency to include terrorists in discourse, which they find somewhat atypical: "To give the enemy such a material, dynamic grammatical profile through the transitivity selections is often not the choice of leaders speaking of political enemies". Churchill's pattern in this speech, in fact, is more usual.

Activation/Passivation

Activation and Passivation refer to whether the social actor in question is represented as the agent or recipient of the process described. The rhetorical significance of this would seem to be that it clearly flatters social actors to be represented as the active, dynamic forces in an activity, rather than 'undergoing' the activity, or as being at the receiving end of it (Van Leeuwen, 1996, pp. 43-44). Butt et al. (2004, p. 285) comment that the enemy is "never construed as an Agent that causes the process to occur." They indicate that such a rhetorical strategy gives the impression of the speaker's group being reassuringly in control. We would expect Churchill, therefore, to activate Allied forces and passivate those of the Germans, but this is not borne out by the statistics:

---

[5] If irrealis references to German forces involved in hypothetical invasions are removed, the percentage of Inclusion drops to 28.30%.

Table 5.4. Activation/Passivation.

	Total References	Active (%)	Passive
Allies	47	18 (38.30%)	29 (61.70%)
Germans	31	16 (51.61%)	15 (48.39%)

Unfortunately for his rhetorical purposes, Churchill is more or less compelled to represent the Allied ground forces, defeated in battle and 'saved' by naval intervention, in passive terms:

> 3. Our Army and 120,000 French troops were indeed rescued by the British Navy from Dunkirk
>
> 36. we have successfully brought off the great majority of the troops.

In references, like these, to the Dunkirk evacuation, the ground forces inevitably occupy a passive, Beneficiary role (Halliday & Matthiessen, 2004, p. 293). Similarly, in Churchill's enumeration of the armed forces currently on British soil, the references are in passive voice, with the forces concerned in the role of Attribute (Halliday & Matthiessen, 2004, p. 245):

> 39. We have, therefore, in this Island today a very large and powerful military force.
>
> 41. We have under arms at the present time in this Island over a million and a quarter men.
>
> 42. Behind these we have the Local Defense Volunteers, numbering half a million.

Mitigating the potential negativity of this representational pattern is the fact that the references involved all transmit information with a positive message; i.e., that large numbers of troops were rescued from Dunkirk, that the presence of such troops in Britain increases our readiness to meet an invasion threat, and so on.

Social Actors: appraisal

Van Leeuwen's analytical system also includes the interpersonal aspect of representation, which he terms 'appraisement', meaning those instances where the speaker signals his/her evaluation of a social actor as good or bad, loved or hated, admired or pitied (Van Leeuwen, 1996, p. 58). The Appraisal Framework, however, offers a more comprehensive treatment of such features, covering implicit evaluation as well as explicit, and offering a well-developed taxonomy of such references. The following tables collect references, from the judgement systems to the social actors dealt with by this study, the fighting forces of the two sides:

Table 5.5. Appraisal of British forces: Judgement.

Line	Reference	Appraisal
1	*the French High Command failed to withdraw the northern Armies from Belgium*	t - J capacity
3	*Our Army and 120,000 French troops were indeed rescued by the British Navy from Dunkirk*	t + tenacity
5	When we consider the <u>heroic</u> resistance made by the French Army	+ J tenacity/propriety
5	25 divisions of the <u>best-trained</u> and <u>best-equipped</u> troops	+ J capacity
8	They have suffered severely, but they have <u>fought well</u>.	+ J tenacity
37	Others are still fighting with the French, and fighting with <u>considerable success</u> in their local encounters against the enemy	+ J capacity.
39	We have, therefore, in this Island today <u>a very large and powerful</u> military force.	+ J capacity intens.
40	This force comprises all our <u>best-trained</u> and our <u>finest</u> troops	+ J capacity
40	those who have already measured their quality against the Germans and *found themselves at no disadvantage*	+ J capacity t +J capacity
48	And these <u>very high-class</u> forces from the Dominions	+ J capacity intens.
52	The rest of our forces at home have a fighting value for home defence which <u>will, of course, steadily increase every week that passes.</u>	+ J capacity
72	There should be no difficulty in this, owing to our <u>great superiority</u> at sea.	+ J capacity intens.
86	Our <u>superior</u> naval surface forces	+ J capacity
88	*no invasion on a scale beyond the capacity of our land forces to crush speedily can take place*	t + J capacity
93	But we have a <u>very powerful</u> Air Force	+ J capacity intens.
94	We were accustomed to inflict in the air losses of as much as <u>two and two-and-a-half to one</u>.	+ J capacity

95	In the fighting over Dunkirk, we..gained the mastery of the local air, inflicting here *a loss of three or four to one day after day.*	t+ J capacity
104	Our fighter pilots-these <u>splendid</u> men, this <u>brilliant</u> youth	+ J propriety, + J capacity
125	If invasion has become more imminent, we have <u>far larger and more efficient</u> forces to meet it	+ J capacity intens.
131	the individual aircraft and the individual British pilot have a <u>sure and definite superiority.</u>	+ J capacity

Table 5.6. Appraisal of German forces: Judgement.

| 101 | the extraordinary and unforeseen power of the armoured columns | + J capacity (intens.) |

The dramatic unevenness in representation between Allied and enemy forces illustrates the extent to which German forces are backgrounded in the speech. How could Churchill, the military expert, fail to acknowledge the outstanding feats performed by the Germans in the campaign to conquer France, or recognise that their armoured columns, for example, were far superior to those of the Allies? To refer to the German armed forces at all must be, at least implicitly, to confer praise on them via the judgement: capacity system. Churchill, therefore, prefers not to mention them at all, preferring to concentrate on positive judgements of our social actors. The impression is given that the Germans, far from having nearly conquered France, and in the process almost captured the entire British army, have suffered 'enormous losses' and are 'evidently exhausted' (5). Taken with suggestions that, in fighting still going on, the Allies are enjoying 'considerable success' (37), such references might even suggest that the German victory is in the balance.

References tend to come from the capacity rather than the tenacity system, for all three of the services. Capacity seems relevant for references to the nation's potential for future resistance; the emphasis is on the readiness to meet future challenges. Tenacity references relate to social actors like the ground troops involved in recent battles, stressing their courage and general fighting ability rather than the outcomes of such battles, since these were mainly negative. Where the outcomes were favourable, as in the aerial combat over France, Churchill is happy to stress the capacity of the RAF, since the knowledge of our 'sure and definite superiority' in the air (131) represents a solid reason to view the coming crisis with greater confidence. The armed forces currently in Britain, the Navy and the RAF, are therefore all positively judged, while the references to the tenacity of the troops involved in France also feed into this positive picture. Since most of these troops have been rescued and will be available for any future conflict, their proven tenacity further strengthens the speaker's case–that Britain's military resources are more than adequate to deal with a possible German invasion.

Concluding remarks

This chapter has concentrated on Churchill's representation of social actors in a key speech, given during the early days of the Second World War, and explored possible strategic reasons that might explain Churchill's selections in this area. Although there is no specific expressed opinion for which Churchill is trying to make a case, he does suggest a possible response to the situation in the emotive sphere, which provides a further clue to the speaker's overall rhetorical intention:

> Therefore, in casting up this dread balance sheet and contemplating our dangers with a disillusioned eye, I see great reason for intense vigilance and exertion, but none whatever for panic or despair (132)

This use of the dialogical resource of proclaim asserts the speaker's notion of the wider significance, for the community as a whole, of his own evaluations (White, 2003).[6] The acceptance by the population of the proposal will depend mainly on Churchill's ethos, or the extent to which he is seen as a reliable source of information. He is indicating here what the emotional response of the population ought to be, on the basis of the factual account that he has presented of the forces engaged in the struggle. If the facts are accepted by the population, then the proposal stands a strong chance of establishing itself. In a macro sense, then, the argumentative structure of the speech as a whole could be seen as follows:

Table 5.7. Their finest hour: Argumentative structure.

Data	Warrant	Claim
(because)	(since)	(therefore)
Our forces are superior to the Germans	In war, the strongest side is always victorious	We should be of good courage

[6] White shows this resource at work in the discourse of Norman Tebbit, commenting that he thereby "construes his own, individual, emotional response as having some substantial degree of significance in the wider community". "White, Peter R. 2. Attitude/Judgement". See web references.

Such a structure is, of course, a gross over-simplification of the many complex sub-plots in Churchill's pattern of argument here, but it has the merit of concentrating attention on the possible pragmatic outcome sought by the speaker when he composed and delivered this address. It is backed up, moreover, by Churchill's own words, towards the end of the speech, where he offers the following summary of his message:

> 110. I have thought it right upon this occasion to give the House and the country some indication of the **solid, practical grounds** upon which we base our inflexible resolve to continue the war

What Churchill calls the 'solid, practical grounds', essentially, relate to the perceived differences in the relative strengths of the contending parties that form the body of much of the speech. In terms of the structure of argumentation, such details could all be included as part of the 'Data' column.

It would be logical to ask why, if the Allied forces were so superior, did the Germans emerge victorious during the recent battle in France? There is, in fact, a noticeable tension in the speech between Churchill's determination to paint an encouraging picture and the facts as they must have appeared to the British people at the time. At times credibility is somewhat strained, as he attempts to put a positive slant on the ejection of British forces from the continent:

> If invasion has become more imminent, as no doubt it has, we, being relieved from the task of maintaining a large army in France, have far larger and more efficient forces to meet it

Nevertheless, morale in Britain was greatly stimulated by the rescue of the armies from Dunkirk. The speech can indeed be read as an attempt to cement the morale-boosting effect of those extraordinary events by presenting, as Churchill puts it, the grounds for hope, and for confidence.

It will be seen that Van Leeuwen's system for analysing the representation of social actors can be a useful tool for studying these textual features. In effect, as I have suggested above, and as any historical work on the period will confirm, the German invasion of France was an extraordinary military success, and total catastrophe for the Allies was only averted by the proverbial whisker. The German forces were frighteningly superior to their counterparts, and only by the use of the kind of representational strategies analysed above could Churchill hope to describe events in the theatre of war without creating a state of panic among the population. Being a consummate orator, he was able to use them to stir and rouse his listeners, perhaps, with his own conviction of ultimate victory.

Thus we have seen how argumentation, in the context of modern political rhetoric, may be used to advance subtler expressed opinions, and aim at achieving abstract pragmatic goals (influencing popular opinion, raising morale, pointing out the bright side, etc.) rather than at some specific real-world result. It may be addressed not to the specific audience of, for example, those present in a parliamentary debating chamber, but directly through the wireless to an entire population.

Appendix: Their Finest Hour analysed for representation of social actors

1	I spoke the other day of the colossal military disaster which occurred when the French High Command failed to withdraw the northern Armies from Belgium at the moment when they knew that the French front was decisively broken at Sedan and on the Meuse.	I The French High Command The northern Armies
2	This delay entailed the loss of fifteen or sixteen French divisions and threw out of action for the critical period the whole of the British Expeditionary Force.	15 or 16 French divisions The British Expeditionary Force
3	Our Army and 120,000 French troops were indeed rescued by the British Navy from Dunkirk but only with the loss of their cannon, vehicles and modern equipment.	Our Army 120,000 French troops the British Navy
4	This loss inevitably took some weeks to repair, and in the first two of those weeks the battle in France has been lost.	
5	When we consider the heroic resistance made by the French Army against heavy odds in this battle, the enormous losses inflicted upon the enemy and the evident exhaustion of the enemy, it may well be the thought that these 25 divisions of the best-trained and best-equipped troops might have turned the scale.	We The French Army The enemy
6	However, General Weygand had to fight without them.	General Weygand
7	Only three British divisions or their equivalent were able to stand in the line with their French comrades.	Three British divisions French comrades
8	They have suffered severely, but they have fought well.	They
9	We sent every man we could to France as fast as we could re-equip and transport their formations.	We
10	I am not reciting these facts for the purpose of recrimination.	I
11	That I judge to be utterly futile and even harmful.	I
12	We cannot afford it.	We
13	I recite them in order to explain why it was we did not have, as we could have had, between twelve and fourteen British divisions fighting in the line in this great battle instead of only three.	I We 12 - 14 British divisions/only 3
14	Now I put all this aside.	I
15	I put it on the shelf, from which the historians, when they have time, will select their documents to tell their stories.	I The historians
16	We have to think of the future and not of the past.	We
17	This also applies in a small way to our own affairs at home.	

18	There are many who would hold an inquest in the House of Commons on the conduct of the Governments-and of Parliaments, for they are in it, too - during the years which led up to this catastrophe.	Many Governments/ Parliaments
19	They seek to indict those who were responsible for the guidance of our affairs.	They Those who were responsible..
20	This also would be a foolish and pernicious process.	
21	There are too many in it.	Many
22	Let each man search his conscience and search his speeches.	Each man
23	I frequently search mine.	I
24	Of this I am quite sure, that if we open a quarrel between the past and the present, we shall find that we have lost the future.	I We
25	Therefore, I cannot accept the drawing of any distinctions between Members of the present Government.	I Members of the present government
26	It was formed at a moment of crisis in order to unite all the Parties and all sections of opinion.	It (the government) All the parties
27	It has received the almost unanimous support of both Houses of Parliament.	It Both Houses of Parliament
28	Its Members are going to stand together, and, subject to the authority of the House of Commons, we are going to govern the country and fight the war.	Its members We
29	It is absolutely necessary at a time like this that every Minister who tries each day to do his duty shall be respected; and their subordinates must know that their chiefs are not threatened men, men who are here today and gone tomorrow, but that their directions must be punctually and faithfully obeyed.	Every minister Their subordinates Their chiefs
30	Without this concentrated power we cannot face what lies before us.	We
31	I should not think it would be very advantageous for the House to prolong this Debate this afternoon under conditions of public stress.	I The house
32	Many facts are not clear that will be clear in a short time.	
33	We are to have a secret Session on Thursday, and I should think that would be a better opportunity for the many earnest expressions of opinion which Members will desire to make and for the House to discuss vital matters without having everything read the next morning by our dangerous foes.	We I Members The House Our dangerous foes
34	The disastrous military events which have happened during the past fortnight have not come to me with any sense of surprise.	Me

35	Indeed, I indicated a fortnight ago as clearly as I could to the House that the worst possibilities were open; and I made it perfectly clear then that whatever happened in France would make no difference to the resolve of Britain and the British Empire to fight on, if necessary for years, if necessary alone.'	I The House Britain and the British Empire
36	During the last few days we have successfully brought off the great majority of the troops we had on the line of communication in France; and seven-eighths of the troops we have sent to France since the beginning of the war-that is to say, about 350,000 out of 400,000 men-are safely back in this country.	We The troops
37	Others are still fighting with the French, and fighting with considerable success in their local encounters against the enemy.	Others (troops) The French The enemy
38	We have also brought back a great mass of stores, rifles and munitions of all kinds which had been accumulated in France during the last nine months.	We
39	We have, therefore, in this Island today a very large and powerful military force.	We A..military force
40	This force comprises all our best-trained and our finest troops, including scores of thousands of those who have already measured their quality against the Germans and found themselves at no disadvantage.	This force The Germans
41	We have under arms at the present time in this Island over a million and a quarter men.	We A million and a quarter men
42	Behind these we have the Local Defense Volunteers, numbering half a million, only a portion of whom, however, are yet armed with rifles or other firearms.	Local Defense Volunteers
43	We have incorporated into our Defense Forces every man for whom we have a weapon.	We Our defense forces Every man
44	We expect very large additions to our weapons in the near future, and in preparation for this we intend forthwith to call up, drill and train further large numbers.	We Large numbers
45	Those who are not called up, or else are employed during the vast business of munitions production in all its branches-and their ramifications are innumerable-will serve their country best by remaining at their ordinary work until they receive their summons.	Those not called up
46	We have also over here Dominions armies.	We Dominions armies
47	The Canadians had actually landed in France, but have now been safely withdrawn, much disappointed, but in perfect order, with all their artillery and equipment.	The Canadians

48	And these very high-class forces from the Dominions will now take part in the defense of the Mother Country.	High class forces
49	Lest the account which I have given of these large forces should raise the question: Why did they not take part in the great battle in France?	I These large forces
50	I must make it clear that, apart from the divisions training and organizing at home, only 12 divisions were equipped to fight upon a scale which justified their being sent abroad.	I The divisions 12 divisions
51	And this was fully up to the number which the French had been led to expect would be available in France at the ninth month of the war.	The French
52	The rest of our forces at home have a fighting value for home defense which will, of course, steadily increase every week that passes.	The rest of our forces
53	Thus, the invasion of Great Britain would at this time require the transportation across the sea of hostile armies on a very large scale, and after they had been so transported they would have to be continually maintained with all the masses of munitions and supplies which are required for continuous battle-as continuous battle it will surely be.	Hostile armies
54	Here is where we come to the Navy-and after all, we have a Navy.	We The Navy
55	Some people seem to forget that we have a Navy.	Some people A Navy
56	We must remind them.	We Them
57	For the last thirty years I have been concerned in discussions about the possibilities of oversea invasion, and I took the responsibility on behalf of the Admiralty, at the beginning of the last war, of allowing all regular troops to be sent out of the country.	I The Admiralty All regular troops
58	That was a very serious step to take, because our Territorials had only just been called up and were quite untrained.	Our territorials
59	Therefore, this Island was for several months particularly denuded of fighting troops.	Fighting troops
60	The Admiralty had confidence at that time in their ability to prevent a mass invasion even though at that time the Germans had a magnificent battle fleet in the proportion of 10 to 16, even though they were capable of fighting a general engagement every day and any day, whereas now they have only a couple of heavy ships worth speaking of-the Scharnhorst and the Gneisenau.	The Admiralty The Germans
61	We are also told that the Italian Navy is to come out and gain sea superiority in these waters.	The Italian navy
62	If they seriously intend it, I shall only say that we shall be delighted to offer Signor Mussolini a free and safeguarded passage through the Strait of Gibraltar in order that he may play the part to which he aspires.	Signor Mussolini

63	There is a general curiosity in the British Fleet to find out whether the Italians are up to the level they were at in the last war or whether they have fallen off at all.	The British fleet The Italians
64	Therefore, it seems to me that as far as sea-borne invasion on a great scale is concerned, we are far more capable of meeting it today than we were at many periods in the last war and during the early months of this war, before our other troops were trained, and while the B.E.F. had proceeded abroad.	Me We Other troops The BEF
65	Now, the Navy have never pretended to be able to prevent raids by bodies of 5,000 or 10,000 men flung suddenly across and thrown ashore at several points on the coast some dark night or foggy morning.	The Navy 5 or 10,000 men
66	The efficacy of sea power, especially under modern conditions, depends upon the invading force being of large size;	The invading force
67	It has to be of large size, in view of our military strength, to be of any use.	It
68	If it is of large size, then the Navy have something they can find and meet and, as it were, bite on.	It (invading force) The Navy
69	Now, we must remember that even five divisions, however lightly equipped, would require 200 to 250 ships, and with modern air reconnaissance and photography it would not be easy to collect such an armada, marshal it, and conduct it across the sea without any powerful naval forces to escort it; and there would be very great possibilities, to put it mildly, that this armada would be intercepted long before it reached the coast, and all the men drowned in the sea or, at the worst blown to pieces with their equipment while they were trying to land.	We 200 to 250 ships armada air reconnaissance all the men
70	We also have a great system of minefields, recently strongly reinforced, through which we alone know the channels.	We
71	If the enemy tries to sweep passages through these minefields, it will be the task of the Navy to destroy the mine-sweepers and any other forces employed to protect them.	The enemy The Navy
72	There should be no difficulty in this, owing to our great superiority at sea.	Our great superiority
73	Those are the regular, well-tested, well-proved arguments on which we have relied during many years in peace and war.	We
74	But the question is whether there are any new methods by which those solid assurances can be circumvented.	
75	Odd as it may seem, some attention has been given to this by the Admiralty, whose prime duty and responsibility is to destroy any large sea-borne expedition before it reaches, or at the moment when it reaches, these shores.	The Admiralty Sea-borne expedition
76	It would not be a good thing for me to go into details of this.	Me

77	It might suggest ideas to other people which they have not thought of, and they would not be likely to give us any of their ideas in exchange.	Other people
78	All I will say is that untiring vigilance and mind-searching must be devoted to the subject, because the enemy is crafty and cunning and full of novel treacheries and stratagems.	I The enemy
79	The House may be assured that the utmost ingenuity is being displayed and imagination is being evoked from large numbers of competent officers, well-trained in tactics and thoroughly up to date, to measure and counterwork novel possibilities.	The House Large numbers of competent officers
80	Untiring vigilance and untiring searching of the mind is being, and must be, devoted to the subject, because, remember, the enemy is crafty and there is no dirty trick he will not do.	Untiring vigilance - The enemy
81	Some people will ask why, then, was it that the British Navy was not able to prevent the movement of a large army from Germany into Norway across the Skagerrak?	Some people The British Navy A large German army
82	But the conditions in the Channel and in the North Sea are in no way like those which prevail in the Skagerrak.	I
83	In the Skagerrak, because of the distance, we could give no air support to our surface ships, and consequently, lying as we did close to the enemy's main air power, we were compelled to use only our submarines.	We Air support Surface ships Enemy's main air power Submarines
84	We could not enforce the decisive blockade or interruption which is possible from surface vessels.	We Surface vessels
85	Our submarines took a heavy toll but could not, by themselves, prevent the invasion of Norway.	Our submarines The invasion of Norway
86	In the Channel and in the North Sea, on the other hand, our superior naval surface forces, aided by our submarines, will operate with close and effective air assistance.	Our naval forces Submarines Air assistance
87	This brings me, naturally, to the great question of invasion from the air, and of the impending struggle between the British and German Air Forces.	Me The British and German Air forces
88	It seems quite clear that no invasion on a scale beyond the capacity of our land forces to crush speedily is likely to take place from the air until our Air Force has been definitely overpowered.	Our land forces Our Air force
89	In the meantime, there may be raids by parachute troops and attempted descents of airborne soldiers.	Parachute troops Airborne soldiers

90	We should be able to give those gentry a warm reception both in the air and on the ground, if they reach it in any condition to continue the dispute.	We Those gentry
91	But the great question is: Can we break Hitler's air weapon?	We Hitler
92	Now, of course, it is a very great pity that we have not got an Air Force at least equal to that of the most powerful enemy within striking distance of these shores.	We Air force Most powerful enemy
93	But we have a very powerful Air Force which has proved itself far superior in quality, both in men and in many types of machine, to what we have met so far in the numerous and fierce air battles which have been fought with the Germans.	We Air force The Germans
94	In France, where we were at a considerable disadvantage and lost many machines on the ground when they were standing round the aerodromes, we were accustomed to inflict in the air losses of as much as two and two-and-a-half to one.	We
95	In the fighting over Dunkirk, which was a sort of no-man's-land, we undoubtedly beat the German Air Force, and gained the mastery of the local air, inflicting here a loss of three or four to one day after day.	We The German Air Force
96	Anyone who looks at the photographs which were published a week or so ago of the re-embarkation, showing the masses of troops assembled on the beach and forming an ideal target for hours at a time, must realize that this re-embarkation would not have been possible unless the enemy had resigned all hope of recovering air superiority at that time and at that place.	Anyone Masses of troops The enemy
97	In the defense of this Island the advantages to the defenders will be much greater than they were in the fighting around Dunkirk.	The defenders 'the fighting'
98	We hope to improve on the rate of three or four to one which was realized at Dunkirk; and in addition all our injured machines and their crews which get down safely-and, surprisingly, a very great many injured machines and men do get down safely in modern air fighting-all of these will fall, in an attack upon these Islands, on friendly soil and live to fight another day; whereas all the injured enemy machines and their complements will be total losses as far as the war is concerned.	We The crews Enemy machines, complements
99	During the great battle in France, we gave very powerful and continuous aid to the French Army, both by fighters and bombers; but in spite of every kind of pressure we never would allow the entire metropolitan fighter strength of the Air Force to be consumed.	We The French army Fighters, bombers
100	This decision was painful, but it was also right, because the fortunes of the battle in France could not have been decisively affected even if we had thrown in our entire fighter force.	We Fighter force

101	That battle was lost by the unfortunate strategical opening, by the extraordinary and unforeseen power of the armoured columns, and by the great preponderance of the German Army in numbers.	armoured columns German army
102	Our fighter Air Force might easily have been exhausted as a mere accident in that great struggle, and then we should have found ourselves at the present time in a very serious plight.	Our Air Force We
103	But as it is, I am happy to inform the House that our fighter strength is stronger at the present time relatively to the Germans, who have suffered terrible losses, than it has ever been; and consequently we believe ourselves possessed of the capacity to continue the war in the air under better conditions than we have ever experienced before.	I Our fighter strength The Germans We
104	I look forward confidently to the exploits of our fighter pilots-these splendid men, this brilliant youth-who will have the glory of saving their native land, their island home, and all they love, from the most deadly of all attacks.	I Fighter pilots, splendid men, brilliant youth
105	There remains, of course, the danger of bombing attacks, which will certainly be made very soon upon us by the bomber forces of the enemy.	The enemy
106	It is true that the German bomber force is superior in numbers to ours; but we have a very large bomber force also, which we shall use to strike at military targets in Germany without intermission.	The German bomber force Ours We
107	I do not at all underrate the severity of the ordeal which lies before us; but I believe our countrymen will show themselves capable of standing up to it, like the brave men of Barcelona, and will be able to stand up to it, and carry on in spite of it, at least as well as any other people in the world.	I Our countrymen The brave men of Barcelona Any other people in the world
108	Much will depend upon this; every man and every woman will have the chance to show the finest qualities of their race, and render the highest service to their cause.	Every man Every woman
109	For all of us, at this time, whatever our sphere, our station, our occupation or our duties, it will be a help to remember the famous lines: He nothing common did or mean, Upon that memorable scene.	All of us He
110	I have thought it right upon this occasion to give the House and the country some indication of the solid, practical grounds upon which we base our inflexible resolve to continue the war.	I The House The country We
111	There are a good many people who say, 'Never mind. Win or lose, sink or swim, better die than submit to tyranny-and such a tyranny.'	A good many people A tyranny

112	And I do not dissociate myself from them.	I Them
113	But I can assure them that our professional advisers of the three Services unitedly advise that we should carry on the war, and that there are good and reasonable hopes of final victory.	I Our professional advisers We
114	We have fully informed and consulted all the self-governing Dominions, these great communities far beyond the oceans who have been built up on our laws and on our civilization, and who are absolutely free to choose their course, but are absolutely devoted to the ancient Motherland, and who feel themselves inspired by the same emotions which lead me to stake our all upon duty and honor.	We The self-governing dominions Me
115	We have fully consulted them, and I have received from their Prime Ministers, Mr. Mackenzie King of Canada, Mr. Menzies of Australia, Mr. Fraser of New Zealand, and General Smuts of South Africa-that wonderful man, with his immense profound mind, and his eye watching from a distance the whole panorama of European affairs-I have received from all these eminent men, who all have Governments behind them elected on wide franchises, who are all there because they represent the will of their people, messages couched in the most moving terms in which they endorse our decision to fight on, and declare themselves ready to share our fortunes and to persevere to the end.	We Mr Mackenzie King Mr Fraser General Smuts I These eminent men Their people
116	That is what we are going to do.	We
117	We may now ask ourselves: In what way has our position worsened since the beginning of the war?	We
118	It has worsened by the fact that the Germans have conquered a large part of the coast line of Western Europe, and many small countries have been overrun by them.	The Germans Many small countries
119	This aggravates the possibilities of air attack and adds to our naval preoccupations.	Air attack Naval preoccupations
120	It in no way diminishes, but on the contrary definitely increases, the power of our long-distance blockade.	Our blockade
121	Similarly, the entrance of Italy into the war increases the power of our long-distance blockade.	Italy
122	We have stopped the worst leak by that.	We
123	We do not know whether military resistance will come to an end in France or not, but should it do so, then of course the Germans will be able to concentrate their forces, both military and industrial, upon us.	We The Germans
124	But for the reasons I have given to the House these will not be found so easy to apply.	I The House

125	If invasion has become more imminent, as no doubt it has, we, being relieved from the task of maintaining a large army in France, have far larger and more efficient forces to meet it.	We A large army
126	If Hitler can bring under his despotic control the industries of the countries he has conquered, this will add greatly to his already vast armament output.	Hitler
127	On the other hand, this will not happen immediately, and we are now assured of immense, continuous and increasing support in supplies and munitions of all kinds from the United States; and especially of aeroplanes and pilots from the Dominions and across the oceans coming from regions which are beyond the reach of enemy bombers.	We The United States Pilots from the Dominions Enemy bombers
128	I do not see how any of these factors can operate to our detriment on balance before the winter comes; and the winter will impose a strain upon the Nazi regime, with almost all Europe writhing and starving under its cruel heel, which, for all their ruthlessness, will run them very hard.	I The Nazi regime
129	We must not forget that from the moment when we declared war on the 3rd September it was always possible for Germany to turn all her Air Force upon this country, together with any other devices of invasion she might conceive, and that France could have done little or nothing to prevent her doing so.	We Germany France
130	We have, therefore, lived under this danger, in principle and in a slightly modified form, during all these months.	We
131	In the meanwhile, however, we have enormously improved our methods of defense, and we have learned what we had no right to assume at the beginning, namely, that the individual aircraft and the individual British pilot have a sure and definite superiority.	We The individual British pilot
132	Therefore, in casting up this dread balance sheet and contemplating our dangers with a disillusioned eye, I see great reason for intense vigilance and exertion, but none whatever for panic or despair.	I
133	During the first four years of the last war the Allies experienced nothing but disaster and disappointment.	The Allies
134	That was our constant fear: one blow after another, terrible losses, frightful dangers.	Our fear
135	Everything miscarried.	
136	And yet at the end of those four years the morale of the Allies was higher than that of the Germans, who had moved from one aggressive triumph to another, and who stood everywhere triumphant invaders of the lands into which they had broken.	The Allies The Germans

137	During that war we repeatedly asked ourselves the question: How are we going to win? and no one was able ever to answer it with much precision, until at the end, quite suddenly, quite unexpectedly, our terrible foe collapsed before us, and we were so glutted with victory that in our folly we threw it away.	We No one Our terrible foe
138	We do not yet know what will happen in France or whether the French resistance will be prolonged, both in France and in the French Empire overseas.	We The French resistance
139	The French Government will be throwing away great opportunities and casting adrift their future if they do not continue the war in accordance with their Treaty obligations, from which we have not felt able to release them.	The French Government We
140	The House will have read the historic declaration in which, at the desire of many Frenchmen-and of our own hearts-we have proclaimed our willingness at the darkest hour in French history to conclude a union of common citizenship in this struggle.	The House Many Frenchmen
141	However matters may go in France or with the French Government, or other French Governments, we in this Island and in the British Empire will never lose our sense of comradeship with the French people.	The French Government We The British Empire The French people
142	If we are now called upon to endure what they have been suffering, we shall emulate their courage, and if final victory rewards our toils they shall share the gains, aye, and freedom shall be restored to all.	We They
143	We abate nothing of our just demands; not one jot or tittle do we recede.	We
144	Czechs, Poles, Norwegians, Dutch, Belgians have joined their causes to our own.	Czechs, Poles, Norwegians, Dutch, Belgians, us
145	All these shall be restored.	
146	What General Weygand called the Battle of France is over.	General Weygand
147	I expect that the Battle of Britain is about to begin.	I
148	Upon this battle depends the survival of Christian civilization.	
149	Upon it depends our own British life, and the long continuity of our institutions and our Empire.	Our Empire
150	The whole fury and might of the enemy must very soon be turned on us.	The enemy Us
151	Hitler knows that he will have to break us in this Island or lose the war.	Hitler Us

152	If we can stand up to him, all Europe may be free and the life of the world may move forward into broad, sunlit uplands.	We All Europe The life of the world
153	But if we fail, then the whole world, including the United States, including all that we have known and cared for, will sink into the abyss of a new Dark Age made more sinister, and perhaps more protracted, by the lights of perverted science.	We The whole world The United States
154	Let us therefore brace ourselves to our duties, and so bear ourselves that, if the British Empire and its Commonwealth last for a thousand years, men will still say, 'This was their finest hour.'	Us The British Empire and its Commonwealth Men

Malcolm X vs. Martin Luther King

Introduction

This chapter returns to a focus on patterns of argumentation and evaluation, as used by two of the best-known leaders of the black American community during the 1950s and early 60s, Malcolm X and Martin Luther King. Both used political rhetoric in the classical manner: to persuade their audiences of the correctness of their views, to ward off or exclude alternative solutions, to bring about perlocutionary effects (Aristotle, 1954, p. 90; Perelman & Olbrechts-Tyteca, 1969, p. 45). Each approached the same social problem–racial injustice–from radically different angles, a circumstance which depended to a large extent on their backgrounds. While Martin Luther King was a classically educated Baptist minister, Malcolm X was a prominent spokesman for the radical group the Nation of Islam. He was educated on the streets of Harlem and then in prison (X & Haley, 2001), and advocated the policy of separation preached by his mentor, Elijah Muhammad. Malcolm X's style is punchy, streetwise and provocative; King's is more sober, closer to European schools of rhetoric. The essential difference between the two is in the areas of strategy and objectives; while King sought integration and social equality through non-violent means, X wanted separation "by any means necessary" (Breitman, 1970). Later in his career, King's positions radicalised to a degree, and he was to identify 'the white power structure' as the source of the problem (Fredrik, 2004, p. 205), though still opposing the use of the slogan 'black power' (ibid: 225-6). Likewise, Malcolm X's positions softened towards the notion of integration, especially following his Haj experiences, in the last year of his life (Baldwin & Al Hadid, 2002, pp. 54-55).

Separation or integration are the two opposing terms of what Baldwin and Al-Hadid (2002) term 'the great debate', and both King and Malcolm X were building their positions on consolidated traditions of black American social resistance, whose most notable protagonists in the 19th century were the separationist Martin Delany and the integrationist Frederick Douglass (Baldwin & Al Hadid, 2002, pp. 253-5).

The march on Washington by the negro civil rights movement, in 1963, was one of the most dramatic events in an extraordinary decade, and King's 'I have a dream' address has gone down in history as a masterpiece of modern political rhetoric. Yet, as the life and work of Malcolm X demonstrated, King's integrationist, Gandhian approach did not convince all his listeners, as can be seen by comparing the following extracts from speeches by the two rival orators:

> The Negro is still sadly crippled by the manacles of segregation and the chains of discrimination. One hundred years later, the Negro lives on a lonely island of poverty in the midst of a vast ocean of material prosperity. One hundred years later, the Negro is still languished in the corners of American society and finds himself an exile in his own land. (Martin Luther King: I have a dream)

> How can the so-called Negroes who call themselves enlightened leaders expect the poor black sheep to integrate into a society of bloodthirsty white wolves, white wolves who have already been sucking on our blood for over four hundred years here in America? (Malcolm X: the Black Revolution)

In King's depiction, agency for the suffering of the negro is elided (Trew, 1979, p. 106). There are 'manacles' and 'chains', typical tools of slavery, but no-one applying them to his hands and feet. The negro's poverty might almost be the result of his own choice. In X's discourse, the same social reality is treated differently in a metaphor which assigns blame, and names the enemy. This pattern of framing, I shall suggest, is not accidental, but assists the speakers in developing their systems of argumentation, in demarcating boundaries between 'in' and 'out' group members, and in the persuasive attempt to align listeners with their own positions.

Speech acts, genus deliberativum

In 2000 Ruth Wodak gave a talk on the Austrian Freedom Party, in which she posed three questions:

> How can we explain Haider's success? How important is the rhetoric of the FPÖ? And what could the contribution from Sociolinguistics and CDA be in investigating this complex issue? (Wodak, 2000)

To many linguists, the first two questions would appear remote from their research interests; would appear, indeed, to have nothing to do with the discipline, belonging instead to fields like Sociology or Political Science. The third lays down the terrain of her own research, and indicates the gulf she intends to bridge, between the study of words–linguistics–and the ways people use them in specific social contexts.

As Van Dijk (2009, p. 1) says, contexts of interaction tend to be seen, in linguistic studies, at best as isolated "variables" of the social situation. For him, however, speech act theory can act as a bridge between "utterances as verbal objects and utterances as social acts" (Van Dijk, 1985, p. 6). Elsewhere he explains:

> Thus, the study of speech acts focused on the "action" dimension of utterances, thus going beyond the study of syntactic form and semantic meaning by adding "illocutionary meaning." Utterances, when made in specific situations, are thus defined not merely as expressions of sentences or propositions but also as social acts such as assertions, promises or threats. (Van Dijk T., 2009, p. 13)

The consummation of this process is the actual fulfilment, in the real world, of the promise or threat involved. Renkama (2004, p. 13) glosses Austin's original term, *perlocution*, as the "production of an effect through locution and illocution" (see also Austin, 1962, p. 109).

As has already been mentioned, above, among the genres of traditional rhetoric is the *genus deliberativum*, a label which covers those speeches which aim to achieve real-world effects (the other two are *epideictic* oratory for ceremonial occasions, and *forensic* oratory, which features in courtroom debates). We have seen that such oratory was vital in the classical world, where rhetorical skill could produce immediate effects in the real world. Parliamentary debates today respect the ancient *genus deliberativum* form, but have lost its essential significance, which was to enable the polis to decide what to do. Today's parliamentary speakers seek rewards for their rhetorical performances in terms of the effect on the wider audience–the listening public, which Halmari and Virtanen (2005, p. 7) term the 'ever-present audience'.

In exploring the rhetorical performances of Martin Luther King and Malcolm X, however, the picture is, again, slightly different. Neither were elected politicians with real power. What they had was influence, over the hearts and minds of their community; an influence which they sought to use, to lead the community in the direction they desired. Each advocated diametrically opposed *expressed opinions* (Van Eemeren & Grootendorst, 1984, p. 2) in their speeches: King, that the goal should be a peaceful collaboration with white society, insisting on social equality, and Malcolm X complete separation, by whatever means necessary, including the use of violence. It is therefore possible to trace, in their speeches, something of the traditional, deontic spirit of *genus deliberativum*: this is the situation before the community, here is what should be done about it. To the extent that either of these prominent spokesman was able to sway listeners by his rhetoric, he would be able to give palpable shape to the unfolding social map, to affect events in a tangible sense. The perspective of this chapter, then, is to explore the presence, in the speakers' rhetoric, of these expressed opinions, the linguistic/rhetorical techniques used to give them support, and the way each engaage with, and ward off, the solutions proposed by the other.

Rhetoric vs. dialectics, argumentation

There are problems in attempting to apply insights from the field of argumentation studies to political rhetoric. In the case of pragma-dialectics, for example, argumentation is conceived of in terms of two interlocutors only, which would seem to align the approach with the Greek discipline of *dialectics* more than that of *rhetoric* (Van Eemeren and Houtlosser 2009, p. 2). These authors sketch a gradual picture of historical separation between the two disciplines until in the modern period: "each conform to a different conception of argumentation and [are] generally considered incompatible." (ibid: 3).

Modern political rhetoric clearly involves argumentation, in the Aristotelian sense of *logos*, but there is generally only one speaker, who develops an argument in the absence of any come-back. In the context of real-world argumentation, other factors than those operating at the level of mere logical coherence can be decisive. Consider the following argument, for example:

1 The economic philosophy of Black Nationalism only means that we should own and operate
2 and control the economy of our community. You would never found - you can't open up a black
3 store in a white community. White men won't even patronize you. And he's not wrong. He's got
4 sense enough to look out for himself. You the one who don't have sense enough to look out for
5 yourself. The white man..the white man is too intelligent to let someone else come and gain
6 control of the economy of his community. But you will let anyone come in and take control of
7 the economy of your community, control the housing, control the education, control the jobs,
8 control the businesses, under the pretext that you want to integrate. No, you outta your mind.

The structure of argumentation in this fragment can be analysed as follows:

Table 6.1. Malcolm X: argumentation.

The black community let white men come in and control the local economy
However, SINCE
Economic control and political control are the same thing (Implicit premise)
THEREFORE
We should own and operate and control the economy of our community

In other words, the fragment clearly presents an argument, but it does not fall neatly into convenient categories. For one thing, it begins with the conclusion, "we should own and operate and control the economy of our community" (1-2). The rest of the text develops a sort of supporting 'argument', which can only be understood if its implicit premise is supplied, that economic control amounts to political control. This makes the argument a sort of enthymeme, in Aristotle's terminology (Fahnestock, 2011, p. 376), which is a syllogism with one implicit premise. Again, however, real-world factors intrude, making it hard for the purely rational faculties to operate in this instance. For one thing, the speaker is berating his audience, praising the white man's intelligence and implying (4, 6-8) that his black listeners are being stupid. In two cases, his criticism is overt: "You don't have enough sense to look out for yourself" (4), "you outta your mind" (8). As Brown and Levinson (1990, p. 66) say, verbal actions such as "expressions of disapproval, criticism, contempt or ridicule, complaints and reprimands, accusations, insults" are indications that "the speaker does not care about the addressee's feelings, wants, etc.", including the basic want to be "approved of, understood, liked or admired" (ibid: 64). The apparent paradox, of a speaker attempting to convince his audience by insulting them can best be understood in terms of X's leadership style, which was, as here, straight-talking to the point of abrasiveness. He came over as an appropriate leader for those elements of his community who wanted to stand up to the white man. Such listeners would, presumably, mentally excuse themselves from involvement in X's criticisms, since he was only voicing their own views. They would possibly feel that his abuse was directed either at back-sliders or the unconvinced.

The concluding phrase, "under the pretext that you want to integrate" (8), is a clear thrust in the direction of Martin Luther King and his philosophy of racial integration. X therefore aligns this 'stupid' behaviour of his audience with the views of his most significant adversary. Thus, properly understood, the fragment takes its place in a wider argumentative context, whose expressed opinion would be that "racial separation and not integration is the appropriate policy for our community". Presumably, much of X's audience would have been sympathetic to this position, and his rhetorical attempt is therefore aimed at aligning the unconvinced. The same considerations, naturally apply, in a very similar fashion, to the rallies of Martin Luther King, where the prevailing mood would have been in favour of integration and non-violent resistance.

Features of this speech such as X's emotional tone, his use of insults, his construction of possible patterns of ingroup/outgroup alignment, all make this 'argument' something quite different from the kind of sober analytical reasoning found in dialectics.

Another difference between a fragment of 'real' political argumentation, such as this, and the 'Socratic' kind, is that listeners have no opportunity to express alternative arguments, but are compelled to listen as the speaker monopolizes the dialogic space. Heckling or, as a final resort, walking out, are the only socially accepted forms in which to express disagreement.

Despite these differences, however, it is widely accepted that rhetorical techniques do have a role to play in persuasive rhetoric and argumentation (see, e.g. Charteris-Black 2005, p. 9; Lawrence 2008, p. 123) and both Malcolm X and Martin Luther King were, in their different ways, masters of rhetoric. The fragment above, for example, displays some of Malcolm X's use of some of the rhetorical devices analysed above, in chapter two. He uses *anaphora* in the formula "control the housing, control..., control..., etc." (6-8), *contrast* "a black store in a white community" (2-3), and *analogy* (3-6) when he compares the behaviour of black and white.

Evaluative language and argumentation

The relation between evaluation and argumentation has not yet received much attention, despite recognition of the usefulness of Martin and White's Appraisal Framework, and its application to a wide range of subjects and analytical contexts. Intuitively, one might expect a proportional relationship to exist between the persuasiveness of an argument and the force of the evaluative language used.[1]

To make this point, consider this example from Blair's discourse on Iraq. In the following fragment, he advances an implicitly expressed opinion: *we should not give Saddam more time; rather, we should use military force against him now.* His words were:

> This is not a road to peace, but folly and weakness which will only mean that when the conflict comes, it will be more bloody, less certain and greater in its devastation.

The terms Blair uses to characterise the conflict are marked by their intensity. Less intense lexical alternatives are available, but it suits his rhetorical purposes to avoid them. If he had concluded: *"when the conflict comes, its impact will be slightly worse"*, his audience would probably have concluded that the matter would not justify risking the hazards of war. Evaluative language is also present

---

[1] Readers are referred to my book on argumentation and evaluative language (Ponton, 2011), where these issues are dealt with.

in the way he presents the views of his adversaries, as '*folly and weakness*' (-Judgement: normality; - Judgement: tenacity), and these terms display the same tendency to use strong, rather than median or weak, evaluations.

The force and character of their evaluations, in fact, is one of the striking points of comparison between Malcolm X and Martin Luther King. In the fragments cited above, for example, it is already possible to trace fundamental patterns with contrasting rhetorical effects:

Table 6.2. X and King: evaluation.

Text	Evaluated	AF value
the Negro is still *sadly crippled* by the manacles of segregation and the chains of discrimination. One hundred years later, the Negro lives on *a lonely island of poverty* in the midst of a vast ocean of material prosperity. One hundred years later, the Negro is still *languished in the corners of American society and finds himself an exile in his own land.*	The Negro The Negro The Negro	-Aff: unhappiness -Aff: unhappiness -Aff: unhappiness
How can the so-called Negroes who call themselves enlightened leaders expect the poor black sheep to integrate into a society of bloodthirsty white wolves, *white wolves who have already been sucking on our blood for over four hundred years here in America?*	The Negroes 'enlightened leaders' White people	-J: capacity -J: propriety, intens.

King's rhetoric features the pitiful figure of the Negro, using the Affect system. The negative emotional states are indicated through the evaluative language, which is occasionally explicit ('sadly', 'lonely island of poverty') but also developed allusively, through the description of his poor social condition. Malcolm X, however, prefers judgement, and directs bitter and sarcastic judgements both against the black 'enlightened leaders', the integrationists–i.e., King and his followers–and against the white Americans, wholly absent (*backgrounded*, in the terms of Van Leeuwen (Van Leeuwen 1996) from King's discourse.

Method

The study focuses on argumentation as it appears in a controversial speech given by Malcolm X following the Kennedy assassination, which became known as 'the chickens come home to roost'. The speaker specifically targets the march on Washington, arguing that it was infiltrated by whites to the point where it lost all meaning. The speech is then briefly compared to Martin Luther King's famous address during the march on Washington.

The focus is on the relation between argumentation and evaluative language. Specifically, on the areas of Judgement (evaluations of human behaviour) and Affect (emotional language), as in the instances just discussed. Such discourse, it will be seen, demarcates boundaries of adhesion within the black community, around the mutually exclusive expressed opinions on possible social strategies. To illustrate patterns of argumentation, I use the completer version of Toulmin's (1958) model, which makes it possible to show the role of supporting data. As Van Eemeren (2009, p. 116) points out, there is a striking similarity between Toulmin's model of argumentation and Cicero's classical *epicheirema* (figure one). The Latin terms are from Cicero, the English are Toulmin's equivalents:

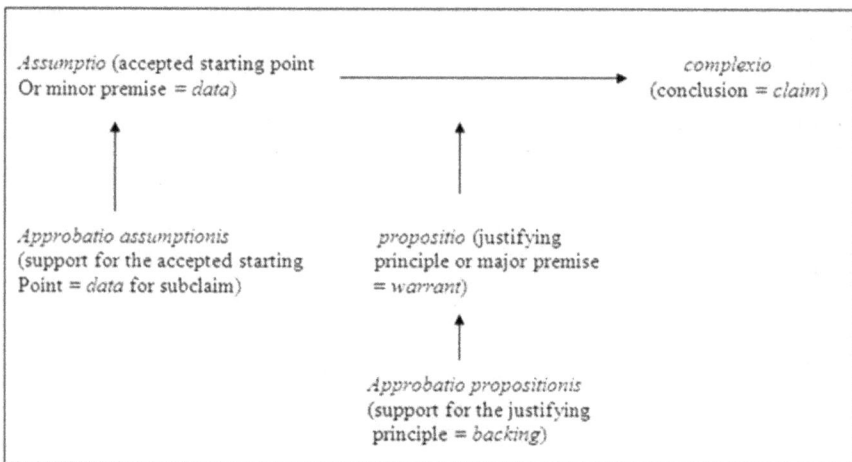

Figure 6.1. Toulmin's and Cicero's models of argumentation.[2]

The model will enable us to appreciate the role of evaluative language in persuasive political rhetoric.

Malcolm X. God's Judgement of White America: Evaluation

In this speech, Malcolm X's rhetoric is directed mainly against the civil rights leaders, as he develops a familiar theme, that separation and not integration is the appropriate course for the black community.[3] The speech was notorious

---

[2] See also Charteris-Black (2005, pp. 8-9).
[3] For the complete text of this long speech, see: "Malcolm X - Speeches God's Judgement of White America". Web references.

for X's remark, in response to a question about the Kennedy assassination, that it was a case of 'the chickens coming home to roost'. The uproar provoked by this led to his suspension from public speaking by Elijah Muhammad. In the speech itself, however, X is, if anything, respectful towards the man he refers to as 'the late president', praising the way he 'controlled' the Civil Rights movement by infiltrating the leadership, and even using the word 'genius' to refer to the Kennedy family's political acumen.

The diagram below (figure two) shows Malcolm X's use of Judgement in this speech, for the various social actors referred to: the black in-group of X's supporters and members of the Nation of Islam; the black out-group including Martin Luther King and other integrationist black leaders and their followers; the white man, a composite collection of social actors including: white America, the white man generally, white liberals, the US government, Republican and Democrat leaders, the ancient Egyptians and Pharaoh, and finally Elijah Mohammad who, as leader of the Nation of Islam, is invoked as an authority.

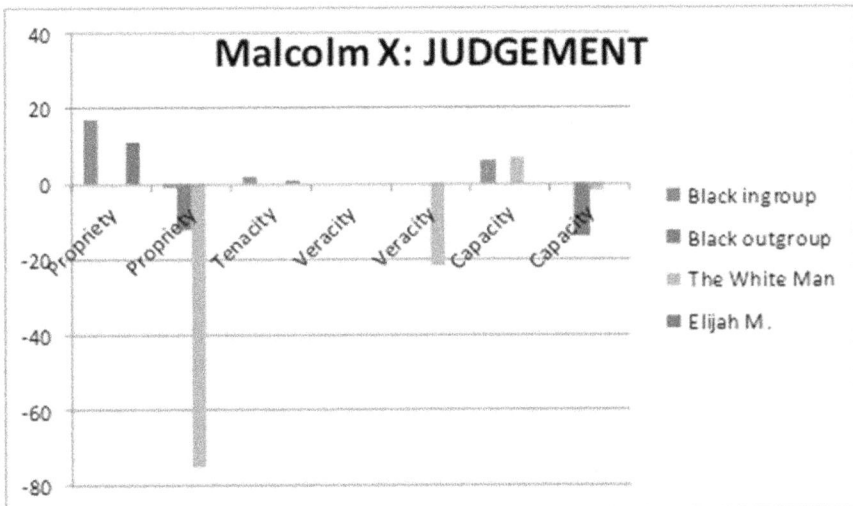

Figure 6.2. God's Judgement on white America: Judgement.

The system most used is that of propriety, which belongs to the realm of judgements Martin and White (2005, p. 52) term *social sanction*, or weighty judgements about truthfulness and ethics. The graph clearly shows the space given to attacks on moral behaviour–both in terms of truthfulness (*veracity*) and ethics (*propriety*) of 'the white man'. For Malcolm X, it needs hardly be said, to be white is to be in an automatic out-group. These social actors are connected by their unethical treatment of the black man. For example:

> We of this present generation are also witnessing how the <u>enslavement</u> of millions of black people in this country is now bringing White America to her hour of judgment (-J: propriety) (4)[4]

Ancient Egypt and Pharaoh are invoked to illustrate, by analogy, the same theme. Just as the negroes in modern America were an enslaved people, so the Israelites were kept prisoner by the ancient Egyptians. According to Malcolm X, Moses said:

> God will destroy you and your entire <u>slave empire</u> from the face of this earth. (- J: propriety)

Elijah Muhammad, leader of the Nation of Islam, X's mentor and chief, is compared to Moses and other biblical heroes of the Israelites:

> This little, <u>meek, humble,</u> inarticulate ex-slave is *a modern Noah, a modern Lot, a modern Moses..a modern Daniel. In fact, he is a modern David* (+ J: propriety, t + J propriety, intens.) (36)

As well as praising his own leader, X makes a significant number of approving references to the behaviour of what I have termed 'the black ingroup', Muslims who are showing fight and initiative:

> The black revolution is the <u>struggle</u> of the nonwhites of this earth against their white oppressors. The black revolution [..] *is sweeping down upon America like a raging forest fire* (+J: tenacity, t + J: tenacity)

The only positive judgements expressed on the White man are grudging tributes to his capacity, as in:

> a <u>shrewd</u> white liberal named Stephen Currier (+ J: capacity) (110).

Alongside these are negative Judgements expressed on the 'Black outgroup', a group including the six leaders of the march on Washington, among them Martin Luther King. These are mocked as 'Uncle Toms', handpicked by the white man:

---

[4] Line references are to the table in the Appendix, which shows analysis for Appraisal.

These *Uncle Tom leaders* do not speak for the Negro majority (t -J: capacity) (80)

The reference is to the lovable negro in Harriet Beecher Stowe's novel Uncle Tom's Cabin, clearly an unflattering portrayal of the integrationists.

A significant aspect of X's use of evaluation relates to intensification. Of this, Martin and White (2005, p. 20) say: "the volume is turned up so that the prosody makes a bigger splash which reverberates through the surrounding discourse". Malcolm X makes frequent use of this resource, multiplying negative tokens in colourful and, at times, alliterative, lists:

the Honorable Elijah Muhammad is turning hundreds of thousands of Americans Negroes away from <u>drunkenness, drug addiction, nicotine, stealing, lying, cheating, gambling, profanity, filth, fornication, adultery,</u> and the many other <u>acts of immorality</u> that are almost inseparable from this <u>indecent</u> Western society (-J: propriety, intens.) (20)

This <u>evil</u> Western world, the white world...a <u>wicked</u> world, ruled by <u>a race of devils,</u> that preaches <u>falsehood,</u> practices <u>slavery,</u> and thrives on <u>indecency and immorality</u> (-J: propriety, intens.) (22)

There are also some instances of Affect, but these are thin on the ground compared to X's extensive use of the Judgement system:

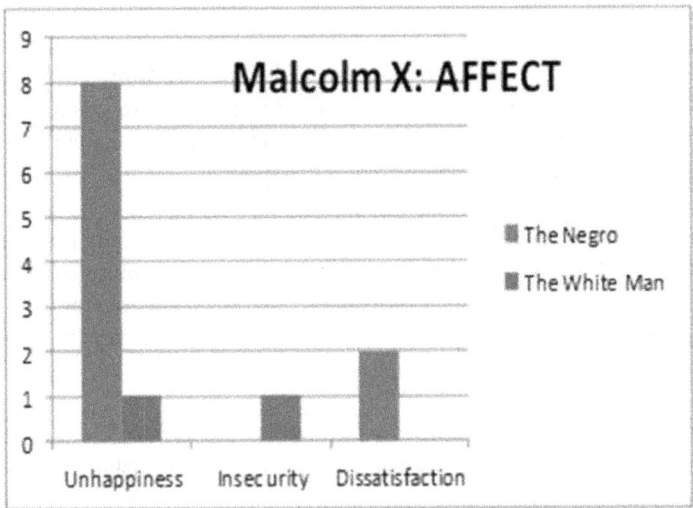

Figure 6.3. Affect.

He uses affect in references that are analogous to those of King, to show the unhappy situation of the negro in his condition of 'modern slavery':

> the black masses are still *without land, without jobs, and without homes* (t -Aff: unhappiness) (121)

The relatively few instances of this resource, however, suggest that X's rhetorical purposes are better served by his use of Judgement, and this can be better appreciated by exploring his use of argumentation.

Malcolm X: Argumentation

There are several different arguments that Malcolm X makes during this speech, among which are:

1) America's power is waning and the hour of its total destruction is at hand

2) Islam is the best religion for America's black population

3) Elijah Muhammad is a modern Moses, standing up to a modern Pharaoh for his oppressed people

4) Both of America's major political parties rely on the Negro vote but care nothing about his condition

5) The Civil Rights movement is in fact controlled by white politicians

However, central to the overall purpose of the speech, supported in different ways by all these different minor instances of argumentation, is the expressed opinion that America's blacks should seek separation rather than integration. X says this explicitly, about the middle of the speech:

> The Honorable Elijah Muhammad warns us daily: The only permanent solution to America's race problem is the complete separation of these twenty-two million ex-slaves from our white slave master, and the return of these ex-slaves to our own land, where we can then live in peace and security among our people.

The expressed opinion is *attributed* (Martin & White, 2005, p. 116) to Elijah Muhammad, an authoritative figure within the Nation of Islam, its leader and spiritual head, for whom many in X's audience will have feelings of respect. Of the operation of this resource, Martin and White say that "high credibility can be implied via the use of sources who have a high status in the field" (Martin &

White, 2005, p. 116). There are frequent references to Elijah Muhammad, always in glowing terms, with an excess of positive evaluation (lines 20, 21, 36-38, 95-96). Thus, the speaker's references to Muhammad as 'a great man of God' (95), as 'a modern Noah, Lot, Moses, Daniel and David' (36) all give credibility to the central expressed opinion, as if the speaker intended to invest Elijah Muhammad with the authority of an authentic prophet.

The figure of Muhammad as Allah's messenger is given further credibility by X's extended use of argument by analogy, as he develops a picture of slave empires, enjoying periods of historical supremacy before being inevitably destroyed by God:

> The Honorable Elijah Muhammad teaches us that as it was the evil sin of slavery that caused the downfall and destruction of ancient Egypt and Babylon, and of ancient Greece, as well as ancient Rome, so it was the evil sin of colonialism (slavery, nineteenth-century European style) that caused the collapse of the white nations in present-day Europe as world powers.

Whatever Elijah Muhammad teaches, then, can be seen–according to Malcolm X–as Allah's word to his people. It is, naturally, persuasive to the extent that his listeners share his own elevated evaluation of the group's leader.

The diagram below shows the role of evaluation in the argumentation in the speech, using the Toulmin model:

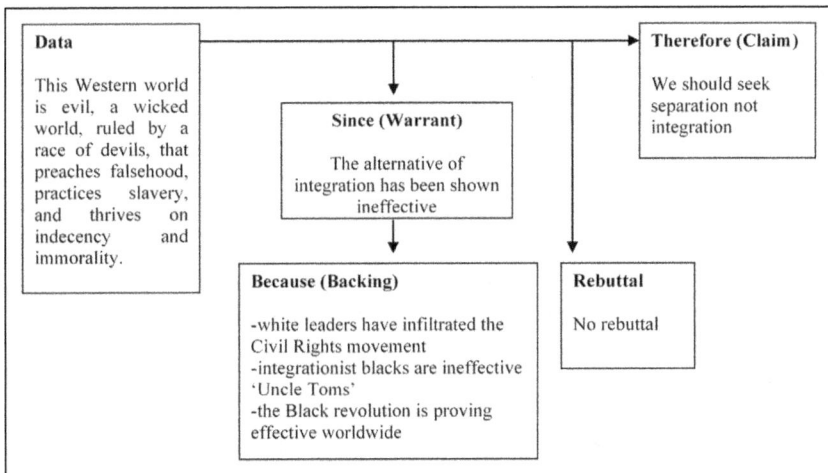

Figure 6.4. God's judgement on white America: argumentation.

Toulmin (1958, p. 90) thinks of the data section as the "information on which the claim is based" or, more colloquially, "what have you got to go on?" Potentially, here, it could include all of X's negative propriety Judgements on white social actors, as well as the negative Affect references with their depiction of negro suffering. In other words, the picture that he paints–in this and in many other speeches–is one of hapless black men at the mercy of this 'race of devils', the white exploiter, the slave master, immoral, depraved, grasping, cunning, and vicious. This is the basic, ideational picture that represents the 'Problem' element of the 'Problem/Solution' pattern (Hoey, 1994, p. 26). Providing an appropriate solution for it occupies the rest of the rhetorical space of the speech.

The warrant stage 'builds bridges' (Toulmin, 1958, p. 91) towards the Claim, or the 'expressed opinion', the favoured solution. In this case, X's dismissal of the integrationists' position sets up an 'either/or' opposition. To the extent that listeners are convinced by X's arguments against the integrationists, support for his own solution will be strengthened. The warrant is further supported by his arguments in the Backing section, about the weakness of the Civil Rights leaders, the 'Uncle Tom' collaborationists, the 'Black bourgeoisie', a minority of the black community who find it convenient to integrate:

These Uncle Tom leaders do not speak for the Negro majority; they don't speak for the black masses. They speak for the "black bourgeoisie", the brainwashed, white minded, middle-class minority who are ashamed of black, and don't want to be identified with the black masses, and are therefore seeking to lose their "black identity" by mixing, mingling, intermarrying, and integrating with the white man.

Thus, X's speech constructs borders around a black 'ingroup' and 'outgroup' (Reisigl & Wodak, 2001, p. 45), which is a still more pertinent distinction than that between black and white. In the former group, which X calls the 'black masses' are the Nation of Islam Muslims and, in short, any black citizen of the US who participates in episodes of civil unrest, to whom he makes approving reference as 'rampaging' negroes (104). In the outgroup are those blacks who want to integrate, and above all, their leaders, for whom he reserves some of his most bitter, sarcastic invective. As well as the disparaging reference to Uncle Toms, he claims that the 'Big Six', prominent leaders of the black community, including Martin Luther King, were used by the Kennedy administration to cap the black protest movement before it got out of hand, and even suggests that they were on the government's payroll:

According to the August 4 edition of The New York Times, $800,000 was split up between these six Negro civil rights leaders on June 19 at the Carlysle Hotel, and another $700,000 was promised to be given to them at a later date after the march was over, if everything went well with the march.

Analysis of each of the stages of Toulmin's model, then, shows that evaluation has a key role to play in the persuasive force of the argument. In the data stage, for example, it is only because the negro's situation is so desperate–a situation conveyed through high-intensity evaluations of the white man's cruelty and the negro's plight–that it is necessary to find a solution. In the warrant, it is X's invective against King's position–which is, again, conveyed through evaluative language–that rules out the alternative solution. To weaken X's evaluations at any of these stages would crucially weaken his overall argument. For example, if, instead of referring to the white man as 'a race of devils' he had used more moderate language, discriminating, perhaps between 'good' and 'bad' white men, his argument would be deprived of much of its emotional force and rhetorical impact. It is evaluative language, moreover, that permits X, with his firebrand rhetorical style, to exploit the common ground between himself and his audience, their common sense of historical outrage and current frustration. This means that the argument advanced is not necessarily the most persuasive or coherent from a rational perspective; rather, as was mentioned above, it appears that emotional factors can be used, by a skilful orator, to colour argumentation and make it more persuasive.

Comparison of X's speech with 'I have a dream'

It is not my intention to provide a detailed analysis of Martin Luther King's speech, something that has already been done by several authors (e.g. Gill & Whedbee, 1997; Shannon, 2007). Rather, I wish to use it to illustrate my general points, which concern the structure of political argumentation and the role within it, and in the construction of in- and out-groups, of evaluative language.

King's upbringing and education led him to approach the same data that Malcolm X deals with in a vastly different way. He learned, from Gandhi, that non-violence could represent a potent political force and, like him, believed that it was the best course to follow from a strategic point of view as well as a moral one:

> In the event of a violent revolution, we would be sorely outnumbered. And when it was all over, the Negro would face the same unchanged conditions, the same squalor and deprivation - the only difference being that his bitterness would be even more intense, his disenchantment even more abject. Thus, in purely practical as well as moral terms, the American Negro has no rational alternative to non-violence (Carson, 2006, p. 266)

In his great speech at the Lincoln memorial, King expressed his vision, using patterns of evaluation that contrast dramatically with those of Malcolm X. In fact, as Gill and Whedbee (1997, p. 180) point out, there is no harangue of the white man for his crimes against the negro; only a single instance of negative propriety judgement, one that condemns Alabama's governor and its 'vicious racists'. Elsewhere, the references to the negro history of enslavement locate it in some indefinite past period, the result of impersonal, historical processes. A few references, from the beginning of the speech, will suffice to make this point clear:

1)   millions of Negro slaves who had been seared in the flames of withering injustice.

2)   It came as a joyous daybreak to end the long night of their captivity.

3)   But one hundred years later, the Negro still is not free.

4)   One hundred years later, the life of the Negro is still sadly crippled by the manacles of segregation and the chains of discrimination.

5)   One hundred years later, the Negro lives on a lonely island of poverty in the midst of a vast ocean of material prosperity.

6)   And so we've come here today to dramatize a shameful condition.

7)   In a sense we've come to our nation's capital to cash a check

The white man's agency as the instrument of the black man's suffering, that burns so insistently in Malcolm X's speech, is elided here by impersonal phrases such as 'the flames of withering injustice' (1), 'the long night of their captivity' (2), and 'the manacles of separation' (4). Use of the past perfect tense (1) pushes the historical context farther from the present day. The use of the cheque metaphor, too, reduces the emotional temperature to that of a sober transaction, across a counter, between black and white. Metaphorically, it is worlds away from X's 'race of devils', his 'growling wolf', and 'smiling fox'. Comparing the two speakers on the subject of police brutality towards the negro, for example, confirms their radically different techniques of re/presentation:

We can never be satisfied as long as the Negro is the victim of the unspeakable horrors of police brutality. (King): - Affect: unhappiness, intens.

The police dogs and police clubs and the high-pressure water hoses were brutalizing black women and children and babies (X): - J: propriety: intense

In King's version, an impersonal phrase 'the unspeakable horrors of police brutality' uses grammatical metaphor, seemingly for the purposes indicated by Ho (2010, p. 6), who says that these might include "making everyday experience inaccessible and remote". X, however, indicates the agents performing these same actions, using a verb 'to brutalize', which also allows him to specify the recipients, expanding the group from King's generalised 'Negro' to include the most vulnerable members of this group (see Richardson, 2004, p. 57), for a discussion of these issues of representation).

While King focuses on the emotional sphere and foregrounds the Negro's unhappy condition, using intensification to increase the impact of this fragment, X uses intensification to whip up anger and resentment in his audience at the white actors' cruel behaviour. King develops a quite different expressed opinion, found in the following passage:

In the process of gaining our rightful place, we must not be guilty of wrongful deeds. Let us not seek to satisfy our thirst for freedom by drinking from the cup of bitterness and hatred. We must forever conduct our struggle on the high plane of dignity and discipline. We must not allow our creative protest to degenerate into physical violence.

Thus, the pattern of King's argumentation is quite different to that of Malcolm X:

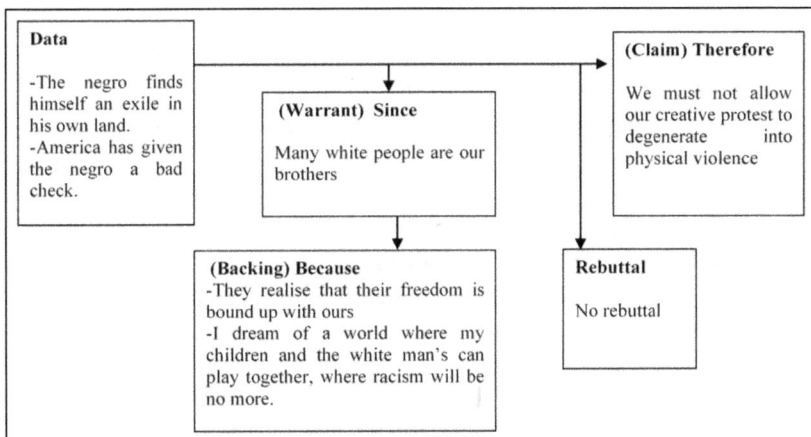

Figure 6.5. Argumentation in 'I have a dream'.

There is, then, no demonization of the white man. Rather, there is an attempt to diminish his responsibility, to distinguish between whites who are 'our brothers' and the few bad apples, represented by the 'vicious racists' of Alabama. The vision of an integrated future allows King's rhetoric to soar, in its famous climax, to a utopian vision in which white and black both gain their 'freedom'. Evaluation in his closing peroration dissolves racial differences, evoking the common humanity of X's 'oppressor' and 'oppressed':

> All of God's children, black men and white men, Jews and Gentiles, Protestants and Catholics, will be able to join hands and sing in the words of the old Negro spiritual:
>
> *Free at last! free at last!*
> *Thank God Almighty, we are free at last.* (t + Affect: happiness, intens.)

Neither King nor Malcolm X uses the dialogically expansive resource, the 'rebuttal clause', for obvious reasons. Both speakers, effectively, are using a 'there is no alternative' (TINA) strategy. Malcolm X's case would be crucially weakened by a qualification, along the lines of 'we must separate from the white man UNLESS you would prefer to integrate with him', and the same goes for King's message. Both are inextricably bound up in an implicit conflict with the other. Malcolm X's greatest 'enemy', apart from the white man, is Martin Luther King, whose prestige among the black community threatens his own, and makes it harder for him to mobilise that community in the sort of social action he favours. The same is true for King, who knows that non-violent social action is only effective if it is performed unanimously. Thus, while both apparently contest the racial injustice their community has suffered at the hands of the white man, their real target is the other, and their real intention is to bring over to their cause as many of the black community as possible.

Concluding remarks

In shaping the Civil Rights Movement, both Malcolm X and Martin Luther King played important roles, as the most prominent representatives of diametrically opposed strategic solutions to the same ideational realities. Their rhetoric was not simply a matter of scoring political points off the other side, as is the case with much modern political debate. Rather, it shared something of the old spirit which animated political debate in the classical period, the *genus deliberativum*, which advocated specific solutions to real-world problems. Had Malcolm X's rhetoric triumphed over the more integrationist philosophy favoured by King, history would look back on very different events in American social history.

The study showed how evaluative language is involved in argumentation, and how both relate to processes of alignment around the speakers' expressed opinions, in the process demarcating borders of in- and out-group identification. In order to be a member of the ingroup, King was implicitly engaged in delineating, it was not even necessary to be black; it was sufficient to believe in the policy of integration and the strategy of non-violence. In this perspective, a black person who contemplated violence, such as Malcolm X, would be excluded from King's ingroup. The same applies to X's ingroup, where, as we saw, black integrationists were sarcastically mocked. Audience members, as the speaker's discourse progressed, would classify, or categorise, themselves into one or the other of the groups, according to how they responded to the message (see Oakes, Haslam, & Turner, 1994; Turner et al., 1987) for further explanation of these cognitive processes).

The analytical model I have been developing in this book, in this chapter, is present in its more complete form, which is to say that it uses five of Toulmin's categories: Data, Warrant, Claim, Backing and Rebuttal. No rebuttal was in fact present but, as was stated in the analysis, neither King nor X admits alternatives, and this is an analytical point which is captured by the inclusion of the Rebuttal category in the model. The essential features of the model should, by now, be clear, and further chapters will explore other nuances in its application to modern political rhetoric.

The model still omits consideration of many components of persuasive rhetoric whose contribution may be considered highly significant, such as the mainly non-linguistic factors dealt with by Atkinson (1984). A principled account of political persuasion should no doubt pay more attention to such resources, and also to *delivery*, the factor famously identified by Demosthenes as the single most important for the would-be rhetorician (Kennedy, 1994, p. 80).[5] Malcolm X and Martin Luther King were both compelling speakers whose performances commanded attention. Both were figures who enjoyed considerable *ethos*, another Aristotelian component of political persuasion necessarily neglected in this exploration of *logos*. The role of *pathos*, however, has at least been touched upon. We have seen from this chapter, indeed, how the contribution of pathos makes its presence truly felt. It is hard to think clearly when under the stimulus of a powerful emotion such as rage, resentment or hatred, and Malcolm X was certainly adept at playing on these emotions in his listeners. King's abilities, I have suggested, led him to represent the same underlying realities in a different way, in accordance with his different ideology, and different overall social vision.

---

[5] Some of these issues are dealt with in Ponton (2016), especially features of non-verbal communication.

Appendix: God's Judgement of White America: Evaluation

	Text	Evaluation	Evaluated
1	the **evil sin** of slavery	-J: propriety	The white man
2	the **evil sin** of colonialism (slavery, nineteenth-century European style)	-J: propriety	The white man
3	**Unbiased** scholars and **unbiased** observers	+ J: veracity	Scholars
4	the **enslavement** of millions of black people in this country	-J: propriety	White America
5	*her downfall as a respected nation*	-J: propriety	White America
6	White America too will be utterly destroyed by her own **sins**	-J: propriety	White America
7	White America must now pay for her **sins**	-J: propriety	White America
8	White America's worst crimes her **hypocrisy** and her **deceit**.	-J: veracity	White America
9	White America **pretends** to ask herself	-J: veracity	White America
10	four hundred years of **cruel bondage**	-J: propriety	White America
11	*We, [..] believe whole-heartedly in the God of justice*	+J: propriety	Muslims
12	*We believe in the Creator*	+J: propriety	Muslims
13	*We believe in the all-wise Supreme Being*	+J: propriety	Muslims
124	*We do not believe in the Trinity*	+J: propriety	Muslims
15	*We who are Muslims call God by his true name*	+J: propriety	Muslims
16	*We who are Muslims believe in this religion*	+J: propriety	Muslims
17	It gives us the **moral discipline** [..] path of **truth and righteousness**	+J: propriety	Muslims
18	complete **submission** and **obedience** to God's will.	+J: propriety	Muslims
19	Many of the **weak, backsliding** Muslims who come to this country	- J: propriety	Muslims
20	the Honorable Elijah Muhammad is turning hundreds of thousands of Americans Negroes away from **drunkenness, drug addiction, nicotine, stealing, lying, cheating, gambling, profanity, filth, fornication, adultery**, and the many other acts of **immorality** that are almost inseparable from this **indecent** Western society.	+J: propriety -J: propriety, intens.	Elijah Muhammad Western society
21	*The Honorable Elijah Muhammad has restored our cultural roots*	+J: propriety	E. Muhammad

22	this **evil** Western world, the white world...a **wicked** world, ruled by a **race of devils**, that preaches **falsehood**, practices **slavery**, and thrives on **indecency and immorality**	-J: propriety/ veracity, intens.	Western world
23	this present **evil** world	-J: propriety	(western) world
24	the **evil** seeds of **slavery** and **hypocrisy**	-J: propriety	White America
25	the harvest of **unjust** seeds	-J: propriety	White America
26	their own **wickedness and lust for evil** [..] the flood of their own **evil deeds**	-J: propriety, intens.	the wicked (biblical) world
27	the **wicked** world of the Sodomites[..] their **evil** deeds	-J: propriety	the Sodomites
28	their own **lowly** passions	-J: propriety	the Sodomites
29	House of **Bondage**, or Land of **Slavery**	-J: propriety	the Egyptians
30	**false** promises of integration with you	-J: veracity	Pharaoh
31	we can [..] practice **righteousness**, and live in **peace**	+J: propriety	The Israelites
32	your entire **slave** empire	-J: propriety	Pharaoh
33	Pharaoh's wealth and power made him too **proud** to listen	-J: propriety	Pharaoh
34	Six **puppets** who have been trained by the whites in white institutions	-J: capacity	Negro leaders
35	*These handpicked spokesmen do nothing but parrot for the whites*	-J: capacity	Negro leaders
36	This little, **meek, humble**, inarticulate ex-slave is a modern **Noah**, a modern **Lot**, a modern **Moses**...a modern **Daniel**	+J: propriety, intens.	Elijah Muhammad
37	stones of **truth**, this modern David	+J: /ver/prop.	E. Muhammad
38	The Honorable Elijah Muhammad's gospel of **truth**	+J: veracity	E. Muhammad
39	We **practice prayer**	+J: propriety	Muslims
40	We make **charitable** contributions	+J: propriety	Muslims
41	*We practice fasting*	+J: propriety	Muslims
42	*pilgrimage to the Holy City Mecca*	+J: propriety	Muslims
43	to atone for her **sins** against God's people	-J: propriety	America
44	our white **oppressor**	-J: propriety	the white man
45	a savior to the **oppressed**	-Aff: unhapp.	The Negro
46	the **wicked slave master**	-J: propriety	the white man
47	so **deaf, dumb, and mentally blind**	-J: capacity	The Negro

48	these American Negroes for their **sinful, ignorant** behavior.	-J: propriety	The Negro
49	The **independence** and **power** of the dark world [..] is rising in **wealth, power, prestige,** and **influence**	+J: capacity	the dark world
50	white man loses his **power**	-J: capacity	the white man
51	His world is **on its way down**; it is **on its way out**	-J: capacity	the white man
52	the evil white man's **unjust** rule	-J: propriety	the white man
53	those who led others into **captivity**	-J: propriety	Those
54	those who **killed** others with the sword	-J: propriety	Those
55	the **wicked** slave master	-J: propriety	the white man
56	the **evil** seeds of slavery he has planted	-J: propriety	the white man
57	the **innocent** from the **guilty**	+J: propriety, -J: propriety	The negro, The white man
58	the **righteous** from the **wicked**	+J: propriety, -J: propriety	The negro, The white man
59	the **oppressed** from the **oppressor**	-Aff: unhapp. -J: propriety	The negro, The white man
60	the **exploited** from the **exploiter**	-Aff: unhapp. -J: propriety	The negro, The white man
61	the **slaves** from the **slave master**	-Aff: unhapp. -J: propriety	The negro, The white man
62	**sinful** white world of **colonizers, enslavers, oppressors, exploiters, lynchers**.	-J: prop. intens.	The white man
63	America as number one among the **guilty** that would be too proud	-J: propriety	America
64	her **corrupt** government, the **crooked** politicians	-J: propriety	ancient Egypt
65	They have been hired by this white government	-J: propriety	Negro leaders.
66	our white **slave master**	-J: propriety	The white man
67	the **crooked** politicians in the government	-J: propriety	The white man
68	The **greedy** politicians	-J: propriety	W. politicians
69	In this **deceitful** American game of power politics	-J: veracity	The white man
70	the liberal is more **deceitful** than the conservative [..] more **hypocritical**	-J: veracity	white liberals
71	the white liberal [..] **posing** as the Negro's friend and benefactor	-J: veracity	white liberals
72	**false** promises of integration	-J: veracity	white liberals
73	*the willing cooperation of the Negro civil rights leaders*	-J: propriety	Negro leaders

74	These leaders **sell out** our people	-J: propriety	Negro leaders
75	*These leaders are satisfied with token victories*	-J: prop./cap.	Negro leaders
76	**false** promises of integration	-J: veracity	W. politicians
77	the black bourgeoisie [..] with **no racial pride**	-J: propriety	Black outgroup
78	the **downtrodden** black masses	-Aff. unhapp.	Black ingroup
79	*the Negro leadership that has been handpicked for them*	-J: capacity	Negro leaders
80	These **Uncle Tom** leaders	-J: capacity	Negro leaders
81	the "black bourgeoisie," the **brainwashed, whiteminded**	-J: cap./prop.	Black outgroup
82	**mixing, mingling, intermarrying, integrating** with the white man	-J: propriety	Black outgroup
83	the **downtrodden, dissatisfied** black masses	-Aff. unhapp.	Black ingroup
84	their ability to **deceive** and to **exploit** the Negro	-J: ver./prop.	White liberals
85	the Negro will then be able to see and **think for himself** (irrealis)	+J: capacity	the Negro
86	the white man's **crooked** game of "power politics."	-J: veracity	The white man
87	the **tricky** strategy used by white liberals	-J: veracity	White liberals
88	The **crooked** politicians in Washington, D.C	-J: propriety	W. politicians
89	*these same Negro civil rights "leaders" are then used by white liberals*	-J: capacity	Negro leaders
90	white politicians who **pose** as liberals, who **pose** as friends	-J: veracity	W. politicians
91	The white liberals are more **dangerous** than the conservatives	-J: propriety	White liberals
92	the **growling** wolf, the [..] smiling fox	-J: propriety	W. politicians
93	these **foxy** white liberals	-J: veracity	White liberals
94	*The black revolution has swept white supremacy out of Africa*	+J: capacity	Black ingroup
95	This **great man of God**	+J: propriety	E. Muhammad
96	he **will not compromise** in any way	+J: tenacity	E. Muhammad
97	the **wrongs** this government has inflicted upon our people	-J: propriety	The white man
98	the white **fox**	-J: veracity	The white man
99	**police dogs, police clubs**, and fire hoses **brutalizing** defenseless black women, children, and even babies	-J: propriety, intens.	The white man

100	these **moderate** Negro leaders	-J: capacity	Negro leaders
101	the **weak** image of the Negro civil rights leaders	-J: capacity	Negro leaders
102	Martin Luther King's image had been **shattered**	-J: capacity	M. Luther King
103	The other civil rights leaders had also become **fallen idols**	-J: capacity	Negro leaders
104	the **rampaging** Negroes	+J: tenacity	Black ingroup
105	white government of America **doesn't believe in God!**	-J: propriety	The white man
106	the **police dogs** and **police clubs** and the high-pressure water hoses were **brutalizing** black women and children and babies	-J: propriety, intens.	The white man
107	Negroes in Birmingham **exploded** and began to defend themselves	+J: tenacity	Black ingroup
108	This **frightened** the entire white power structure.	-Aff. disinclin.	The white man
109	political **genius** with which the Kennedy family was ruling this country	+J: capacity	the Kennedies
110	a **shrewd** white liberal named Stephen Currier	+J: capacity	Stephen Currier
111	civil rights leaders began **to fight publicly among themselves**	-J: capacity	Black leaders
112	*$800,000 was split up between these six Negro civil rights leaders*	-J: propriety	Black leaders
113	**skillfully** projected them as the leaders of the March on Washington	+J: capacity	The white press
114	those blacks are so **dissatisfied, disenchanted**, and **angry** (irrealis)	-Aff.: unhapp., -Aff. dissat.	Black ingroup
115	the **shrewd** politicians in Washington	+J: capacity	W. politicians
116	its **hypocrisy** on civil rights	-J: veracity	Kennedy govt.
117	The late President's **shrewd** strategy	+J: capacity	Kennedy
118	give the late President an **Oscar** for the "Best Producer of the Year	+J: capacity	Kennedy
119	the four white liberals who participated should get an **Oscar**	+J: capacity	White liberals
120	Negro civil rights leaders should go and **Oscar** for the "Best Supporting Cast	+J: cap. (ironic)	Black leaders
121	the black masses are still **without land, without jobs, and without homes**...their Christian churches are still **being bombed, their innocent little girls murdered**.	-Affect: unhappiness, intens.	Black ingroup

122	the black masses are still **unemployed, still starving, and still living in the slums**....and, I might add, getting **angrier and more explosive every day**	-Aff. unhapp. intens, -A: dissat	Black ingroup
123	the **crimes** she has committed	-J: propriety	The white man
124	the evils she has **brutally** and **mercilessly**	-J: prop. intens.	White America
125	her **deceitful** offers of integration	-J: veracity	America
126	*we can live in peace and harmony with our own kind (irrealis)*	+affect: happ.	Black ingroup
127	this white government is **afraid** (irrealis)	-Affect: insec.	W. government
128	this **wicked** race that **enslaved** us	-J: propriety	The white man
129	this **race of devils**	-J: propriety	The white man
130	its **sins** against our people	-J: propriety	The white man

Chapter 7

Information structure in Gerry Adams' speech on disarming the IRA, April 6th, 2005

Introduction

The context of what are generally termed, in British political and newspaper discourse 'the troubles' in Northern Ireland, arose for historical reasons, provoked by England's political and military hegemony over neighbouring territories. The history of conquest and colonisation dates back as far as Tudor times. In the 20th century, bitter sectarian rivalry between Protestants, descended mainly from Presbyterian Scottish settlers, and the Catholic minority left in the Northern counties after partition in 1921, was a constant feature of life in the new Irish state (Cottrell, 2005). The Irish Republican Army had played a prominent role in events leading up to the achievement of partial Irish independence from the British crown, and it surfaced again in the late 1960s, when sectarian violence in the counties led to British troops returning to Belfast in large numbers. On the political scene, Sinn Fein represented the views of the republican community, but during the 1970s and 1980s, they were refused access to mainstream political debate, because of their perceived connection to an outlawed terrorist organisation. In Ulster, the IRA's campaign of terror was matched by unionist paramilitary bodies such as the Ulster Defence Force, and for decades the province was characterised by tit-for-tat murders, pub bombings, and other acts of reciprocal violence that poisoned the political and social climate. The troubles witnessed, in short, "one of the longest running, and most brutal, terrorist campaigns the world has ever seen" (Morrison, 2013, p. 175).

Sinn Fein leader Gerry Adams comes from a family with a proud history of membership of the IRA, and the opinion that he is a leading member of the organisation, though denied by the man himself, is widely accepted (see Adams, 2003). Adams' constant denials have been attributed to the fact that an admission would have curtailed his potential for political discussions. Although, for many years, Adams and other prominent Sinn Fein/IRA personalities were denied acceptance in official political circles, secret talks with successive British governments were regular events, especially following the fall of Margaret Thatcher in 1989 (Frampton, 2009, p. 80). These talks began to change the atmosphere during the following decade, when political gains by Sinn Fein made two things apparent: firstly, for the British government under John Major, no useful purpose could be served by continuing to exclude such an important player from discussions on the province's future, and secondly, from the IRA/Sinn Fein point of view, hope began to dawn that progress could, after all, be made by political means rather than by dragging out a military campaign that offered few prospects of eventual victory.

An important breakthrough was the Good Friday agreement, signed on 19th April 1998, which brought an IRA ceasefire, alluded to by Adams in this speech, inaugurating an uneasy period of power-sharing in the Northern Ireland Assembly. This arrangement was only partially successful, with the assembly suspended on various occasions, but the ceasefire generally held. Adams is trying, in this 2005 speech, to prepare the ground for the document entitled the Provisional IRA Statement on Permanent Cessation of Violence, eventually published on 28th July 2005 (Morrison, 2013, p. 175). The speech appears to have the rhetorical aim of achieving a general consensus around the policy favoured by the leadership, and asks members to begin processes of "intense internal consultation". Adams' speech can also be seen as a response to the party's commitment, taken as part of the Good Friday agreement, to push for the decommissioning of IRA weapons (Maillot, 2005, p. 37), an extremely sensitive topic for most republicans.

Unity and consensus are potential problems for any political group, but in the case of Sinn Fein/IRA they have historically been particularly acute. Since its formative years in the wake of the 1916 Easter Rising the party, and its armed sister organisation, have each been riven by internal division that have periodically led to breakaway groups forming new organisations (Ó Broin, 2009, p. 190). The latest episode had seen the formation of the so-called 'Real IRA', (Cottrell, 2005, p. 112), see also (Mooney & O'Toole, 2003), a hard-line group within the IRA that had rejected the terms of the Good Friday agreement and split off to continue its own favoured military activities. Adams, therefore, is well aware that the choice to abandon armed struggle in favour of methods of negotiation is likely to alienate certain factions within the audience, which consists largely of members of IRA/Sinn Fein. There are clear parallels, then, with the situations of Malcolm X and Martin Luther King just discussed where, as we saw, each speaker had to negotiate with rival groups and ideological positionings among their own potential supporters.

There is a tension over the speaker's own identity politics throughout the speech, visible in lines like:

In the past I have defended the right of the IRA to engage in armed struggle (27)

If we accept that Adams, for the whole course of the recent armed struggle, had been a *de facto* member of the IRA, and that all those present were perfectly aware of this, then such formulae become paradoxical. It is natural to wonder at the continual discursive charade, which creates two distinct groups (IRA and Sinn Fein), apparently on different sides of a certain question. The discursive world created by Adams, in fact, is one in which the political body (Sinn Fein) is apparently requesting the military body (the IRA) to renounce its whole *raison-d'être*, and to leave the future resolution of the struggle to the politicians. But if the leadership of the two bodies effectively correspond, the listener might wonder, where is the need for consultation?

Introduction: theme and rheme

In this chapter, we focus on 'information structure' (Arnold et al., 2013), or the way writers organise and present their material at the textual level; what M.A.K. Halliday terms 'the clause as message' (Halliday & Matthiessen, 2004). Following the Prague school, Halliday uses the terms Theme and Rheme, where the former refers to the first element in any clause, and the latter to the remainder (ibid: 64):

> The Theme is the element which serves as the point of departure of the message; it is that which locates and orients the clause within its context. The remainder of the message, the part in which the Theme is developed, is called in Prague school terminology the Rheme

The following phrase, where Theme and Subject correspond, would be an example of what Halliday calls an 'unmarked' theme:

Table 7.1. Unmarked theme.

THEME	RHEME
Sinn Fein	has demonstrated the ability to play a leadership role as part of a popular movement towards peace, equality and justice (40)

A 'marked' theme, on the other hand, is one that is something other than the Subject (ibid: 73), as in:

Table 7.2. Marked theme.

THEME	RHEME
In the past	I have defended the right of the IRA to engage in armed struggle (27)

Using marked themes is one resource speakers have for foregrounding a particular element of the clause and backgrounding others. I shall suggest, below, that one of the rhetorical effects Adams is seeking to create in this speech relates to 'the past', insinuating that, as a strategy, armed struggle belongs there, and he does just that in this sentence.

However, the picture becomes more complex if we consider that the functions of Theme and Rheme may correspond (or not) with another important aspect of the clause as message, the conveying of 'new' information (Halliday & Matthiessen, 2004, p. 87), or information that cannot be inferred from what has already been uttered. The subject matter of most ordinary conversation–or political rhetoric–will generally be *recoverable*, in Halliday's sense, either from what has already been mentioned, or from the general context knowledge of participants (ibid: 91). Fries (1994, p. 233) claims that "writers tend to place New information towards the end of the clause, thus strengthening the correlation of New with Rheme" (see also Los et al. 2012, p. 4). For example:

Table 7.3. Given and new.

THEME	RHEME
Sinn Fein	has demonstrated the ability to play a leadership role as part of a popular movement towards peace, equality and justice (40)

Here, according to Fries, the theme 'Sinn Fein' would represent something 'given', something all listeners know about and recognise; the rest of the sentence, the rheme, would be 'new information', or the message that the speaker wishes to convey to listeners about the theme.

One typical pattern of information structure sees the Rheme of a former clause taken up as the Theme of the successive, as in:

Table 7.4. Theme and rheme.

RHEME
5. Eleven years ago, *the (Irish Republican) Army leadership ordered a complete cessation of military operations.*

THEME
6. *This courageous decision* was in response to proposals put forward by the Sinn Fein leadership where '*this courageous decision*' is now presented as Given information, and thematised.

What precisely is intended by 'New information' can be somewhat problematic at times, however:

23. You asserted the legitimacy of the right of the people of this island to freedom and independence.

We can hardly consider the description in the Rheme as offering new information, since it presents a discursive construction of the republican movement which would be commonplace to Adams' audience. In fact, much of the content of the Rhemes in this speech is taken up by statements containing historical references that are anything but new to Adams' putative audience, as in the following, which blames unionists for past political failures:

14. That agreement perished on the rock of unionist intransigence

or this specimen of partisan propaganda:

11. The Irish Republican Army <u>has kept every commitment made by its leadership</u>

One way of reading this apparently anomalous circumstance, i.e. that Adams' Rhemes are so uncontroversial for his hearers, hence not 'new' in any sense, is to consider his intended audience more closely. Although the speech is explicitly addressed to the IRA, much of its communicative purpose relates to the construction of a positive identity for republicanism generally. The propositions Adams outlines in the Rhemes are not as dialogically inert for global public opinion as they are for listening republicans, although of course they are hardly 'new' to such an audience either. Halliday (2004, p. 91), however, insists that "what is treated as non-recoverable has the meaning: attend to this; this is news." Fries (1994, p. 244) explains that, while Themes serve as "orienters" to the information contained in the clauses, Rhemes "regularly contain information which relates to the purposes of the text". They develop, in other words, those specific features of a speaker's message that distinguish it from other speeches on the same subject. However predictable the discourse in question may be, it is nonetheless a fresh assemblage of points of view on a matter. In the case of this speech by Adams, coincidentally, it also happens to represent the announcement of a genuinely 'new' political stance.

Given information and Theme

Theme, then, tends to be associated with Given information. If we look at the elements constituting the themes in Adams' text, the *contextualizing* function of the Themes is apparent at first glance: references abound to such well-known context features as, for example:

> *republican volunteers/republicans, the IRA, the Irish Republican army, Sinn Fein, the unionists, nationalists, the British and Irish establishments, the two governments*, etc.

A second lexical group is also apparent, of words connected in some way with the concept of struggle:

> *time of great peril, mighty odds, courageous decision, your courage, selflessness and determination, peace process*, etc.

There is also a third group of references to processes that involve the passage of time:

> *eleven years ago, on a number of occasions, the most recent of these, at that time, since then, for over thirty years, in the past, the catalyst for much of this change*, etc.

These things, then, form the basic structural framework of Adams' speech; they are, to put it simply, what his message is *about*. The rest of the message is contained in the various Rhemes.

The Theme performs its orienting function precisely because, as can be seen in the Themes of Adams' speech, such elements constitute 'shared knowledge' for most members of the discourse community; for this reason, the information can be taken as Given. The typical (unmarked) rhetorical pattern is to map Given onto Theme:

Table 7.5. Given/New.

GIVEN THEME	NEW RHEME
23. <u>Many of your comrades</u>	made the ultimate sacrifice

There are variations from this pattern. In line 8, for example, Adams makes a claim:

it was the IRA leadership which authorised a number of significant initiatives to enhance the peace process

This is an example of a 'predicative' theme (Halliday & Matthiessen, 2004, p. 95). Such themes express the semantic feature of *exclusiveness* (it was....and no-one else). This would be an example of a marked theme, emphasising that the content is to be attended to as news.

The mapping of Given/New onto Theme/Rheme as a pattern of textual organisation gives the speaker rhetorical possibilities as s/he "plays with the system" (ibid: 93) to create particular effects. Instead of conforming to the typical pattern, which has a nominal group or pronoun in thematic position, a speaker can place another grammatical constituent there, such as a temporal Circumstance. Such constructions reverse the normal pattern of correspondence between Given and Theme, and New and Rheme:

Table 7.6. New/Given.

NEW THEME	GIVEN RHEME
5. Eleven years ago,	The (Irish Republican) Army leadership ordered a complete cessation of military operations.

Halliday suggests that by means of such disruptions in normal textual patterning,[1] writers can draw attention to certain aspects of their message, creating moments of communicative tension that will serve their overall rhetorical goals. Meanwhile, Fries (1994, p. 247) advances the hypothesis that variations in word order constitute a major tool for writers seeking to compensate for the deficiencies of the written medium, when compared to speech, in signalling prominence.

The following example shows how speakers can exploit such patterns in an attempt to naturalise (see Fairclough, 1996, p. 91) propositions that are, in essence, merely partial versions of reality shaded by the ideology of the speaker:

Table 7.7. Given and new.

Given/Theme	New/Rheme
15. The short-sightedness of the two governments	compounded the difficulties

---

[1] The rhetorical term for this is hyperbaton, which we saw in the Burke speech, above.

Adams has used nominalisation to present a debatable proposition, namely the attributive proposition that 'the two governments *are* short-sighted'. By thematisation, this proposition automatically becomes a part of the 'given' portion of the message. It would be possible, however, to present the same content information in the passive voice, as follows:

> The difficulties were compounded by the short-sightedness of the two governments

In this version, the proposition that the governments were short-sighted, since it occupies the 'new' slot, is clearly cast as a matter for debate. The speaker's actual selection casts the proposition as shared information between speaker and public. If the speech is considered as directed at the IRA alone, of course, Adams' presupposition is a fair reflection of the facts as they appear to the majority of his audience. In terms of its wider reception, though, the formulation will be likely to alienate those with a stake in the social actors implicitly criticised. Chilton (2004, p. 56) gives an analogous example and comments:

> The point of such packaging, and the effect, is that the bits of 'reality' so packaged are made less salient or more taken for granted as common ground for speaker and hearer.

Marked themes

Marked themes, then, are themes which reverse the expected pattern of mapping, of Given with Theme, and New with Rheme. The marked themes, in Adams' speech are shown in the table below.

Table 7.8. Adams, marked themes.

2.	In time of great peril.
4.	Against mighty odds
5.	Eleven years ago
7.	Since then
8.	It was the IRA leadership
9.	On a number of occasions
14.	At that time
15.	The short-sightedness of the two governments

18.	Since then
23.	For over 30 years
30.	In the past
32.	Now
62.	Now is the time

The marked themes are found to consist, to a significant degree, precisely in those references to temporal processes indicated earlier; to *the past,* to *now,* and to *moments in past time.* Foregrounding *chronos* in this way emphasises the possibility that society itself is in a state of flux, that situations, even the most rigid and seemingly entrenched, are also subject to change. What was an appropriate response thirty years ago may not, in the nature of things, be appropriate today.

Examining some of these clauses in terms of their constituents (Halliday & Matthiessen, 2004, p. 168) will offer more clues as to the rhetorical significance of these thematic choices:[2]

Table 7.9. In time of great peril.

CIRCUMSTANCE: contingency	ACTOR	PROCESS: MATERIAL	GOAL
2. In time of great peril	You	stepped	into the Bearna Baoil, the gap of danger.

Table 7.10. Against mighty odds.

CIRCUMSTANCE: contingency	ACTOR	PROCESS: MATERIAL	GOAL
4. Against mighty odds	You	held the line (and) faced down a huge military foe,	the British Crown Forces and their surrogates in the unionist death squads.

In both these examples, the heroism of the republicans is emphasised by thematising the circumstances of contingency. The peril and the odds are

---

[2] The interested reader is referred to Halliday's text for a full explanation of these terms, typical of Systemic Functional Linguistics; however, an intuitive grasp of their meanings will be sufficient for present purposes.

stressed in these instances of hyperbaton. Fronting the first sentence with the temporal circumstance appears to locate the events in a sort of mythical past space. The effect is rather similar to that of a fairy story beginning *Once upon a time..*, an effect heightened, for non-Gaelic speakers at least, by Adams' use of the Gaelic phrase 'the Bearna Baoil'. The Bearna Baoil is a reference to an episode during a heroic defeat in the long saga of anti-English rebellion. It has passed into legend, into the Irish national anthem and other songs that are still sung today.

In the following examples, temporal effects are once more in evidence. The IRA is again the Actor, and the Circumstance of time is thematised:

Table 7.11. Eleven years ago.

CIRCUMSTANCE: Extent	ACTOR	PROCESS: VERBAL	SCOPE
5. Eleven years ago	the Irish Republican Army leadership	ordered	a complete cessation of military operations

Table 7.12. For over 30 years.

CIRCUMSTANCE: Extent: duration	ACTOR	PROCESS: MATERIAL
23. For over 30 years	the IRA	showed that the British government could not rule Ireland on its own terms

One effect here is to background the Actor slightly: the IRA is represented as having been an influence on events, but thematisation of time functions to associate it with the past. There are other such references in the text, sufficient to create an effect of semantic prosody (Baker, 2006, p. 87) in this sense (e.g. lines 2, 3, 4, 5, 27, 37, 39, 43, 54). Of course, Adams is not trying to suggest to his IRA audience that they are to be seen as 'yesterday's men'. Rather, the marked themes underscore his general message, which is that changing times require changing strategies, and that to continue with violent methods in today's context is to remain somehow trapped in the past. Line 51 makes this plain, as Adams re-evokes the Bearna Baoil but places it firmly in a modern, democratic context, thus uniting past and present:

Table 7.13. Now is the time.

CIRCUMSTANCE: Extent	ACTOR	PROCESS: VERBAL	CIRCUMSTANCE: Manner	CIRCUMSTANCE: Manner
51. Now is the time	(for) you	to step into the Bearna Baoil again	not as volunteers risking life and limb	but as activists in a national movement towards independence and unity.

The present time (now) is thematised, and the heroic military associations of the Bearna Baoil are re-contextualised in terms of democratic activity.

Argumentation and evaluation

In terms of evaluative language, the speech has a fairly predictable pattern in terms of ingroup legitimisation and outgroup de-legitimisation (figure eight, below):

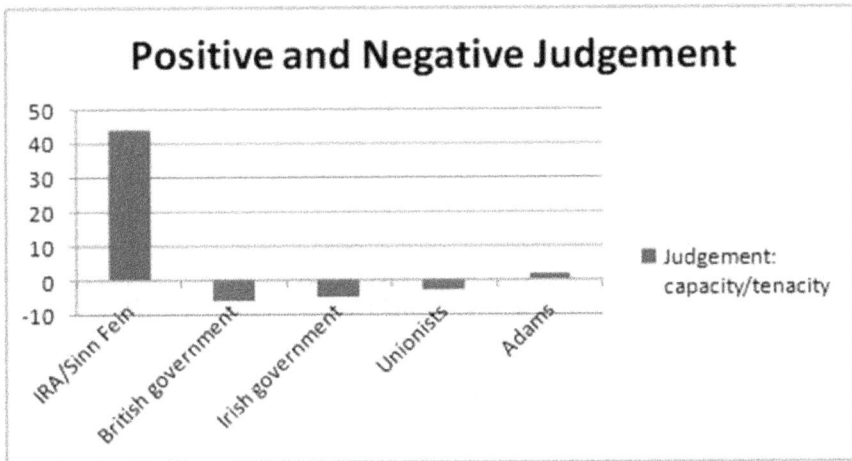

Figure 7.1. Adams' speech: positive and negative judgement.

Social actors belonging to the Adams groups–IRA, Sinn Fein, the Irish people–are represented with positive judgements while the opponents receive negative ones. Adams emphasises, in particular, the past courage of the IRA in its military campaign:

Against mighty odds you held the line and faced down a huge military
foe (i), *the British Crown Forces and their surrogates in the unionist
death squads (ii)* (4)

    i.   + J tenacity intensified

    ii.   t - J propriety

These references to the past have a subtle link with those to the future, as
Adams goes on to suggest that it is precisely the quality of courage (rather
than, for example, negotiating skills) that will be required in the years ahead:

Now is the time for you *to step into the Bearna Baoil again (i);* not as
volunteers risking life and limb (ii) but as *activists in a national
movement towards independence and unity (iii).* (51)

    i.   t + J tenacity

    ii.   t + J tenacity

    iii.   t + J tenacity

Again, with this second reference to the 'Bearna Baoil', Adams connects past
and future and underlines a sense of continuity in the activities of the
volunteers in the very different contexts. He thus attempts to reassure the
more hard-core elements in his audience that they will not be redundant
when the group embarks on its new pathway.

In terms of argumentation, the expressed opinion appears to be that, since
the movement finds itself at a 'defining moment' (58), where a peaceful
approach will bear fruit in terms of achieving its long-term goals, it is more
necessary than ever that the movement unite around a policy based on
permanent ceasefire. It is noticeable that, in the structure of this argument,
there is an implicit warrant (table nine):

Table 7.14. Argumentation.

Data	Warrant	Claim
(because)	(since)	(therefore)
	Implicit warrant	
There is a strong possibility for achieving our goals through peaceful means	(The old ways of armed struggle were ultimately ineffective)	We should try to achieve our aims by purely political and democratic activity

Relevant textual references:	Relevant textual references:	Relevant textual references:
• Sinn Fein has growing political influence (18, 46) • It is possible for the struggle to move forward by peaceful means (25) • I know this is possible because of the special knowledge of my position (26) • There is an alternative to violence (29,30) • The way forward is by building political support for republican and democratic objectives (31) • The 1994 ceasefire demonstrated Sinn Fein's ability to lead by example (38) • Sinn Fein has demonstrated the ability to play a leadership role (39) • Republicans have a key role in the process (49)	• Ireland is a very different place from 15 years ago (42-43)	• The way forward is by building political support for republican and democratic objectives across Ireland and by winning support for these goals internationally (31); • courageous initiatives which will achieve your aims by purely political and democratic activity (33)

For the reasons which have already been mentioned, it is not Adams' intention to alienate any of his listeners by suggesting that their services, in the changing context of modern Ireland, will no longer be required. On the contrary, he is at great pains to point out the immense value of their contribution to the current favourable situation (2-4, 21-24, 27-28, 50-53). And yet it has been observed that Sinn Fein/IRA found itself drawn to the negotiating table, during the nineties, as much by a sense that the armed struggle was dragging on indefinitely with no sign of achieving its ends, as by any other fundamental factor (Frampton, 2009, p. 84). To draw too much attention to the redundancy of the military approach here, however, would be politically inexpedient, and for this reason, Adams prefers to use positive evaluation to flatter and reassure his listeners.

Concluding remarks

This chapter has combined Hallidayan analysis of the information structure with the more familiar resources, for this book, represented by argumentation and the persuasive force of evaluative language. It shows, in other words, how it is possible to integrate other tools from the wide field of linguistics with the basic model, where these will serve a useful analytical purpose. As we have seen, questions of thematic organisation are anything but random, and permit the speaker to construe a range of nuances which contribute to his overall rhetorical design.

We have seen, for example, how thematisation of temporal components assisted Adams in creating an impression that times had changed, and thereby insinuating that new responses might be necessary for the new realities of the situation. Thematisation also assists in processes of naturalisation, in which the speaker attempts to pass off possibly contentious propositions as matters of fact, as we saw above in the example of the short-sightedness of the two governments. Another instance occurs in line 6, where Adams speaks of the decision to abandon the IRA's military campaign, referring to it as:

This <u>courageous</u> decision (+J: tenacity)

The decision can fairly be termed courageous, because, as we have seen, it entailed a completely new departure for the organisation Sinn Fein/IRA, with no guarantee that success would ensue. It ran the risk of alienating rank and file members, possibly provoking a movement among the unconvinced to join the Real IRA or, in an extreme case, to form yet another breakaway para-military group. Over the years of armed resistance, of clandestine violence, of embittered social relations that disfigured the province of Ulster, the IRA soldiery had become used to its routines. To many, abandonment of the armed struggle would have smacked of betrayal, and it required all the prestige/ethos of Gerry Adams, backed by his lieutenant Martin McGuinness, to make the ceasefire happen.

The proposition which Adams advances is not straightforward, however. As mentioned above, there are some points of analogy with the debate played out in the preceding chapter, between supporters of Martin Luther King and those of Malcolm X. Malcolm X, for example, would no doubt have argued that a courageous response to social oppression must involve some form of violent struggle, and would see negotiation for eventual integration as a form of cowardice. By its very nature, the IRA is much closer to the positions of Malcolm X than those of Martin Luther King. By including this nexus of possible conflict in the theme, Adams is able to associate it with matter-of-factness, due to the potentialities of its place as the 'Given' element of the information structure. Attempts to rhetorically naturalise propositions that are in reality debatable is a typical feature of much political rhetoric, and this chapter has, I hope, illustrated the role information structure can play in the process.

Appendix: Adams' speech 06/04/2005

1.	I want to speak directly to the men and women of Oglaigh na hEireann, *the volunteer soldiers of the Irish Republican Army.*	t+ J capacity/ tenacity
2.	In time of great peril *you stepped into the Bearna Baoil, the gap of danger.*	t + J tenacity
3.	When others stood idly by, you and your families gave your all, in defence of a risen people and in pursuit of Irish freedom and unity.	- J tenacity + J propriety
4.	Against mighty odds you held the line and faced down a huge military foe, *the British Crown Forces and their surrogates in the unionist death squads.*	+ J tenacity intensified t - J propriety
5.	*Eleven years ago, the (Irish Republican) Army leadership ordered a complete cessation of military operations.*	t + J propriety
6.	This courageous decision was in response to proposals put forward by the Sinn Fein leadership *to construct a peace process, build democratic politics and achieve a lasting peace.*	+ J tenacity t + J propriety
7.	*Since then - despite many provocations and setbacks - the cessation has endured.*	t + Affect: Happiness, Cheer
8.	And more than that, when elements within the British and Irish establishments and rejectionist unionism delayed progress, it was *the IRA leadership which authorised a number of* significant *initiatives to enhance the peace process.*	- J propriety t + J capacity + App Valuation
9.	On a number of occasions, commitments have been reneged on.	- J propriety
10.	These include commitments from the two governments.	
11.	The Irish Republican Army has kept every commitment made by its leadership.	+ J propriety
12.	The most recent of these was last December when *the IRA was prepared to support a* comprehensive *agreement.*	t + J propriety + App: Valuation
13.	At that time, the army leadership said the implementation of this agreement would allow everyone, including the IRA, to *take its political objectives forward by peaceful and democratic means.*	t + J: propriety
14.	That agreement perished on the rock of unionist intransigence.	- J propriety
15.	The shortsightedness of the two governments compounded the difficulties.	- J capacity
16.	Since then, there has been a vicious campaign of vilification against republicans, driven in the main by the Irish government.	- J propriety
17.	There are a number of reasons for this.	
18.	The *growing political influence* of Sinn Fein is a primary factor.	t + J capacity

19.	*The unionists also for their part, want to minimise the potential for change, not only on the equality agenda but on the issues of sovereignty and ending the union.*	t - J propriety
20.	*The IRA is being used as the excuse by them all not to engage properly in the process of building peace with justice in Ireland.*	t - J propriety
21.	*For over 30 years, the IRA showed* that *the British government could not rule Ireland on its own terms.*	t + J capacity t - J capacity
22.	*You asserted the legitimacy of the right of the people of this island to <u>freedom and independence</u>.*	t + tenacity + J propriety
23.	Many of your comrades <u>made the ultimate sacrifice</u>.	+ J propriety
24.	Your <u>determination, selflessness</u> and <u>courage</u> have brought the freedom struggle towards its fulfilment.	+ J propriety
25.	That <u>struggle</u> can now be taken forward by other means.	+ J tenacity
26.	*I say this with the authority of my office as president of Sinn Fein.*	t + J capacity
27.	In the past I have defended *the right of the IRA to engage in armed struggle.*	t + J propriety/tenacity
28.	I did so because there was no alternative for *those who would not* bend the knee, or *turn a blind eye to oppression,* or for those who wanted a national republic.	t + J propriety t + J tenacity
29.	Now there is an alternative.	
30.	I have clearly set out my view of what that alternative is.	
31.	The way forward is by *building political support* for republican and democratic objectives across Ireland and by winning support for these goals internationally.	t + J tenacity
32.	I want to use this occasion therefore to appeal to the leadership of Oglaigh na hEireann *to fully embrace and accept this alternative.*	t + J propriety (intens.)
33.	Can you take courageous initiatives which will achieve your aims *by purely political and democratic activity?*	+ J tenacity t + J propriety
34.	I know full well that such truly historic decisions can only be taken in the aftermath of intense internal consultation.	+ ApValuation
35.	I ask that you initiate this as quickly as possible.	
36.	I understand fully that the IRA's most recent <u>positive</u> contribution to the peace process was in the context of a <u>comprehensive</u> agreement.	+ J: propriety +ApValuation
37.	But I also hold the <u>very strong</u> view that republicans need <u>to lead by example.</u>	+Ap Valuation + J capacity
38.	There is no <u>greater</u> demonstration of this than the IRA cessation in the summer of 1994.	+J tenacity (intens.)

39.	Sinn Fein has demonstrated the <u>ability</u> to play a leadership role *as part of a popular movement towards peace, equality and justice.*	+ J capacity t + J propriety
40.	*We are totally committed to ending partition* and to *creating the conditions for unity and independence.*	t + J tenacity (intens.) t + J propriety
41.	Sinn Fein has the <u>potential and capacity</u> *to become the vehicle for the attainment of republican objectives.*	+ J capacity t+Aff Happiness, Cheer
42.	The Ireland we live in today is also a <u>very different</u> place from 15 years ago.	+Ap Valuation
43.	*There is now an all-Ireland agenda with <u>huge</u> potential.*	t + Aff, Happiness, Cheer +Ap Valuation
44.	Nationalists and republicans have a <u>confidence</u> *that will never again allow anyone to be treated as second-class citizens.*	+ Aff Security, Confidence t + J tenacity
45.	<u>Equality</u> is our watchword.	+ J propriety
46.	The catalyst for much of this change is the <u>growing</u> support for republicanism.	+Ap Valuation
47.	Of course, *those who oppose change* are not going to simply roll over.	t - J propriety
48.	It will always be a battle a day between *those who want maximum change* and *those who want to maintain the status quo.*	t + J propriety t - J propriety
49.	*But if republicans are to prevail, if the peace process is to be successfully concluded and Irish sovereignty and re-unification secured,* then *we have to set the agenda* - no-one else is going to do that.	t + J tenacity t + Aff Happiness, Cheer t + J tenacity
50.	So, I also want to make a personal appeal to all of you - the women and men volunteers who have <u>remained undefeated in the face of tremendous odds</u>.	+ J tenacity (intens.)
51.	Now is the time for you to *step into the Bearna Baoil* again; not *as volunteers risking life and limb* but as *activists in a national movement towards independence and unity.*	t + J tenacity t + J tenacity t + J tenacity
52.	Such decisions will be <u>far reaching and difficult</u>.	+Ap Valuation
53.	But you never lacked <u>courage</u> in the past.	+ J tenacity
54.	Your <u>courage</u> is now needed for the future.	+ J tenacity
55.	*It won't be easy.*	t + J tenacity
56.	*There are many problems to be resolved by the people of Ireland in the time ahead.*	t + J tenacity

57.	Your ability as republican volunteers, to <u>rise to this challenge</u> will mean that *the two governments and others cannot easily hide from their obligations and their responsibility to resolve these problems.*	+ J capacity t - J tenacity
58.	Our struggle has reached a <u>defining</u> moment.	+ Ap valuation
59.	I am asking you to join me in <u>seizing this moment</u>, *to intensify our efforts, (to rebuild the peace process) and decisively move our struggle forward.*	+ J tenacity t + J tenacity t + J tenacity

Chapter 8

From Bears to Wolves: Republican rhetoric in the Cold War and the War on Terror

Introduction

In the last two chapters of this book, we approach the topic of metaphor, and its connection with persuasive political discourse; the final chapter will deal with the right-wing British political party UKIP and its verbal and visual metaphors for Europe, while this one explores metaphor in political films produced by the US Republican Party. While the other chapters have looked mainly at persuasive discourse in its textual form, the last two attempt to trace persuasive techniques at work in visual and other multimodal features.

This study explores Republican framing in two recent episodes; the celebrated 'there's a bear in the woods' video which President Ronald Reagan used in his election campaign in 1984, and, twenty years later, an advertisement showing wolves in a forest, used by G.W. Bush for his 2004 election campaign, during the so-called war on terror. The aim is to account for these artefacts in terms of a theory of persuasive political rhetoric that sees framing as central, and also involves cultural allusions and metaphor.

The first video was made for Reagan's 1984 re-election campaign, at a time when America and the Soviet Union were vying with each other for supremacy in the field of nuclear armaments. The question of being–or appearing to be–strong or weak in international terms was crucial, and in the latter stages of the Cold War, this consideration had a major impact on the US defence budget. Reagan had to show that he, rather than Democrat rival Walter Mondale, would spend more on America's nuclear arsenal, thus guaranteeing safety for voters. The short video shows a large bear walking, at first on a hillside, then among trees. We hear a voice-over speaking of 'a bear in the woods'. Some people can't see it, others say it's tame. The text develops a simple proposition: "Since no-one knows whether the bear is tame or dangerous, doesn't it make sense to be as strong as the bear?" Finally, the camera cuts to a photo of President Reagan, smiling above the slogan: 'Preparing for peace'. Reagan was known as 'the great communicator', and this short film is another among many publicity triumphs during his period in the White House. It is impossible to gauge the precise impact of this electoral message, but the implicit message (vote for a president who believes in spending as much on nuclear weapons as our enemy) is persuasively insinuated.

In 2004, the Republican Party decided to release a similar video in order to drive home the party's message during America's struggle with the Islamic terrorist Osama Bin Laden and the Iraqi dictator Saddam Hussein. The setting and general design of this second film are very similar. The main difference is that, while the voiceover in the bear video makes no overt reference to the political context, the latter begins by denouncing Democrats' plans for cuts in defence spending. The film ends with a shot of five wolves that are beginning to move in a menacing fashion towards the camera. The voice announces: "weakness attracts those who are waiting to do America harm". Thus, while the film's message in the first is left implicit, in the second it is spelled out. Viewers are told, in other words, how they should interpret the film's symbolism.

Methodology

This chapter focuses on the persuasive function of the videos, and attempts to account for it in terms of two factors; firstly, an understanding of the role of the bear and the wolf in popular culture, and secondly, the persuasive powers of metaphor, which has traditionally played a key role in political rhetoric of all kinds. The model of argumentation in political rhetoric which has so far featured in this book is backgrounded; instead, the notion of discourse framing will be invoked as an overarching concept that carries the main persuasive charge of these videos. Framing, as a general notion in cognitive science, derives from work by Bateson (1954) and Goffman (1974). According to Norris et al. (2003, p. 11), the essence of framing is selection, "to prioritize some facts, images or developments over others, thereby unconsciously promoting one particular interpretation of events". Though this is widely accepted, a critical perspective would question, in this definition, how far it is correct to call the processes involved 'unconscious'. To the extent that the 'prioritisation of facts or images' are conscious, the promotion of a particular interpretation of events would also be conscious. This is no secret to those who work in media, in advertising, or in politics, where image consultants (otherwise known as 'spin doctors') have become well-established figures over the past few decades. Perhaps more to the point is that the promotion of interpretations operates at an unconscious, subliminal level, and this is the perspective on framing that is adopted here. For instance, in the Bear in the Woods video, framing refers to the participants, processes, events and multimodal features involved in the video, all of which are not unconscious but rather the result of deliberate choices on the part of political advisers collaborating with expert media professionals such as script-writers, editors, directors, actors, and so on, in order to create a product which has a specific aim.

The bear and the wolf are clearly employed as visual metaphors, but in order to understand their persuasive impact, I suggest, we need to understand something of the role of both in popular, especially American, culture. In order to understand the differing impacts of both films, finally, we will need some of the tools and techniques of Multimodal discourse analysis (Baldry & Thibault, 2006), (Kress & Van Leeuwen, 1996).

Metaphors

As in advertising discourse, persuasive political messages attempt to hide the fact that their intentions are, in fact, persuasive at all. As Halmari and Virtanen observe:

> While the need to persuade is as old as humanity, the linguistic forms of persuasion do not constitute a stable, monolithic phenomenon. The very nature of persuasion requires that its forms need to be kept implicit. Few like to be persuaded against their will and, hence, the best kind of persuasion is often implicit persuasion (Halmari & Virtanen, 2005, p. 239)

The Republican video 'A Bear in the Woods' falls into this category of subtle persuasion, where the message is insinuated through a variety of semiotic means rather than spelled out in so many words. In the Wolves video too, though the message is more explicit, the real strength of the message is not so much in the verbal part but in the images and the subliminal web of associations which they activate. These associations involve a consideration of the persuasive force of metaphor.

Metaphor was traditionally thought of simply as a decorative rhetorical device, and as such it is considered by Aristotle, in his *Poetics*; however, modern approaches have revised this view. In an influential summary of rhetorical devices, Perelman and Olbrechts-Tyteca (1969) shed new light on the role of metaphor in argumentation. When Lakoff and Johnson published their work, *Metaphors We Live By* (1980), they opened the way for metaphor to be viewed as a cognitive resource fundamental to the way we organise our experience. They argue that cognition rests on foundations acquired in earliest infancy, that it consists of conceptual metaphors such as 'Up is Good' and 'Down is Bad'. They connect such cognitive structures to bodily functions such as crawling, attempting to stand, falling over, and so on, and suggest that these metaphors are 'wired in' to the growing child, forming the basis of unconscious adult evaluations and behaviour.

From this perspective, Charteris-Black (2005, p. xi) calls metaphor "a highly effective rhetorical strategy for combining our understanding of familiar experiences in everyday life with deep-rooted cultural values that evoke powerful emotional responses".

In order to appreciate the relevance for persuasive political discourse, we will need to take a step back, to the traditional, Aristotelian perspective on metaphor. Metaphors, says Aristotle, "consist in giving the thing a name that belongs to something else on the grounds of analogy". One of his examples is as follows:

> Pericles said that the young manhood killed in the war vanished from the city as though someone took the spring from the year.

Metaphor, as has been pointed out at several points in this book, compares something about which we know little to something which we know well, perhaps with the aim of helping us to come to terms with the unknown. Lakoff and Johnson (1980, p. 246) speak of mapping one conceptual domain onto another. In Aristotle's example, there is an attempt to come to terms with sudden death, with the absence of familiar faces in the community. Pericles does this by comparing the vanished youth with something as well-known and rooted in human experience as the spring. When we say that 'life is a journey', we do something similar. Journeys are familiar to everyone; they have beginnings, middle parts and endings. Life, on the other hand, has mysterious aspects but, apparently, it too has these same components. These correspondences, between the *source* of the metaphor (the journey) and the *target* (life) are known as the *grounds* of the metaphor and in this case, it may seem apparent that the metaphor is used to compare birth to the start of a journey, death to its end, and so on. Zinken and Musolff (2009, p. 6), however, suggest that it is no easy matter to determine the precise grounds on which metaphors should be interpreted, and quote scientific research which suggests that even such a conventional metaphor as this has no generally agreed meaning.

Politicians have frequently exploited the profound forces involved in metaphor to gain support for their policies, as the following examples illustrate:

Table 8.1. Some political metaphors (mostly from Charteris-Black (2005).

Metaphor	Used by	Force of metaphor
"The dark curse of Hitler"	Winston Churchill	Hitler compared to an evil magician. To strengthen public feeling against him.
"The road to victory may not be so long as we expect."	Winston Churchill	To encourage listeners by making them feel they have nearly reached their 'destination'.

"Mad dog Gheddafi"	Ronald Reagan	To gain support for eliminating Gheddafi (mad dogs are put down).
"A journey of change"	Tony Blair	To characterise his drastic reforms of the Labour Party (New Labour jettisoned many of its core values such as support for the working classes, nationalisation and close ties with Trade Unions).
"The price of indifference"	G.W. Bush	From economics. Bush argues that non-action against Saddam Hussein will 'cost' the U.S. a high price in the future.
"Chains of discrimination"	Martin Luther King	Although the negro no longer has actual 'chains', the fact that discrimination is still to be found shows that he is not fully free yet.

Ronald Reagan's 'mad dog' metaphor for the Libyan leader Gheddafi serves to illustrate the role of metaphor in persuasive political discourse. It is well-known that mad dogs, perhaps infected with rabies, can be extremely dangerous for humans, therefore the usual course is to put them to sleep. By thus referring to Gheddafi, whose actions were certainly unpredictable, violent and dangerous to America's interests, Reagan insinuates that he too should be put to sleep. In fact, the United States organised an attempted assassination of the Libyan leader. Charteris-Black (2005, p. 13) explains the persuasive force of such a metaphor:

> Metaphor influences our beliefs, attitudes and values because it uses language to activate unconscious emotional associations and it influences the value that we place on ideas and beliefs on a scale of goodness and badness. It does this by transferring positive or negative associations of various source words to a metaphor target.

In this case, the negative associations of mad dogs are transferred to the Libyan leader. Note that Reagan does not openly advocate that the United States should engage in political assassinations. This might raise uncomfortable questions, possibly alienating both allies and some of his own electoral base. Rather, he chooses to refer to Gheddafi with a metaphor which might have the effect of smoothing the way for the policy his administration has chosen to enact.

In much the same fashion, the choice of a bear and wolves for the political videos are dictated by metaphorical considerations. Russia is a Bear is the first metaphor; Terrorists are Wolves is the second. Since both the bear and the wolf are dangerous wild animals, clearly one implicit meaning of the videos relates to notions of protection from potential sources of harm. However, I suggest below that, in order to appreciate nuances in the meaning of the two videos, we need to understand both the specific political context at their time of release, and cultural associations of the two species of animal.

The bear and the wolf in popular (American) culture

In the Bear video, the source is the bear in the woods, and the target the Russians; in the Wolves video, the source is the wolf and the target anti-American terrorists. The message designers' intention, we may safely presume, is that qualities of the former will be transferred to the latter by viewers.

In order to understand the impact of a phrase like 'there's a bear in the woods', however, it is necessary to understand something of what the figure of the bear has meant, culturally, for Americans. There is a difficulty here, which is akin to another difficulty in discourse analysis, that of knowing how much context information to bring to the analysis of any particular text, and what circumstances might be relevant in any one case. Clearly, the bear belongs to the category of 'scary wild animal', and there have been many films, some recent, in which it appears as such: The Bear (L'Ours, Jean-Jacques Annaud 1988), and Grizzly Man (Werner Herzog 2005), for example. But the bear is also the archetypal cuddly toy, the 'teddy bear', and beloved to generations of American children through Disney films–Baloo the bear in The Jungle Book (1966) and Winnie-the-Pooh (1971). Both bears are positive figures, anthropomorphised and rendered suitable for stardom in movies, and both have had an enormous impact on the popular imagination in America. The difficulty, then, relates to the question of selection. It would seem that, if we wish to appreciate the persuasive force of the Reagan 'Bear in the Woods' video, we need to have some conception of what the image of the bear will mean, for viewers, in terms of their own likely responses to the figure. I suggest, below, that in selecting a bear for their video, Reagan's film-makers were not simply selecting, at random, a member of the wild animal category. Rather, they were tapping into a matrix of cultural associations whose ramifications are complex and not entirely predictable. I suggest, below, that the choice of animal was deliberate, and that a picture of the place of the bear in popular culture is, in fact, necessary to appreciate the persuasive nuances of the video itself.

The same is true, naturally, for the wolf, one of the archetypes of danger for many of the European countries which provided America with its immigrant populations during the 19th and 20th centuries. Packs of wolves roamed the forests in the Middle Ages and the wolf became, over the centuries, a metaphorical symbol for greed, cruelty, rapaciousness and even aggressive male sexuality (Pluskowski, 2006). It left its mark on several of the best-known and loved children's fables, among them the *Three Little Pigs* and *Little Red Riding Hood* (Dundes, 1991). Other wolf-figures are found in American popular culture, for instance in the novels of Jack London, *The Call of the Wild,* and *White Fang* (London, 2000), while in terms of Hollywood the wolf became a global star through the Kevin Costner film *Dances with Wolves* (1990).

In short the wolf, like the bear, represents a nexus of conflicting cultural attitudes, values and themes which cannot be reduced simply to membership of a category of 'dangerous animals'. To align the figure of the bear with Soviet Russia, and to compare terrorists to a pack of wolves, is to launch a message that cannot simply be interpreted in a linear or simplistic fashion. On the contrary, films are complex semiotic artefacts, whose images, music and words activate all kinds of responses on many different levels.

There's a bear in the woods. Ronald Reagan 1984

Context

Ronald Reagan was, in some commentators' opinions, one of the most influential Republican presidents of the twentieth century. He gave his name to a brand of right-wing, free-market economic policies (*Reaganomics*), and advanced policies that are now the staple of the Republican Party, such as tax reductions to stimulate economic growth, tight fiscal control to combat inflation, economic deregulation and cuts in government spending. Like many Republicans, he supported capital punishment and was bullish in his dealings with international problems such as terrorism and the Cold War. He allowed Libya to be bombed in 1986 in an assassination attempt on dictator Colonel Gheddafi, and was the president during the first days of the collapse of the Soviet Union.

Though not a politician by profession, Reagan's successful career in movies served him well when it came to appearances in front of the cameras, speech-making and the public presidential debates, as we have already seen. These qualities earned him the nickname of 'the great communicator', and helped him succeed in national politics, despite his advanced age. During his first term in office, Reagan survived an assassination attempt, the only U.S. president to do so. He began to reverse his predecessor Jimmy Carter's policy of *détente* with the Soviet Union, ordered a massive build-up in America's armed forces and nuclear capabilities and, together with British Prime Minister Margaret Thatcher, denounced the Russians in ideological terms. In 1983, he coined the phrase 'the evil empire' to describe the Soviet Union. In the same year, Reagan introduced his 'Strategic Defence Initiative', a policy of using ground and space-based missiles to detect and shoot down enemy nuclear devices. There were doubts whether this was technologically feasible, and the policy became known as 'star wars'. However, some commentators have claimed that it was Soviet anxiety over such an ambitious defensive programme that hastened the end of the Cold War.[1]

Reagan's electoral success in 1980 was due to the fact that he had managed to attract support from traditional democrat voters unconvinced by their own party, the so-called 'Reagan Democrats'. When the 'Bear in the Woods' documentary was released, it was during the run-up to the 1984 election, one of its aims was to target these same Reagan Democrats in order to keep their allegiance. It encapsulated, in a very simple electoral message, one of the core questions of the whole campaign. Reagan had, effectively, pursued a policy, not just of keeping pace with Soviet spending on armaments, but outspending them by a considerable margin, during the past four years. Therefore the election was an opportunity for the nation to express its assessment of whether his strongman policy in the international arena was good for national security.

There's a bear in the woods. The video

The video was the work of prominent advertising executive Hal Riney, who provided the voiceover in the rich, reassuring, avuncular voice familiar from many TV commercials. In the terms of Van Leeuwen's work on voice quality, this would be a 'personal' tone, using a soft, relaxed voice at low pitch and volume. The tone denotes a relationship of 'close friendship' (Van Leeuwen, Speech, Music, Sound, 1999, p. 191). It is soft and moderate, with significant pauses and use of a falling intonation on sentence-ends. As Wardhaugh (2006, p. 321) points out, the association of this pattern with 'firm statements' conveys a sense of reassurance and security. To analyse the videos, some of the perspectives of the emerging field of Multimodality are used (Baldry & Thibault, 2006; Kress, 2010).

The voiceover is accompanied by a rhythmic beating pattern on a drum of some kind, which creates a sense of tension, perhaps suitable to the implied menace in the words. When the shot of Reagan appears in the final clip, the backing sound has become music, with some muted but strong, vaguely patriotic, stirring violin music.

The text itself is extremely simple, and the running time of only 30 seconds means that this is a short, sharp message, an effect heightened by the simple sentence pattern:[2]

---

[1] "McCarry, Charles. Star Wars and the Soviet Collapse". See web references.

[2] I use the transcription conventions of Jefferson, as set out in Schiffrin (1994, pp. 422-33), with the procedures of Brown and Yule (1983, p. xii) for pauses, with a dash [-] used for "short pauses", a plus sign [+] for "longer pauses" and two plus signs [++] for "extended pauses".

Table 8.2. there's a bear in the woods.[3]

1	There's a bear in the woods (↓) (-) for some people, the bear is easy to see (↓) (+) others don't
2	see it at all (++) some people say the bear is tame (+) others say it's vicious (+) and dangerous
3	(+) since no one can really be sure who's right (+) isn't it smart to be as strong as the bear?
4	(++) if there is a bear

The following table shows the shot sequence in the video:

Table 8.3. There's a bear in the woods. Sequence.

Shot number		Voiceover	Action
1		"There's a bear in the woods.."	The bear appears, not in the woods but in front of the woods in a clearing, on a slight hill
2		"For some people the bear is easy to see.."	Close-up of the bear focusing on its size
3		"Others don't see it at all."	At this point the bear moves back into some trees

---

[3] "Avmorgado. Ronald Reagan TV Ad: the Bear." See web references.

4		"Some say the bear is tame. Others say it's vicious.."	The bear walks through a stream
5		"..and dangerous."	The bear climbs a hill, in the open now
6		"since no one can really be sure who's right, isn't it smart to be as strong as the bear?"	It walks along the brow of a hill, as if going somewhere
7		"If there is a bear."	A man appears at right picture. Seeing him, the bear stops and draws back slightly.
8			Still of a smiling Reagan appears

As Kress and Van Leeuwen (1996, p. 2) say, in their introduction to a work that deals with the interpretation of non-linguistic features:

> Like linguistic structures, visual structures point to particular interpretations of experience and forms of social interaction. To some degree these can also be expressed linguistically. Meanings belong to culture, rather than to specific semiotic modes. And the way meanings are mapped across different semiotic modes, the way some things can, for instance, be 'said' either visually or verbally, others only visually, again others only verbally, is also culturally and historically specific.

The film-maker's choices in the areas of composition, of colour, setting, light and shade, filter, camera angle and of backing music, in other words, can be interpreted as contributing to the film's overall message, to the same degree as that of the text itself. Words are only another semiotic component in the film's overall meaning, alongside all these other features.

The relation between the text and these other compositional features is at times harmonious, but elsewhere appears to be in contrast. For example, in the first sequence (shot one), the text says 'there's a bear *in* the woods', while the picture shows a bear not in the woods at all, but in front of them. Together with the menacing backing music, this could indicate that the bear is already emerging from the woods, could be on its way to attack someone. The active potentialities of the bear are somehow emphasised; if there is one in the woods, it is clearly not confined to them. In the second shot, there is a closer connection between text and image. The bear is 'easy to see' for some, and the shot is a close-up of the bear, the only occurrence of close-up in the short film. This shot underlines the favoured interpretation of the message designer - there *is* a bear, and it is plain to see. The only point at which the bear returns, briefly, into the woods, is in shot three, where the text says "Others don't see it at all." The bear is momentarily screened behind some branches. However, he soon emerges, to full view, walking through a stream, to the accompaniment of the commentary: "Some say the bear is tame. Others say it's vicious.." The bear's existence, which some have doubted, is confirmed by these formulations: while some say the bear is tame and others that it is vicious, no-one says that there is no bear. 'The bear is tame' is an existential process (Halliday & Matthiessen, 2004, pp. 256-9), a formula which recognises the ontological status of the phenomenon in question. The next section again shows the bear, in full view, out in the country, walking along a ridge, apparently heading somewhere. This is one of the longer shots of the film, accompanied by the voiceover: "since no one can really be sure who's right, isn't it smart to be as strong as the bear?" In the penultimate shot, a man now appears on the right of the picture, apparently unarmed, standing still. The bear, on noticing him, stops too, and draws back slightly. The inferences of body-language from man and bear are a) that the man, knowing himself to be as strong as the bear, has no fear, and b) that the bear, realizing that this man is as strong as him, is afraid and stops to consider his position.

In a subtle touch, the text only now takes up again the hypothetical aspect of the bear's existence, in the phrase '*if* there is a bear'. Having just watched this bear moving in and out of the woods, through streams, across open country and now confronting a human being, the viewer can be in little doubt that–at least in the film-maker's perspective–there is a bear. Thus, the film only appears to open dialogical space to the doubters, while the overwhelming force of the non-textual aspects of the message denies alternative views on the bear's existence. Textual message and visual message, then, intertwine in a complex web of meanings concerning the existence (or not) of a bear in the woods, and the nature of this possibly existent, possibly non-existent, bear. However, as they say, "seeing is believing": viewers are firmly positioned alongside the textual voice with its declaration at the outset: "There's a bear in the woods", and against the doubters. The concluding rhetorical question maintains the tension by returning to the question of the bear's hypothetical existence:

> since no one can really be sure who's right, isn't it smart to be as strong
> as the bear? If there is a bear

Here the viewer may be 'tricked' into assenting to the rhetorical question when what s/he is actually doing is providing a sort of cognitive reflex that resolves not the rhetorical question but that posed by the final conditional - i.e., is there a bear or isn't there?

The text performs a classic instance of flawed political logic, when it advances the proposition that 'no-one can really be sure who's right' (shot six). It helps, in analysing such arguments, to reduce them to their barest components, to what Damer (2005) calls the 'standard form' for propositions:

> SINCE Some say the bear is dangerous, and some say it's tame
>
> AND SINCE
>
> No-one can really be sure who's right
>
> THEREFORE
>
> It makes sense to be as strong as the bear

In this form, it becomes fairly easy to spot the flaw in the syllogism. Apart from the fact that it pre-supposes the bear's existence, so that a first step in resolving the dilemma over how the bear should be treated should be to determine whether or not there actually is one, this could be an instance of what Damer calls a 'missing evidence' fallacy (Damer, 2005, p. 241). No evidence is provided for the crucial supporting proposition ('no-one can really be sure who's right'). The solution, actually, pre-supposes the correctness of one of the alternatives presented by the initial proposition, i.e. that the bear is dangerous. But, supposing the bear to be tame, then the effort spent on becoming as strong as the bear is clearly wasted.

If we transfer this discussion from the metaphorical sphere to the actual, the stakes are high. In order to become 'as strong as the bear', the Reagan administration spent a fortune on nuclear weapons and the military generally, money which could have been spent differently, for example on social programmes to improve the lives of ordinary American citizens. Since the cost of becoming as strong as the bear was so great, it could be argued, what ought to have been done was to invest (a much lesser sum of) money in diplomatic and cultural initiatives to ascertain whether the bear was tame or not.

The final shot, of a smiling President Reagan, associates the leader with the strong man shown confronting the bear in the preceding image. The slogan 'prepared for peace' underlines, once more, the implicit belief of the Republican party which commissioned the film. In other words, that peace comes about through military strength, that only if a nation is militarily strong can it expect its potential enemies to come to peaceful agreements.

The Bear in the Woods film is a classic example of a successful political advertisement, which makes a point persuasively and with a minimalist style and economy. The fact that Russia has traditionally been known as 'the bear' makes the metaphor even easier to appreciate. The video was repeatedly broadcast in the days and weeks before the election, and Reagan was re-elected in a landslide. How far the video in question contributed to this victory is, of course, impossible to determine. But Reagan's crushing victory shows that most Americans believed his foreign policy was correct, and the bear video was key in communicating that policy.

G.W. Bush and the war on terror

Context

The War on Terror, also known as the Global War on Terrorism (GWOT) is a term applied to an international military campaign that the USA started, in retaliation for the 11 September 2001 terrorist attacks on the United States. It refers to an international military campaign to eliminate al-Qaeda and other militant organizations. The United States and many other NATO and non-

NATO nations such as Pakistan participated in the conflict. The chief among America's allies was Britain, whose leader Tony Blair was a prominent supporter. British support was crucial for the Bush administration as it sought to get the UN to pass resolutions in favour of military intervention in Iraq and Afghanistan. In the end, the USA and Britain decided on unilateral military action against Saddam Hussein without UN support, and the invasion of Iraq went ahead in 2003.

It was president G.W. Bush who first used the phrase "War on Terror". It was perhaps suggested to Bush's speech-writers by veteran TV journalist Tom Brokaw who, watching the collapse of the twin towers, pronounced the phrase: "Terrorists have declared war on America". The phrase has been used by the Bush administration and western media, to refer to a global military political campaign directed against terrorist organizations and regimes accused of supporting them. These organizations and regimes have tended to be of Muslim persuasion, as was the case with America's primary target, the al-Qaeda group led by Osama Bin Laden.

The years that followed saw levels of public opposition to their governments, especially in the US and Britain, at unprecedented levels. The campaign to drum up support for America's and Britain's policy of invading Iraq involved leaks of incorrect security information about Saddam's weapons of mass destruction, false claims by government and media respecting the Iraqi dictator's links with Al-Qaeda, and a deliberate flouting of UN procedures that threatened the future credibility of the organisation itself. The UN, in fact, had weapons inspectors inside Iraq searching for Saddam's illegal weapons, but they were hastily withdrawn when it became apparent that the Anglo-American invasion was imminent.

The techniques used by the terrorists, who hi-jacked airliners and flew them as guided missiles to destroy targets in America, meant that security procedures of civilian aviation have needed to be tightened up beyond all recognition. Passengers around the world have had to submit to these lengthy and, at times, humiliating procedures.

Because of all these factors, there was a real need at the time for the government to use media outlets to broadcast America's message, to explain to citizens why sacrifices of time and comfort had to be made, and to attempt to bring their hearts and minds on board with the government's aggressive foreign policy. The situation was analogous, in fact, to that faced by the Republican party in 1984. In that instance, as we have seen, the significant features of the international situation were the Cold War with Soviet Russia and the need to win support for a policy of public spending on the military.

However, though there are similarities between the two contexts, there are also crucial differences. The Cold War had been a reality in American cultural life since the Second World War. Russia had been a visible enemy, a presence in the world that spurred America on at all levels. From the space race and competition for Olympic medals to the global extension of two empires founded on antithetical ideologies, Russia had become effectively branded as America's 'public enemy number one'. After the terrorist attacks, however, American people felt a sense of insecurity that they had not felt for generations. The attacks have been compared to the Japanese attack on Pearl Harbour, the last military attack on American territory. But Pearl Harbour was an island in the Pacific Ocean, at a distance of thousands of miles from the homeland. The Al-Qaeda attack had destroyed the twin towers, landmarks on the Manhattan skyline and global symbols of America's power, presence and national identity. There was a palpable sense of national vulnerability.

The Wolves video emerges from this social context, as G.W. Bush attempts to communicate the government's message to the people. It built on the success of the Bear video, which it follows in style.

The wolves video

Between the two films, the similarities are so obvious that the latter film is clearly intended to be viewed in an intertextual relationship with its predecessor. Meanings of the first are recalled by many features of the composition, including setting, human and animal characters, length, music and theme. This is pointed out by an article on the Political Advertising Resource Centre website,[4] which comments that the Republicans may have hoped to draw on Reagan's popularity as president, that something of this would accrue to G.W. Bush by association. They also illustrate points of similarity in the international situation, i.e. that in both contexts, America is threatened by a powerful foreign enemy. Just as Republican voters bought into the message of the bear video to produce a massive landslide for Reagan in 1984, so the film-makers hoped to create a similar surge of support for Bush. The video was released just a week before the 2004 general election, a circumstance which helps account for the most obvious contrast with the bear video, the explicit reference to Bush's opponent Kerry and his plans for defence cuts.

---

[4] "2004 - Wolves". See web references.

Table 8.4. Wolves. Sequence.

Shot number		Voiceover	Action
1		In an increasingly dangerous world	Dark shots of trees and plants inside a forest
2		Even after the first terrorist attack on America	More trees, a split-second glimpse of a wolf moving
3		John Kerry and the liberals in Congress	Wide angle shots of trees inside forest
4		voted to slash America's intelligence	Again, a wolf glimpsed for a second before the camera shoots up to see trees against the sky

5		operations	A split-second shot of the wolf's face...more trees..another brief shot of the wolf in motion
6		By 6 billion dollars...Cuts so deep they would have weakened America's defences.	Camera angle now outside the wood. The message stays for 4 seconds
7		And weakness attracts those who are waiting to do America harm.	The wolves scatter and approach the camera menacingly
8		I'm George W. Bush and I approve this message.	The president in an office speaking on the phone

By contrast with the first film, in the Wolves video, the opening occurs inside the wood, and shots of a recognisable forest interior feature strongly in the first half. The bear, it will be remembered, was generally outside rather than inside the woods. Another point of contrast is that, while in the first film the bear was generally to be seen, in this video the wolf or wolves are hard to detect, at least in the first part (shots 1 - 5). They are glimpsed momentarily and lost again. The shot of the wolf's face (shot five), with its menacing yellow-eyed stare, is shown so fleetingly that the technique seems akin to that of a horror film, which may present a disturbing image in a distorted sequence, a brief flash. This may symbolise a crucial fact about terrorists, the intended target of the metaphor, that they are extremely difficult to locate. They skulk in dark places, in remote caves in distant and inaccessible countries like Iraq and Afghanistan, and only emerge to carry out swift and deadly attacks.

In the case of Russia, the target of the Bear metaphor, there is a clear difference. Everyone knows where Russia is, who are its public figures, how they can be contacted, and so on. The question in the former video regards the bear's intentions; is it tame or dangerous? Here, there is no doubt. Terrorists have shown how dangerous to America they can be. But the overall message is the same: strength is the key to bringing about a satisfactory resolution of a problem for America. And this strength is quantifiable in terms of dollars spent on defence. However, the wolves video does not mention Bush's commitment to spend more on the military; rather, it accuses Kerry of planning a massive cut. The text about Democrats' plans remains visible for fully four seconds of the video's thirty seconds running time. It is followed by the crucial scene of the film, which shows a pack of wolves rising and moving in a menacing fashion towards the camera, while the voiceover declares: "weakness attracts those who are waiting to do America harm." There can be no doubt about the film's intended meaning: if you vote for Kerry and the Democrats, their defence cuts will put America at risk of a terrorist attack.

The voiceover is significantly different from the bear video, which focused on the question of whether or not there is a bear in the woods and, if there is, what it is like. Here, there is no mention of wolves in woods, nor any existential doubts. It is taken for granted that there is something dangerous in the woods, as the voiceover begins "In an increasingly dangerous world" (shot one). The woods, therefore, are intended to be read, metaphorically, as standing for the world, whose dangers have not yet been eliminated by following the policy of being as strong as the bear. Unfortunately, it seems, the bear was not the only danger in the woods. And the film offers glimpses, in the brief shots of the wolf or wolves, of what this new danger might be.

The voiceover, though similar in pace and also in its use of significant pauses (table five), also presents points of contrast with the former video:

Table 8.5. Wolves video.

1	In an increasingly dangerous world (↓) (+) even after the first terrorist attack on America
2	(+) John Kerry and the liberals in Congress voted to slash America's intelligence operations
3	(++) by 6 billion dollars (++) cuts so deep they would have weakened America's defences
4	(++) and weakness attracts those who are waiting (+) to do America harm (+) I'm George
5	W. Bush and I approve this message

To begin with, the reader has a female voice. The tone is tense, low-pitched, and quiet. Though the intonation pattern of the first utterance (1) is falling on the last word, and is thus comparable with that of the bear video, the content belies the sense of re-assurance associated with this pattern. And thereafter the pattern is at a constant pitch, which keeps the listener in a state of tension until the very last four words "to do America harm" (4), which are pronounced emphatically. This message, for American listeners, is the opposite of reassuring. Though a softly-pitched female voice, perhaps, could sound intimate and sensual, the effect is eerie and disturbing, an effect heightened by the dramatic pauses, the aggressive and violent lexis (terrorist attack / slash / cuts so deep / weakness / harm), and by the weird electronic music, which would also not be out of place in a horror movie. As the speaker reads the last four words, over a musical crescendo, the wolves rise to their feet. Sound and image work together; the sound ends on a note of resolution and the images take over. Cause and effect are perfectly symbolised; if we cut defence, we become weak; if we become weak, the wolves will move in.

A final difference is that, in this film, we have two voices. Instead of simply a photo of Reagan, there is an action shot of President Bush, standing with phone in hand, saying that he approves of this message. The comment can probably best be understood if we remember the electoral contest. His rival, John Kerry, is named in the ad, and probably Bush is present to balance this up: Vote Bush is therefore another of the film's subliminal messages. The logical structure is plainly designed to support this message:

SINCE John Kerry and the liberals voted to cut America's defence spending by $6 billion

And SINCE this would make America vulnerable

(And SINCE) weakness attracts those who wish to do America harm

THEREFORE voters should not vote for Kerry but should vote for Bush

The inference is that Bush and the Republicans will spend more on defence, or at least will oppose such cuts. The logical structure, effectively, appears more solid than in the former video.

Discussion

It is not the purpose of this chapter to evaluate the two films, to say which is 'better' in terms of some theory of communication. Rather, it is to compare them in terms of the linguistic and semiotic toolkit outlined in the methodological part of the chapter. Both use metaphor and logical argument as well as a wealth of semiotic resources to communicate a persuasive message which regards aspects of the social context of modern America.

The bear in the woods film, I suggested, was an example of completely successful political communication. Part of its success derived from the use of the ready-made bear = Russia metaphor, but its virtues can also be better understood by comparison with the later film. Its argumentative structure is grounded in a sort of folk-wisdom, in the realm of Aesop's fables, and of proverbial statements regarding animals such as "a bird in the hand is worth two in the bush" (no pun intended), "turkeys don't vote for Christmas", and so on. The suggestion it is making is a universal one–if there's a bear in the woods, it makes sense to be as strong as the bear. There is no overt reference to the Russian enemy, to defence spending, nor to the other party's politics. Thus, it would be possible for a viewer who knew nothing of international politics to enjoy the film on its own level, and to take something from it. The wolves video by contrast, with its specific attack on a named political opponent, John Kerry, can only refer to that specific political context, to that specific historical moment. There is no interpretative effort required from the viewer, for whom the meaning is explicitly spelled out.

In terms of the cultural associations, too, there are key differences. I suggested, above, that the bear is one of the most popular and well-loved among America's wild animals, thanks to the teddy bear and the anthropomorphising process, to what could be termed *Disneyfication*. There are violent elements in the bear too, but nevertheless, his image is generally a positive one. He features, in the film, in close-up shots, lumbering about the place, splashing through a stream, quite an amiable bear, certainly if contrasted with the sinister shots of the wolf. When he meets an unarmed man, he stops in his tracks and draws back. There are no shots of a terrifying grizzly roaring. Not only this, but the text of the voiceover gives explicit recognition to the possibility that the bear might actually be 'tame', thus aligning it with the kind of tame bears we are used to encounter in zoos or circuses. In fact, before its numbers declined and it became a protected species, the bear had a long tradition of being kept for human amusement, in the cruel medieval practise of bear-baiting, or dancing to an accordion or fiddle.

Viewers, essentially, are primed to love bears, whether in the playful guise of Baloo or in the humdrum, cuddly figure of Winnie-the-Pooh. This is why the transition to the smiling figure of Ronald Reagan is so effective. Reagan appears, with an animal trainer's complacent grin, above the slogan 'Preparing for Peace'. He is the strong man, the man who can tame the bear, to unleash its friendly, lovable qualities for the amusement of the paying public.

The international context gives further clues to understanding the film's effectiveness. Reagan, in point of fact, was already coming from a position of relative strength when compared to the Soviets, whose financial resources had been drained to breaking point by the effort of keeping military spending up to American levels. In a few short years, their empire was to collapse under its own weight. Though the collapse, when it came, was a surprise to many, the American secret service cannot have been completely in the dark. Something of this certainty can, arguably, be traced in this film, particularly in the closing sequence where an unarmed man confronts this supposedly dangerous beast and makes it draw back. The man, who instantly morphs into Ronald Reagan, must have secret, invisible sources of strength that give him the confidence to behave in this way.

Summing up the message of the bear video, it appears to convey a sense of security to viewers, through the use of intonation, the positive associations of the bear, the structure and composition of the film, and so on. Vote for Reagan, the bear tamer, the film seems to say, and all will be well. Man's natural superiority over the bear will emerge, and the bear's positive potentialities will all be realised.

The situation is quite different in the wolves film. Here there are no attempts to exploit positive associations of the wolves, for example, those present in the Costner movie. The wolves are framed as savage creatures lurking in the woods, in cinematic techniques that highlight their sinister and terrifying aspects. The disturbing music, the haunting yellow-eyed stare, the split-second flashes, the dramatic pauses of the female narrator; all these features align the wolves in question with the predators who terrorised villagers throughout the Middle Ages, and the deadly villains of folk tale and fable.

By comparison with the rich associative and metaphorical picture in the bear film, the latter appears to be a somewhat crude attempt by the Republican party to stimulate the emotion of fear in its viewers. This is, of course, one of the oldest tricks in the political book. Politicians use rhetoric to create a sense of fear in the population, and simultaneously present themselves as having the right policies to protect their populations from whatever dangers they have described. Tony Blair used this tactic many times during the Iraqi crisis, most notably when he claimed that Saddam's weapons of mass destruction could be deployed within forty-five minutes, a claim which by the time it had been mediated to the British public was being used to suggest that Britain was in imminent danger of being attacked by the Iraqis. The invasion of Iraq, to eliminate the threat of Saddam, was proposed as the solution to the problem. In the wolves film, Bush is presenting himself as the better of the two candidates to protect viewers from these terrible wolves, since his political opponents have decided to make cuts in military spending.

Concluding remarks

I have suggested that the differences in these two apparently similar films can best be explicated using a methodology that mixes traditional linguistic and metaphorical analysis with an approach to the broader semiosis of message construction, and a consideration of the cultural context.

In political terms, it is of interest that the bear video, which, I have suggested, paradoxically transmits a sense of security to viewers, was followed by an unprecedented electoral success for President Reagan, who went on to have the satisfaction of being president at the time of Russia's capitulation in the forty-year-old Cold War. Of course, it is impossible to claim, with any conviction, that this success at the polls was in any way due to the film's qualities. But Reagan, the Republican Party, and the USA, in that historical period, were in a position of strength, and something of this can be detected in the overall composition of this film. By contrast, G.W. Bush's victory in the 2004 election, just a week after the wolves video was released, was the narrowest ever recorded by an incumbent president. The undecided, mainly Democratic supporters, who had voted *en masse* for Reagan in 1980 and again in 1984, largely because of his foreign policy, were less convinced by Bush.

Again, it is impossible to connect the election result with the film's effect. Perhaps, though, the use of terror as a persuasive means proved less appealing to voters than the security of the former film. People preferred to vote for the bear tamer than for the man who claimed that the other guy was exposing us to attack by wolves. Reagan was shown, via the man representing him in the film, as standing up to the bear, unarmed, on a hillside path. Bush is shown in an office, at some distance from the forest, telephoning somebody to say that he approves of the message. But who, in this scenario, is standing up to the wolves as they emerge from their forest? In the film, they are simply shown approaching. Thus, while Bush gives viewers the message that Kerry is cutting expenditure on the military, there is no symbolic representation, at the level of the film itself, of a Republican strongman standing up to the attack, protecting the citizens from the terrorists. Bush, the film suggests, may be good at criticising his political opponents. In a crisis, he might make telephone calls. But, in the case of another terrorist attack like September 11th, voters might feel that more decisive action would be necessary.

Chapter 9

Time to get our country back? UKIP visual and verbal metaphors for Europe

Introduction

The UK Independence Party (UKIP) has been called a "populist party that defines itself by opposition to the European Union" (Gifford, 2006, p. 880). Formed in 1993, it has drawn its support from across the political spectrum, tapping into a rich vein of Euroscepticism, a sentiment of mistrust towards Europe and the EU project which has become a well-established feature of the British political landscape (George, 1998). Especially since the recent global financial crisis, levels of Euroscepticism have been rising across the continent (Harmsen and Spiering 2005; Statham et al. 2010) but, although Brussels directives have the same impact on all member states, other nations do not seem to experience the same degree of tension as Britain (Pfetsch & Eschner, 2010, pp. 167-9). The forthcoming in-out referendum, promised by Conservative Prime Minister David Cameron, is a testimony to the central role played by this trend in current British politics; and, in a way, represents an indirect tribute to the efficacy of UKIP's campaign.[1]

UKIP was dismissed by many observers in its early days as just another fringe party, and famously described in an off-the-cuff comment by Cameron, in 2006, as a 'bunch of fruitcakes, loonies and closet racists'.[2] Today, however, it has consolidated its position as the principal mouthpiece of anti-European sentiment in Britain. It represents a real threat to the establishment in Westminster, with twenty-four MEP's, three members of the House of Lords, and one MP in the Commons. In an attempt to gain more widespread electoral credibility, it has diversified its political platform to include a range of social and economic measures, but its chief policy remains that of bringing Britain out of the EU: as UKIP puts it in many publicity posters, to 'take back control of our country'.

---

[1] This chapter was written before Brexit became a reality.
[2] "UKIP demands apology from Cameron". See web references.

This chapter explores the language of UKIP's leader, Nigel Farage; specifically, the way he uses evaluation and rhetorical devices such as metaphor to construct a persuasive anti-European message which builds on Britain's historical fund of Euroscepticism. Farage's texts form the main content of a Daily Express webpage, *Farage on Friday*, a convenient locus for exploring the construction of a Eurosceptic narrative. As well as verbal metaphors for Europe, the paper examines the metaphors in UKIP's electoral posters.

Metaphors, verbal and visual

We have seen that Metaphor means understanding and experiencing one thing in terms of another (Lakoff & Johnson, 1980, p. 5). It is that rhetorical trope, identified and discussed by Aristotle, which transfers a word (the *source, vehicle,* or *focus*) into a context (the *target, tenor,* or the *frame*) that is not the word's natural or common context (Christ'l, 2009, p. 61). In the Shakespearean metaphor 'in my mind's eye', 'eye' is the source, and 'mind' the target. The writer is thereby able to communicate a complex aspect of cognition–something about which little is known–in terms of everyday experience. As already mentioned, since the appearance of Lakoff and Johnson's book, *Metaphors We Live By* (1980), metaphor has been the subject of extensive study, and its merely decorative function re-thought considerably.

The role of metaphor in persuasive discourse has received attention, especially in the political context (e.g. (Beer & Landtsheer, 2004; Charteris-Black, Politicians and rhetoric: the persuasive power of metaphor, 2005; Halmari & Virtanen, 2005). In certain contexts, metaphor can be used to epitomise a politician's entire argument, producing persuasive effects that may be hard to account for with precision, but which arguably leave deeper traces than anything else s/he may have said. Some examples include Margaret Thatcher's appearance with a broom at a party conference, Ronald Reagan's use of the 'mad dog' metaphor for Colonel Gheddafi, and G. W. Bush's 'war on terror'. As Hart (2010, p. 127) says, in the political context, metaphor can be both 'strategic' and 'ideological'. When Reagan used the phrase 'mad dog' to characterise Gheddafi, his intent was probably strategic, to prepare public opinion for the imminent attempt to assassinate the Libyan leader. When Mrs Thatcher appeared at a party conference brandishing a broom and declaring "we're going to sweep the country clean of Socialism", the metaphor was primarily ideological, since it aligned socialism with rubbish and Conservative policies with a cleansing agent. It also, however, played a part in Thatcher's strategy of casting herself in the role of strong party leader, aiming to strengthen her support amongst those present. In this sense, the metaphor served to make explicit in-group and out-group connections at an ideological level: participants in any party conference tend to be the committed only, but there are factions within every group. In the Conservative party these factions have lately tended to divide along Europhile/Eurosceptic lines; in Thatcher's day there was talk of so-called 'wet' and 'dry' Tories, between those who supported Thatcher's radical social agenda (the dries) and those who favoured the old-style policies of social consensus associated with Ted Heath (the wets). Via the implicit reference to the well-known British proverb 'a new broom sweeps clean', then, Thatcher was making a pitch for a more radical style of leadership and government, attempting to align members of the audience with her own positions.

Political persuasion via metaphor is not to be thought of as an instantaneous, cause/effect device that produces an immediate impact on an audience. Rather, as in the case of the 'war on terror', the phrase can be taken up and repeated by mass media, entering the zeitgeist through constant repetition, until it makes its presence felt in a perlocutionary sense. As Geary (2011, p. 3) says, "metaphorical thinking influences our attitudes, beliefs, and actions in surprising, hidden, and often oddball ways." Metaphors can be verbal as in the Shakespearean example just quoted, but they can also be non-verbal/visual, as is the case with Thatcher's broom. The UKIP posters are typical examples of visual metaphor, whose purpose is to favour the conditions for the subliminal acquisition, by viewers, of a political ideology and a specific political message.

Methodology

Ruth Wodak's discourse-historical method (Wodak, 2000; 2001), which has been discussed to a degree in earlier chapters of this book, proposes a research paradigm that attempts to situate intra-textual meanings in a broader, diachronic cultural spectrum. Her notion of context encompasses:

The immediate, language or text internal co-text;

The intertextual and interdiscursive relationship between utterances, texts, genres and discourses;

The extralinguistic social/sociological variables and institutional frames of a specific context of situation (middle range theories);

The broader sociopolitical and historical contexts, which the discursive practices are embedded in and related to (grand theories) (Wodak, 2001, p. 93)

This broad model allows for trends in public opinion to be related not just to the current social context, but to manifestations of analogous content in a relatively distant historical period. As Wodak writes, the discourse historical method "explores the ways in which particular genres of discourse are subject to diachronic change" (Wodak, 2001, p. 65). While much work in Critical

Discourse Analysis probes the connections between discourse as text and underlying ideologies or discourse structures, concentrating on exposing the power structures implicit in current linguistic practices, Wodak's approach goes beyond the synchronic context. It has an interdisciplinary emphasis, requiring triangulation with data from fields like history, economics, geography and sociology. Thus, Farage's anti-European rhetoric is persuasive to the extent that it represents a modern, mediated version of a traditional sub-text within Britishness (in particular, within Englishness). Not only is it necessary to consider jingoistic British exceptionalism (Garland & Rowe, 1999), which represents a historical-cultural dimension in the origin of Euroscepticism, but more general sociological data must also be considered. According to Medrano and Gray (2010, p. 207), for example, the British media are more than twice as likely to assess the EU's impact in negative terms as their European counterparts. Data from the 2006 Eurobarometer, meanwhile, a periodical statistical check of public attitudes within Europe, shows that only 34% of British citizens at that time believed the EU was a good thing, compared with 53% in Europe as a whole (Eurobarometer 66, 2006).

The discourse-historical approach, then, provides the basic methodological framework within which the data is analysed. The aim is to study the visual and verbal metaphors in UKIP discourse from a perspective that sees them as persuasive tools which, by feeding into a groundswell of popular/populist public opinion, construct an anti-European message. Visual metaphors are taken from the UKIP posters, exemplified by the most notorious one showing an escalator positioned on the white cliffs of Dover. Verbal metaphors for Europe come from their leader Nigel Farage's column in the Daily Express, and are compared with metaphors on the same subject taken from the 'British News Corpus' found in articles from several of the UK's most prominent newspapers.[3]

Multimodal discourse analysis is a relatively new field, but has already produced tools that assist in analysis of the contribution to meaning-making of non-textual elements such as colour and spatial organisation (Kress & Van Leeuwen, 1996; Baldry & Thibault, 2006; Kress, 2010), etc.; some of these are used to analyse the UKIP posters.

Finally, the Appraisal Framework is used to register some of Farage's evaluative language on the topic of Europe.

------

[3] The metaphors were collected from the first 1000 hits for 'Europe' in the British News corpus, which consists of 200 million words from each of four major British newspapers: Guardian/Observer, Independent, Telegraph and Times for the year 2004: "A collection of English corpora". See web references.

British Euroscepticism and the European project

Britain's Euroscepticism can be seen as the manifestation of an insular attitude, fostered by its geographical characteristics and the course of its history. As one of the continent's oldest democracies, unconquered by a foreign power since 1066, it has remained a detached observer of movements on the continent. Its foreign policy has been shaped above all by the strategic use of alliances to maintain the balance of power (Jovanovi Miroslav, 2013, pp. 95-6). In recent memory, moreover, participation in the First and Second World Wars has led to Europe, and especially Germany, being associated with deep national trauma. An extreme strand of Eurosceptic discourse even has it that the whole European project is nothing more than a German plot to win the Second World War by peaceful means (see, e.g. Beddowes & Cippolini, 2014). This may seem an isolated absurdity; however, such discourse is not entirely absent from the British political mainstream. In 1990, during the public debate leading up to ratification of the Maastricht treaty, no less a personage than Nicholas Ridley, the United Kingdom's Trade and Industry secretary, said that giving up sovereignty to the European Commission was "tantamount to giving it to Adolf Hitler", and that moves toward European Monetary Union were a "racket designed to take over the whole of Europe" (Medrano & Gray, 2010, p. 214).

British Eurosceptics frequently evoke the scenario of a super-state, whose politicians and bureaucrats can dictate laws to Britain, over which parliament has no right of decision (Teubert, 2001). This question of sovereignty can be traced back to Winston Churchill, who believed in some form of European political body, but said:

> If I were asked, would you agree to a supranational authority which has the power to tell Great Britain not to cut any more coal or make any more steel, but to grow tomatoes instead?" I should say, without hesitation, the answer is "No."[4]

This position clashes with that of the EU's founding fathers, Jean Monnet and Robert Shuman. Speaking in Strasbourg in 1949, for example, Shuman said:

---

[4] "Schuman plan". See web references.

Our century, that has witnessed the catastrophes resulting in the unending clash of nationalities and nationalisms, must attempt and succeed in reconciling nations in a supranational association.[5]

Margaret Thatcher expressed some characteristic features of British Euroscepticism in her notorious 'Bruges speech' in 1988, notably in the passage where she speaks of "dominance from Brussels" and a "European super-state".[6] Her remarks had an impact on the future development of Britain's relations with the EU, and also had their weight in successive political events within the Conservative party that led, eventually, to the foundation of UKIP.

Origins of UKIP

Britain's entry into what was then called the 'Common Market', in 1973, was the achievement of Conservative Prime Minister, Edward Heath. Although the entry decision was sanctioned, in 1975, by a 'Yes' vote in a referendum, it was later argued, by euro sceptics, that the British people had been ill-informed about the nature of the Common Market. Opposition to entry never really died away in the following decades, and re-surfaced in a big way during the 1990s following the 1992 Maastricht treaty, which definitively revealed the intention to create a political and monetary union in Europe. A prominent Anglo-French businessman, Sir James Goldsmith, formed his 'Referendum Party' to push for a new referendum on Europe, contesting the 1997 general election and proposing the following question for the new referendum:

Do you want the United Kingdom to be part of a federal Europe or do you want the United Kingdom to return to an association of sovereign nations that are part of a common trading market?

Goldsmith's question, therefore, exposed an equivocation that had seen the Conservative Party, all-powerful during the 80s under Margaret Thatcher, split over Europe under John Major. The question focuses on the nature of the community itself, posing two alternative visions that, it was suggested, had not been appreciated by the British electorate in 1972. The inference is that a project of creeping political union had been foisted on the British public, which had been led by Heath to believe it was joining an economic free trade area. As Tory MP John Butcher claimed, in 1992:

---

[5] "Schuman project". See web references.
[6] "Thatcher, Margaret. Speech to the college of Europe". See web references.

Our people have always been in favour of a Europe-wide free trading area. They have never been in favour of the gradual and surreptitious building of a European state (Gifford, 2006, p. 875)

UKIP was founded in 1993, by Alan Sked, a professor at the London School of Economics, as a cross-party movement opposed to Maastricht ratification. It initially attracted several Conservative euro sceptics, but Goldsmith's Referendum Party was a more successful proponent of Euroscepticism, performing better than UKIP in the 1997 elections. However, on Goldsmith's death in 1997, his party disappeared; UKIP took over as the mouthpiece for British Euroscepticism, and won three seats in the EU elections in 1999. Since then it has made steady gains, culminating in by-elections which saw Douglas Carswell and Mark Reckless, rebel Tory MPs, become its first members of the House of Commons.[7] It is currently pushing on with its agenda, taking votes from both major parties and looking likely to make a significant impact on the British political landscape. In 2013, during an appearance on the Andrew Marr TV show, leader Nigel Farage summed up the party's basic position:

We want our country back from Brussels–that's number one– otherwise, we can't govern ourselves. We want to control our borders because whilst we've got no prejudice against anybody immigration has been hopelessly out of control for the last decade and a touch more.[8]

The party, therefore, expresses a nationalist point of view, similar to the kind of anti-immigration rhetoric traditionally found among parties of the far right. Farage's disclaimer 'we've got no prejudice against anybody' is an instance of a well-known linguistic strategy (Van Dijk T., 1991, p. 136) to anticipate and ward off potential accusations of racism (the most serious of Cameron's accusations, mentioned above). Because it attracts extremists and xenophobes, UKIP must always be wary of such pitfalls, and the extreme anti-immigration position of the British National Party, indeed, rests on an identical perception that immigration is 'hopelessly out of control'. By means of such disclaimers, Farage hopes to position his party as a more moderate voice on the issue.

---

[7] Reckless later lost his seat, in the 2015 election.
[8] "Farage, Nigel. The Andrew Marr Show Interview". See web references.

Data (i) Visual Metaphors: The UKIP posters

Political posters have a consolidated role in carrying a party's message at key times, such as local or national elections (Seidman, 2008). They can operate at a subliminal level, reinforcing the persuasive effects of traditional political discourse (Charteris-Black, 2009, p. 101). Some of the most successful in Britain in recent times have been those produced by advertisers Saatchi and Saatchi for the Conservative party.[9] Their success in transferring the techniques of product advertising into the political sphere epitomise a post-modern 'commodification of politics' (Mancini, 2011, p. 25) that sees commercial processes such as branding ever-more present in the political sphere.

UKIP's posters continue this development, proposing a series of verbo-pictorial metaphors in Forceville's terms (2009, p. 383). Their success in influencing the public debate can be partly inferred from the fact that they have spawned a host of derisory spoofs, such as the following:

Figure 9.1. Spoof UKIP poster.

This poster copies the rather garish colours found in UKIP posters, especially the purple and yellow that are key features of the party's brand. The significance of colour as a semiotic resource has been explored by Kress and Van Leeuwen (Kress & Van Leeuwen, 2002), who cite Kandinsky's descriptions of the effects of each colour. Though yellow is generally warm and appealing, it also has a less appealing quality: "Yellow, if steadily gazed

---

[9] See, for example, the poster of Harold Wilson's pipe, used by Labour in 1966, or the snaking dole queue used by the Conservatives under Margaret Thatcher in 1979. "Administrator, Mirror". See web references.

at in any geometrical form, has a disturbing influence, and reveals in the colour an insistent, aggressive character" (Kandinsky, 2008, p. 82). As for purple, the painter apparently cannot even bear to name it, commenting merely that the mixture of red and blue creates: "a dirty colour, scorned by painters of today" (ibid: 86). The poster carries a prominent, xenophobic message that characterises UKIP as crudely anti-immigrant. More subtly, the sub-text refers to 'chaps at the golf club', positioning UKIP supporters as affluent, middle/upper-middle class/traditional Conservative voters. The party is aligned with fascist dictatorships by the message on the right, 'the police will visit you if you laugh at UKIP'.

The most notorious of UKIP's posters to date is arguably that featuring the White Cliffs of Dover, which seem to stand, in a metonymic sense, for Britain itself:

Figure 9.2. UKIP White Cliffs poster.

Like the works of surrealist painter René Magritte, the poster acts, arguably, at a deeper cognitive level than that of mere language. The message at the textual level, carried in the small print, is simply that: *the EU has made it easier for immigrants to enter the UK. 4,000 people per week are coming in.* But in the context of a written genre such as a newspaper report, a letter, email or political pamphlet, the impact of such a message could be slight. Such genres have a limited readership, and readers may have become desensitised to their impact, a circumstance which is also true of oral genres such as the political speech, the interview, or the party political broadcast. The poster operates in a much more powerful way. It is not necessary to be a newspaper reader to receive the message, which will inevitably reach everyone passing within eyeshot of billboards, prominently positioned around Britain's town centres, every day. Whether they like the message or not, viewers will feel "the cumulative effect of repeated exposures" (Taylor et al., 2006, p. 1), see also Burns (2011, p. 301).

Again, like Magritte's works, the image presents a paradoxical conjunction of normally incompatible elements, a signal that it is intended to be received as a visual metaphor (Kaplan, 2005, p. 169). The famous White Cliffs, once a natural entry-point for the returning traveller or foreign visitor, represent not only a natural border but represent everything associated with what Blake called England's green and pleasant land. The crude addition of an escalator–a technological device for conveying people up slopes in public spaces–forcibly suggests ideas of violation, of imposition, and of entry from Europe, the source of the frontal camera shot.

The left/right division (Kress & Van Leeuwen, 1996, p. 57) is also worthy of comment. It is noticeable that the escalator neatly runs down the very centre of the image. According to Kress and Van Leeuwen, this division would correspond to the textual features of Theme and Rheme in Halliday's system, with Given information presented on the left, New on the right (see chapter six). The message designers assume as common ground the circumstance expressed in the printed text, that Britain's borders have been abolished by the EU. The New section consists of the headline text 'No Control', and a much smaller detail '4000 people every week'. Britain is pictured as powerless, lying prone, having 'no control' over the moment when the escalator will start to move.

The left/right distinction also operates in the juxtaposition of the image with the accompanying UKIP banner to the right. In this case, however, the most appropriate underlying cognitive pattern could be that of Problem - Solution (Hoey, 1994, pp. 26-46), with the immigration discourse as the former, and voting UKIP as the latter.

The image's persuasive force thus cuts across political categories, conveying the powerful Eurosceptic message that Britain's borders have been abolished by Brussels, and floods of unwanted immigrants will be - or already are - the result.

Data (ii) Verbal Metaphors: Farage on Friday

The data consists of Farage's columns in the Daily Express, *Farage on Friday*, all the back issues that can be obtained by googling 'Farage on Friday' from 2013 and 2014 (about 13,000 words). Metaphors for Europe are shown, with instances, in the table below (table one):

Table 9.1. Metaphors for Europe, from Farage on Friday.

N.	Text	Metaphor
1	one of the most senior figures in *EU-land*	The EU = a theme park
2	Mr Barroso has *doggedly* pursued Euro-federalism	Barroso = a dog
3	*at the helm* whilst all of this has been going on has been Jose Manuel Barroso	The EU = a ship
4	yet another *barrage* of erroneous law-making	EU laws = missiles
5	to satisfy *Brussels' growing hunger* to harmonise all legislation across Europe	The EU = a hungry person
6	stop the *travelling circus* between Brussels and Strasbourg	The EU = a circus
7	*Euro-fanatics* have very little economic sense	EU enthusiasts = religious extremists
8	Despite criticising the EU for *furring the arteries of economy* to the point of sclerosis	The EU = cholesterol
9	small businesses buckle under *the burden of regulation*	EU laws = burdens
10	*riding roughshod* over complex political and cultural situations	The EU = a horse-rider
11	speaking time when *the big players* are in the chamber	EU politicians = gamblers
12	you are marginalised ruthlessly by *the Brussels machine*	The EU = a machine
13	Next week *the travelling EU circus* once again	The EU = a circus
14	*open door* migration across Europe	The EU = a house
15	anything else the UK may wish to block post November can be *trampled* by countries wishing to move in a completely different direction	EU countries = a herd of beasts
16	Lisbon Treaty that enshrined every other major treaty into *one big ball of control*	The Lisbon treaty = a ball

Since the dominant ideological characteristic of UKIP is its opposition to Europe, one would expect to find negative evaluative patterns in Farage's metaphors (Koopmans, Erbe, & Meyer, 2010, p. 91). This is, in fact, the case, as the EU is compared to a theme park (1), an enemy firing missiles (4), a hungry man (5), a travelling circus (6,14), a religious fanatic (7), cholesterol (8), a burden (9), a runaway horse (10) and a machine (12). It is impossible to trace a systematic attack on the EU; apart from the 'travelling circus', all these metaphors have just a single instance. Their rhetorical effect depends upon the reader recognising the relevant features of the source in each case. In the case of the travelling circus example, relevant context information is that the

EU has important centres in Brussels and Strasbourg; the former hosts the European Commission and the European Parliament, while Parliament also meets in Strasbourg. There is considerable movement of diplomatic, bureaucratic and political staff between the two centres, the costs of which must be met by the European tax-payer. Travelling circuses presumably have high running costs; however, the metaphor also mocks the EU by comparing them to trained animals that entertain the public, to jugglers, fire-eaters and clowns–the whole enterprise, in other words, is characterised as an expensive charade, rather than as a serious political project.

To respond favourably to such a metaphor, the reader must share the writer's implicit ideology. As with the examples discussed above, the metaphors are cues that activate an in-group response from Farage's Eurosceptic readers and political supporters. The party leader is flag-waving, via these negative evaluations of familiar UKIP targets, re-affirming the group's ideological positions. They signal attitudes to Europe in a concentrated form, engaging with readers, aligning them for or against Farage's positions.

If we compare Farage's metaphors for Europe with metaphorical reference to the keyword 'Europe' in a corpus of British newspapers, the rhetorical function of Farage's metaphors becomes plainer (table two):

Table 9.2. 'Europe' in British Press corpus.

	Text	Metaphor
1	might say recklessly so, yet Europe seems impotent to respond, apparently conte	Europe = impotent person
2	spection trip to Thailand, announced that Europe will not take any risks with publ	Europe = careful gambler
3	world will soon be knocking on Western Europe's door, United Nations officials	Europe = a house
4	drug use, the Netherlands has always been Europe's hub for liberal loving, living	Europe = a wheel
5	swarthy mob that are storming Fortress Europe, the southern horde that will toppl	Europe = a fortress
6	over the emergence of a two-speed Europe. At the launch of Ireland's six-month	Europe = a vehicle
7	threatens to create a two-tier Europe. EU citizens should be equal, and the right t	Europe = a building
8	of this I am not running away from Europe. I'm going to finish my course there	Europe = something scary

9	described as the collective suicide of Europe. The cult of martyrdom cannot but r	Europe = a suicide
10	unless the EU wakes up to making Europe a global competitor." As a man who h	Europe = a business
11	that it needed "only a spark to set Europe alight". The England team were certai	Europe = a fire
12	Europe and Japan both have a duty to shoulder more of the burden of global secu	Europe = a workman
13	been an obvious time to say goodbye to Europe and head back home. But things t	Europe = a person
14	relations remain fraught, and mistrust between Europe and the US is still high. B	Europe = a person
15	must give an example "because" Europe cannot always go at the speed of the sl	Europe = a vehicle
16	he said, while acknowledging that Europe carries a "heavy burden of guilt". Jew	Europe = a guilty person
17	Just as Europe does, Japan needs to assume more responsibilityfor its own natio	Europe = an adolescent
18	homesearch.co.uk. While Britain tops Europe for DIY (bricolage in French) wit	Europe = a list
19	Asian central bank policies. So Europe's tummy upset is set to continue, unless t	Europe = a sick person
20	US recovery really is. The other is why Europe has been so slow to join the party	Europe = a party-goer
21	suddenly find themselves worse off. Europe loses, then, on two counts: deteriorat	Europe = a loser
22	he stresses the fact that "all Europe was complicit with Franco. For 40 years, he	Europe = a plotter
23	I 'm not sure sluggish continental Europe would agree. It is in danger of being pu	Europe = a sleepy person

A common feature of some of these references is personalisation (1,2,9,12,13,14,16,17,19,20,21,22,23), as Europe is variously characterised as a person with impotency, as a gambler, a suicide, a workman, etc. Unlike Farage's use of metaphor, however, here there is little trace of an underlying Eurosceptic ideology. Europe is mainly used as a convenient proxy for the geographical units that comprise it. For example, (14) develops a metaphor that compares Europe and the US to a couple in a long-term relationship, which is currently 'fraught' with 'mistrust'. In (11), Europe is compared to a 'fire', that needs only the 'spark' of some great British performance by the soccer team to 'set alight'. Such references exemplify a decorative prose style, typical of the newspaper article genre. In no sense could they be construed as carrying a negative, anti-Brussels position. The metaphors that deal more closely with the specific political and economic sense of Europe, meanwhile (1,6,7,10,15,19,20,21,23), seem neutral with regard to the phenomenon they describe. The EU, in (6) and (7) is potentially criticised as 'two-speed' or 'two-tier', in (20) as 'slow' to recover, in (23) as 'sluggish'; but these are criticisms of the way the institutions of Europe operate, rather than fundamental objections to its existence, as we find in Farage. The same could even be said for (1), the 'impotent' metaphor, probably the most striking. The writer could, arguably, even be pro-European, though opposed to its current behaviour in the specific context.

Discussion

In Farage on Friday the writer's metaphors for Europe, when they occur, tend to encapsulate his ideological position vis-a-vis Europe as a political entity. In some, the ideological traces are signalled by explicit negative evaluation (table three):

Table 9.3. Farage's metaphors, evaluation (based on Martin and White (Martin & White, 2005).

2	Mr Barroso has doggedly pursued Euro-federalism	-J: tenacity
4	yet another barrage of erroneous law-making	-J: capacity
7	Euro-fanatics have very little economic sense	-J: propriety
8	Despite criticising the EU for furring the arteries of economy to the point of sclerosis	-J: capacity
9	small businesses buckle under the burden of regulation	-J: capacity
10	riding roughshod over complex political and cultural situations	-J: propriety
12	you are marginalised ruthlessly by the Brussels machine	-J: propriety
15	the UK may wish to block post November can be trampled by countries wishing to move	-J: propriety
16	Lisbon Treaty that enshrined every other major treaty into one big ball of control	-J: propriety

Thus, in (4) the underlying Eurosceptic ideology is signalled by the negative evaluation of 'erroneous', added to the implicit negative charge conveyed by the metaphorical term 'barrage', which compares the EU regulations' arrival in Britain to that of explosive missiles, such as the doodlebugs, sent over by Hitler in 1944/5. In (7), the writer exploits the current anti-Islamic vogue to characterise EU supporters as religious fanatics, bent on imposing their unwanted, outdated systems and ideas. In (2), the evaluation is somewhat paradoxical, since to pursue something doggedly is at least to do so in a committed fashion. The choice of dogged rather than a positive evaluative term such as resolute, however, confirms this as another case of Farage revealing his ideological positions. The reader knows that, for Farage, Euro-federalism is the last goal he would wish to pursue, and therefore identifies Barroso as an embodiment of an out-group ideology.

To read Farage on Friday, however, is not to encounter the kind of anti-European tirade that one might expect; indeed, there are many columns in which Farage makes no specific reference to Europe, or does so in neutral terms. The column, then, does not seem to be a locus used by Farage to push his anti-European agenda more widely, to engage with readers of all persuasions in an ongoing debate over the EU's merits. Rather, it seems to be written with a fairly restricted readership, of UKIP supporters and Daily Express readers, in mind. The metaphors signal the party's ideology, construing agreement on core positions between writer and reader, rather than engage with the unconvinced in a sustained attack on the EU. Where UKIP does use metaphor with a macro-persuasive intent, attempting to bring over to its positions a significant number of the voting public, is in its poster campaigns. Here, there are no generic limits to the recipients of the message; the posters, as said above, will reach vast numbers of the British population, and will have the effects that accrue in cases of repeated exposure. To the extent that people are concerned about immigration to the UK, they will respond to the message; to the extent that they are also Eurosceptic, they can hardly fail to connect the two phenomena in a cause/effect relation. They are, therefore, primed to activate a problem/solution response, and to see voting UKIP as a potential solution to the problem which concerns them. As outlined above, the white cliffs metaphor, and those in other UKIP posters, activate deep responses because they tap into reserves of cultural and historical knowledge in a direct way, in a way that reaches across political divides. This latter phenomenon has precedents in the EU context: during the 1975 referendum on Europe, the 'No' campaign was led by maverick Tory MP Enoch Powell, who teamed up with the socialist politician Tony Benn, two figures whose political views on most topics could hardly have been further apart. However, Euroscepticism provided a common bond in their case, and today it still provides the fertile soil in which the seed of UKIP's message lands amongst the British population.

Concluding remarks

Euroscepticism is, in Wodak's terminology, the relevant macro-topic (Wodak, 2001, p. 93) of the UKIP discourse under examination. Farage's distrust of Brussels can be seen alongside Churchill's, cited above, while it is instructive to see the attitudes of both against an underlying populist discourse of British national identity. Farage, on the Greek crisis, said:

> Greece isn't a democracy now, it's run through a troika - three foreign officials that fly into Athens airport and tell the Greeks what they can and can't do.[10]

Meanwhile, in his study of Englishness, Featherstone (2009, p. 2) reports the following song, sung by drunken English fans at the 2005 Ashes Test:

> With St George in my heart keep me English / With St George in my heart I pray / With St George in my heart keep me English / Keep me English till my dying day.

Although Farage is ostensibly dealing with the Greek situation, his real concern–and the real political point of this remark–relates to the UK. It is an argument by analogy; the fear is that one day, bureaucrats may land at Heathrow and start telling the British what they may and may not do. This was precisely Churchill's objection. However sympathetic he may have been towards what he himself called the United States of Europe, he stopped short of any concession of British sovereignty to the new body. Churchill preferred to think of a united Europe as a continental power block which would serve to thwart Soviet expansionism.

The song, meanwhile, indicates how, at a popular level, Englishness is seen as a vital index of collective identity, an identity whose historical dimension is evoked here by the appeal to the patron saint. However, as Featherstone says, the song also resonates within the discourses of contemporary Euroscepticism and national sovereignty:

> The singer, it implies, might one day wake up as someone else - not English, without nationhood or, most worryingly of all perhaps, of another nation.

---

[10] "Nigel Farage Quote". See web references.

As this chapter has suggested, there is a connection between patriotism and Euroscepticism, and the anti-European rhetoric of UKIP can therefore tap into a powerful groundswell of public opinion. Such attitudes constitute the essential climate for the transmission of the Eurosceptic 'meme' (Chilton, 2005; Mazar, 2010, p. 568) within the British speech community.

UKIP's recent electoral successes have brought Euroscepticism to the forefront of the British political agenda, and Farage to the brink of success. It will be interesting to observe, in the coming period, how this populist movement shapes Britain's future relations with Europe.

Post scriptum

Since this chapter was written, the British people have voted to leave Europe, thus fulfilling everything the euro sceptics have fought for since 1972, and consecrating Farage's position as that of a politician who has achieved his stated political goal. It is too early to say whether Brexit will prove to be a good or a bad thing, nor is this the purpose of this chapter, after all. However, Brexit provides sufficient evidence that the above descriptions of euro-sceptical attitudes both among Britain's politicians and, more significantly, at a popular level, were justified, by the most reliable of tests. It is no longer possible to maintain a fiction that sees British Euroscepticism as a phenomenon that concerns a small, politicised minority; on the contrary, it is a strong current of opinion in Britain that has forced itself to the foreground of events.

Again, it is worth repeating that there is no reliable measure of the effectiveness of any instance of persuasive discourse, whether it is carried out through verbal or visual metaphors, or some other means. There is no way of establishing the contribution to the Brexit vote of this or that campaign, poster, debate or any other manifestation of persuasive discourse. However, Farage and UKIP will feel that the techniques they have used, for conveying their message, have been successful. In the run-up to the vote on 23rd June 2016, indeed, there was controversy about another UKIP poster, the so-called 'Breaking Point' poster, which appeared just before the vote. It showed a seemingly endless line of refugees crossing the Croatia-Slovenia border, above the slogan 'the EU has failed us all', thus playing on the fears, described above, of Britain's loss of control over immigration. Whatever the rights and wrongs of this latest poster campaign, Farage and his colleagues will again feel that they were able to get their message out.

As in the preceding chapter, no use has been made of the model for argumentation I have been outlining in this book; rather, we have explored aspects of current political communication, engaging with resources (visual and verbal metaphors) that develop subtler forms of persuasive discourse. In the last chapter, I shall attempt to draw together some of the threads.

Chapter 10

Conclusion

At various points throughout this work, it has been stressed that there is not, at present, any single approach to political discourse analysis that enjoys general acceptance. Some of the deficiencies and omissions from the model outlined in these pages have also been indicated from time to time. I shall try, in this last chapter, to briefly remedy some of these omissions, as well as present a succinct summary of the model.

Not much has been said about *ethos*, or the respect due to a speaker's character. Aristotle, indeed, goes so far as to say that this may be the most important persuasive device a speaker may possess. Of course, although some modern politicians have a consistent presence in the mass media, there is a difference between knowing a politician in such contexts and knowing what they are really like, when the cameras are not running. However, over time, a politician may acquire a reputation for ethical behaviour, efficiency in government, practical abilities, kindness, social concern, self-sacrifice, or some other virtue. Such a politician, of whom it is still possible to find examples, will enjoy support because people appreciate these qualities. The term 'integrity' is perhaps a modern version of Aristotle's original concept. To a degree, the practical effectiveness of a speaker's ethos will depend on the political ideologies of the hearers. Clearly, a Labour politician with a reputation for integrity will appeal less to Conservative listeners than to a Labour public, and *vice versa*. There is some evidence that a Labour politician like the late Tony Benn, for example, was able to cross party lines to some extent in this respect. For an extreme example of the persuasive force of ethos, consider the example of Gandhi, when at the height of his influence as India's leader. For his supporters, he could do no wrong, and a word from him was almost a command, against which no formal argument, however coherent from the logical perspective, would have had much chance of prevailing.

Naturally, this factor also explains the reverse; certain politicians become associated with negative character traits, which may be reflected in nicknames with negative connotations (among many possible examples, consider 'tricky Dicky' for Richard Nixon and the nicknames of Margaret Thatcher, who was known both as 'the Iron Lady' and the 'milk snatcher'). In recent times, the ethos of politicians as a category has plummeted to rock bottom, and the phenomenon has led to the emergence of 'anti-politics' in various global contexts.

I have not devoted much space, in the book, to the purely rhetorical skills associated with what Atkinson (1984) termed 'spell-binding oratory'. Here a speaker is able to draw their public along with them, to sweep them off their feet with the sheer brilliance of the delivery; to engage their sympathies, to amuse, to move them to the point of tears, to enrage them with accounts of injustice, and the like. Such a speaker will draw at will on the resources described above in the chapter on Burke, and be persuasive not because of any logical consistency but simply through the old-fashioned magic of *ars bene dicendi*. Again, such responses are affected by party loyalties; left of centre listeners will favour Tony Benn, Barack Obama and (probably, Bill) Clinton; on the right choices may feature Ronald Reagan, Margaret Thatcher, Nigel Farage.

The model outlined in this book might be used to study a political speaker in the terms proposed, and integrate such other, 'supra-logical' features that might present points of interest in the specific context. However, that is to move beyond the scope of this particular work, which was to outline a model for approaching the textual/discursive aspects of persuasive political rhetoric, whose focus is essentially on the logical relations involved in the argumentation. In other words, the main focus is on what Aristotle termed 'logos'. Figure One, below, summarises what has been said on this topic during the course of the book:

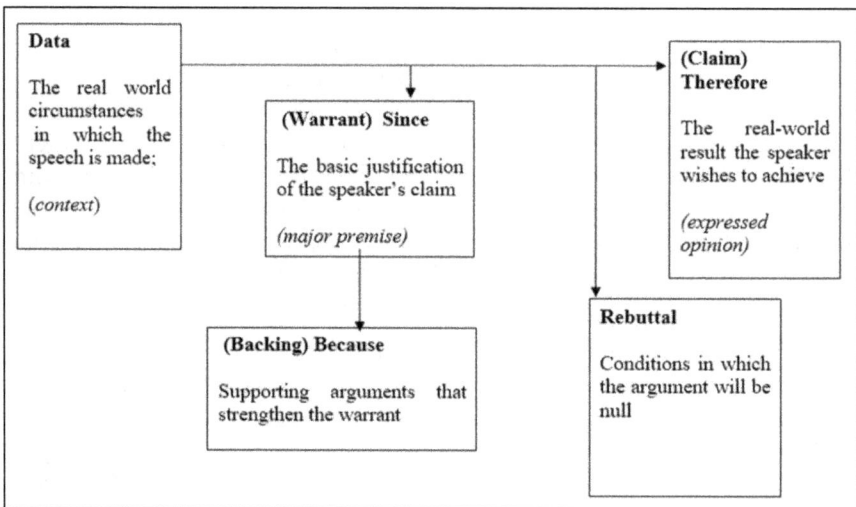

Figure 10.1. A basic model of argumentation.

These terms come from Toulmin (1958), and indeed, the structure of the model itself is closely based, as acknowledged above, on Toulmin's work. I am making no claim to originality in this sense; however, Toulmin's original work refers to argumentation in the context of individual dialogues, and this focus is not untypical of later research conducted within argumentation theory. As far as I know, the model has not yet been systematically applied to political argumentation, and I hope the content above has demonstrated the usefulness of this approach.

In each of the chapters, as the model was progressively presented, different facets of linguistic description were explored, and an attempt was made to show how the elements might combine in actual text analysis. Most of the chapters were followed by an appendix which showed the actual analysis performed by the author, using the tools described. As I hope to have illustrated throughout the book, core linguistic concepts such as speaker evaluation, stance, discourse semantics, epistemic and deontic modality, pragmatics, information structure, pronoun reference and presupposition may all be relevant to the analysis of political argumentation. It is hoped that this book will enable would-be analysts to adapt their own favoured linguistic approaches to the practical work of linguistic analysis, or to borrow some of the tools outlined here. Such researchers are naturally invited to deepen their knowledge of the many linguistic issues touched on, above, through follow-up studies of the texts in the bibliography.

References

Adams, G. (2003). *Hope and history: making peace in Ireland.* Kerry: Brandon.

Aristotle. (1954). *The rhetoric and the poetics of Aristotle.* New York: Random House.

Arnold, J., Kahn, J. M., Kim, L. K., & Kaiser, E. (2013). Information structure: linguistic, cognitive, and processing approaches. *Advanced Review*, 403-413.

Atkinson, M. (1984). *Our masters' voices.* London and New York: Methuen.

Austin, J. (1962). *How to do things with words.* London: Oxford University Press.

Baker, P. (2006). *Using corpora in discourse analysis.* London and New York: Continuum.

Bakhtin, M. (1994). *The Bakhtin Reader: selected writings of Bakhtin, Medvedev and Voloshinov.* (P. Morris, Ed.) London: Arnold.

Baldry, A., & Thibault, P. (2006). *Multimodal transcription and text analysis.* London and Oakville: Equinox.

Baldwin, L. V., & Al Hadid, A. Y. (2002). *Between cross and crescent: Christian and Muslim perspectives on Malcolm and Martin.* Gainsville: Florida University Press.

Barbalet, J. (2006). Emotions in politics: from the ballot to suicide terrorism. In S. Clarke, P. Hoggett, & S. Thompson, *Emotion, politics and society* (pp. 31-58). Basingstoke and New York: Palgrave Macmillan.

Bateson, G. (1954). A theory of play and fantasy. In G. Bateson, *Steps to an ecology of mind* (pp. 117–193). New York: Ballantine.

Bayley, P. (2004). Introduction: the whys and wherefores of analysing parliamentary discourse. In P. Bayley, *Cross-cultural perspectives on parliamentary discourse.* Amsterdam: John Benjamins.

Beddowes, D. J., & Cippolini, F. (2014). *The EU: the truth about the fourth reich: how Adolf Hitler won the Second World War.* Paris: Les Editions de la Resistance.

Beer, F. A., & Landtsheer, C. D. (2004). Metaphors, politics and world politics. In F. A. Beer, & C. D. Landtsheer, *Metaphorical world politics* (pp. 5–52). East Lansing: Michigan State University Press.

Bermejo-Luque, L. (2011). *Giving reasons: a linguistic-pragmatic approach to argumentation theory.* Dordrecht, Heidelberg, London and New York: Springer.

Biber, D., Conrad, S., & Reppen, R. (2004). *Corpus linguistics: investigating language structure and use.* Cambridge and New York: Cambridge University Press.

Breitman, G. (1970). *By any means necessary: speeches, interviews, and a letter by Malcolm X.* New York: Pathfinder Press.

Brown, G., & Yule, G. (1983). *Discourse analysis.* Cambridge: Cambridge University Press.

Brown, P., & Levinson, S. C. (1990). *Politeness: some universals in language use.* Cambridge and New York: Cambridge University Press.

Burns, N. (2011). Point of involvement, purchase and consumption: the delivery of audience engagement. In N. M. Burns, T. Daugherty, & M. S. Eastin, *Handbook of research on digital media and advertising: user generated content content consumption* (pp. 300-313). Hershey and New York: Information Science Reference.

Butt, D., Lukin, A., & Matthiessen, C. M. (2004). Grammar, the first covert operation of war. *Discourse and Society, 15*(2-3), 267-290.

Caldas-Coulthard, C. R. (1994). On reporting reporting: the representation of speech in factual and factional narratives. In M. Coulthard, *Advances in written text analysis* (pp. 295-320). London: Routledge.

Carson, C. (2006). *The autobiography of Martin Luther King.* London: Abacus.

Charteris-Black, J. (2005). *Politicians and rhetoric: the persuasive power of metaphor* (1 ed.). Basingstoke and New York: Palgrave-MacMillan.

Charteris-Black, J. (2009). Metaphor and political communication. In A. Musolff, & J. Zinken, *Metaphor and discourse* (pp. 97-115). Basingstoke and New York: Palgrave Macmillan.

Chilton, P. (2004). *Analyzing political discourse: theory and practise.* London and New York: Routledge.

Chilton, P. (2005). Manipulation, memes and metaphors: The case of Mein Kampf. In L. de Saussure, & P. Schulz, *Manipulation and ideologies in the twentieth century.* Amsterdam and Philadelphia: John Benjamins.

Chilton, P., & Schaffner, C. (1997). Discourse and Politics. In Van Dijk, Teun (ed). In *Discourse studies: a multi-disciplinary introduction. Vol. II. Discourse as structure and process* (pp. 206-230). London: Sage.

Chilton, P., & Schäffner, C. (2002). *Politics as text and talk: analytic approaches to political discourse.* Amsterdam and Philadelphia: John Benjamins.

Christ'l, D. L. (2009). Collecting political meaning from the count of metaphor. In A. Musolff, & J. Zinken, *Metaphor and discourse* (pp. 59-78). Basingstoke and New York: Palgrave Macmillan.

Cienki, A. (2004). Bush's and Gore's language and gestures in the 2000 US presidential debates: A test case for two models of metaphors. *Journal of Language and Politics, 3*(3), 409-440.

Conley, T. M. (1990). *Rhetoric in the European tradition.* Chicago and London: Chicago.

Cottrell, R. C. (2005). *Northern Ireland and England: the troubles.* Philadelphia: Chelsea House Publishing.

Coulthard, M. (1994). On analysing and evaluating written text. In M. Coulthard, *Advances in written text analysis* (pp. 1-11). London and New York: Routledge.

Damer, T. E. (2005). *Attacking faulty reasoning.* Toronto: Thomson.

Dundes, A. (1991). Interpreting Little Red Riding Hood psychoanalytically. In J. M. McGlathery, *The Brothers Grimm and Folktale* (pp. 16-49). Chicago: University of Illinois Press.

Fahnestock, J. (2009). Quid pro nobis. Rhetorical stylistics for argument analysis. In F. H. In van Eemeren, *Examining argumentation in context:*

fifteen studies on strategic maneuvering (pp. 191-220). Amsterdam: John Benjamins.

Fahnestock, J. (2011). *Rhetorical style: the uses of language in persuasion.* Oxford: Oxford University Press.

Fairclough, N. (1996). *Language and power.* Harlow: Pearson.

Fairclough, N. (2000). *New Labour, new language.* London: Routledge.

Fairclough, N. (2001). Critical discourse analysis as a method in social scientific research. In R. Wodak, & M. Meyer, *Methods of critical discourse analysis* (pp. 121-139). London, Thousand Oaks and New Delhi: Sage.

Fairclough, N. (2003). *Analysing discourse: textual analysis for social research.* London and New York: Routledge.

Featherstone, S. (2009). *Englishness: twentieth-century popular culture and the forming of English identity.* Edinburgh: Edinburgh University Press.

Fidler, D. P., & Welsh, J. M. (1999). *Empire and community. Edmund Burke's writings and speeches on international relations.* Boulder and Oxford: Westview.

Forceville, C. (2009). The role of non-verbal sound and music in multimodal metaphor. In C. J. Forceville, & E. Urios-Aparisi, *Multimodal metaphor* (pp. 383-402). Berlin and New York: Mouton de Gruyter.

Fowler, H. W. (2009). *A dictionary of modern English usage.* Oxford: Oxford University Press.

Frampton, M. (2009). *The long march: the political strategy of Sinn Fein 1981 - 2007.* Basingstoke and New York: Palgrave Macmillan.

Fredrik, S. (2004). *Ring out freedom! Martin Luther King, Jr. And the making of the civil rights movement.* Bloomington and Indianapolis: Indiana University Press.

Fries, P. (1994). On theme, rheme and discourse goals. In M. Coulthard, *Advances in written text analysis* (pp. 229-249). London: Routledge.

Garland, J., & Rowe, M. (1999). War minus the shooting?: jingoism, the English press, and Euro 96. *Journal of Sport and Social Issues, 23,* 80-95.

Geary, J. (2011). *I is an other: the secret life of metaphor and how it shapes the way we see the world.* New York: Harper Collins.

George, S. (1998). *An awkward partner: Britain in the European community.* Oxford: Oxford University Press.

Gifford, C. (2006). The rise of post-imperial populism: The case of right wing euroscepticism in Britain. *European Journal of Political Research, 45*(5), 851-869.

Gill, A. M., & Whedbee, K. (1997). Discourse studies: a multi-disciplinary introduction. In T. Van Dijk, *1997. Rhetoric* (Vol. 1). London: Sage.

Goffman, E. (1974). *Frame Analysis.* New York: Harper and Row.

Greenbaum, S., & Quirk, R. (1990). *A student's grammar of the English language.* London: Longman.

Halliday, M. (1994). *Introduction to Functional Grammar (2nd edition).* London and New York: Arnold.

Halliday, M. (2001). New ways of meaning: the challenge to applied linguistics. In A. a. Fill, *The ecolinguistics reader: language, ecology and environment* (pp. 175-203). London and New York: Continuum.

Halliday, M., & Matthiessen, C. M. (2004). *Introduction to functional grammar.* London and New York: Arnold.

Halmari, H., & Virtanen, T. (2005). *Persuasion across genres: a linguistic approach.* London: John Benjamins.

Harmsen, Robert and Spiering, Menno 2005. Euroscepticism and the evolution of European political debate. In Harmsen, Robert and Spiering, Menno (eds). *Euroscepticism: party politics, national identity and European integration.* (n.d.). Amsterdam and New York: Rodolphi.

Hart, C. (2010). *Critical discourse analysis and cognitive science. New perspectives on immigration discourse.* London, Basingstoke and New York: Palgrave Macmillan.

Ho, V. (2010). *Hong Kong Baptist University Papers in Applied Language Studies Vol 14.* Retrieved February 2, 2014, from Grammatical metaphor in request E-mail discourse: http://lc.hkbu.edu.hk/book/pdf/v14_01.pdf

Hoey, M. (1994). Signalling in discourse: a functional analysis of a common discourse pattern in written and spoken English. In M. Coulthard, *Advances in written text analysis* (pp. 26-45). London and New York: Routledge.

Hunston, S., & Thompson, G. (2003). Beyond Exchange: Appraisal systems in English. Editors' Introduction. In S. Hunston, G. Thompson, S. Hunston, & G. Thompson (Eds.), *Evaluation in text: Authorial stance and the construction of discourse.* Oxford and New York: Oxford.

Hyatt, D. (2005). Time for a change: a critical discoursal analysis of synchronic context with diachronic relevance. *Discourse & Society, 16*(4), 515-534.

Hyland, K. (2007). Stance and Engagement: A model of interaction in academic discourse. In T. Van Dijk, *Discourse studies (vol. 3)* (pp. 102-121). London, Thousand Oaks and New Delhi: Sage.

Jakobson, R. (1999). Linguistics and Poetics. In A. Jaworski, & N. Coupland, *The Discourse Reader* (pp. 54–62). Abingdon: Routledge.

James, R. R. (1980). *Churchill speaks 1897-1963: Collected speeches in peace and war.* Leicester: Windward.

Jovanovi Miroslav, N. (2013). *The Economics of European integration.* Cheltenham and Northampton, Mass.: Elgar.

Kandinsky, W. (2008). *Concerning the spiritual in art.* Auckland: The Floating Press.

Kaplan, S. (2005). Visual metaphors in print advertizing for fashion products. In K. Smith, S. Moriarty, G. Barbatsis, & K. Kenney, *Handbook of visual communication. Theory, methods and media* (pp. 167-178). London and Mahwah, New Jersey: Lawrence.

Kecskes, I. (2008). Dueling contexts: A dynamic model of meaning. *Journal of Pragmatics, 40*, 385-406.

Kecskes, I., & Zhang, F. (2009). Activating, seeking and creating common ground: a socio-cognitive approach. *Pragmatics and Cognition, 17(2)*, 331-355.

Kennedy, G. A. (1994). *A new history of classical rhetoric.* Princeton: Princeton University Press.

Kienpointner, M. (1996). *Vernünftig argumentieren. Regeln und techniken der argumentation (Reasonable argumentation. Rules and techniques of discussion).* Reinbek bei Hamburg: Rowohlt.

Koopmans, R., Erbe, J., & Meyer, M. (2010). The Europeanization of public spheres: comparisons across issues, time, and countries. In R. Koopmans, & P. Statham, *The making of a European public sphere: media discourse and politic* (pp. 63-97). Cambridge: Cambridge University Press.

Kress, G. (2010). *Multimodality.* London and New York: Routledge.

Kress, G., & Van Leeuwen, T. (1996). *Reading images: the grammar of visual design.* London: Routledge.

Kress, G., & Van Leeuwen, T. (2002). Colour as a Semiotic Mode: Notes for a grammar of colour. *Visual Communication, 1*(3), 343-368.

Lakoff, G. (1993). The contemporary theory of metaphor. In A. Ortony, *Metaphor and thought (2nd edition)* (pp. 202-251). Cambridge: Cambridge University Press.

Lakoff, G., & Johnson, M. (1980). *Metaphors we live by.* Chicago and London: University of Chicago Press.

Lawrence, S. (2008). The intertextual forging of epideictic discourse: construals of victims in the South Africa truth and reconciliation commission amnesty hearings. In B. Johnstone, & C. Eisenhart, *Rhetoric in Detail. Discourse analysis of rhetorical talk and text* (pp. 113-140). Amsterdam: John Benjamins.

Lock, F. P. (1998). *Edmund Burke.* Oxford: Oxford University Press.

London, J. (2000). *The call of the wild and other Jack London tales.* Boston: State Street Press.

Los, B., Lopez-Couso, M. J., & Meurman-Solin, A. (2012). On the interplay of syntax and information structure: synchronic and diachronic considerations. In B. Los, M. J. Lopez-Couso, & A. Meurman-Solin, *Information structure and syntactic change in the history of English* (pp. 3-20). Oxford: Oxford University Press.

Maillot, A. (2005). *New Sinn Fein: republicanism beyond the IRA.* Abingdon and New York: Routledge.

Mancini, P. (2011). *Between commodification and lifestyle politics: does Silvio Berlusconi provide a new model of politics for the twenty-first century?* Oxford: Reuters.

Mann, W., & Thompson, S. (1987). Rhetorical structure theory: a theory of text organization. In L. Polanyi, *The structure of discourse.* Ablex Publishing Corporation.

Martin, J. R. (2003). Appraisal systems in English. In S. Hunston, & G. Thompson (Eds.), *Evaluation in text: Authorial stance and the construction of discourse.* Oxford and New York: Oxford University Press.

Martin, J. R., & Rose, D. (2003). *Working with discourse.* London and New York: Continuum.

Martin, J., & White, P. R. (2005). *The language of evaluation: the appraisal framework.* Basingstoke and New York: Palgrave Macmillan.

Mazar, R. (2010). Appendix B: Major Research Centers and Institutes. In J. Hunsinger, L. Klastrup, & M. Allen, *International handbook of internet research* (pp. 549-604). London and New York: Springer.

Medrano, J. D., & Gray, E. (2010). Framing the European Union in National Public Spheres. In R. Koopmans, & P. Statham, *The making of a European public sphere. Media discourse and political contention.* Cambridge: Cambridge University Press.

Miles, R. (1989). *Racism.* London: Routledge.

Miller, D. R. (2004). '...to meet our common challenge': engagement strategies of alignment and alienation in current US international discourse. In M. Gotti, & C. Candlin (Eds.), *Textus XVIII, n.1, Intercultural discourse in domain-specific English* (pp. 1-24).

Mooney, J., & O'Toole, M. (2003). *Black operations: the secret war against the real IRA.* Ashbourne: Maverick House.

Morrison, J. F. (2013). *The origins and rise of dissident Irish republicanism: the role and impact of organizational splits.* New York, London, New Delhi, Sydney: Bloomsbury.

Mühlhäusler, P., & Harré, R. (1990). *Pronouns and people: the linguistic construction of social and personal identity.* Oxford: Blackwell.

Norris, P., Kern, M., & Just, M. (2003). *Framing terrorism. The news media, the government and the public.* New York and London: Routledge.

Nöth, W. (1995). *Handbook of semiotics.* Bloomington: Indiana University Press.

Ó Broin, E. (2009). *Sinn Fein and the politics of left republicanism.* London and New York: Pluto Press.

Oakes, P., Haslam, S. A., & Turner. J. (1994). *Stereotyping and social reality.* Oxford US and Cambridge UK: Blackwell.

Oktar, L. (2001). The ideological organization of representational processes in the presentation of us and them. *Discourse and Society, 12* (3), 313-346.

Partington, A. (1998). *Patterns and meanings: using corpora for English language research and teaching.* Amsterdam: John Benjamins.

Perelman, C., & Olbrechts-Tyteca, L. (1969). *The New Rhetoric. A treatise on argumentation.* Paris: University of Notre-Dame Press.

Pfetsch, B., Adam, S., & Eschner, B. (2010). The media's voice over Europe. Issue salience, openness, and conflict lines in editorials. In R. Koopmans, & P. Statham, *The making of a European public sphere. Media discourse and political contention.* Cambridge: Cambridge University Press.

Pluskowski, A. (2006). *Wolves and the Wilderness in the Middle Ages.* Woodbridge: Boydell Press.

Ponton, D. M. (2011). *For argument's sake: speaker evaluation in modern political discourse.* Newcastle: Cambridge Scholars Publishing.

Ponton, D. M. (2016). Movements and meanings: towards an integrated approach to political discourse analysis. Russian Journal of Linguistics (Vestnik RUDN), vol. 2016, p. 122-139.

Reisigl, M. (2009). Rhetorical tropes in political discourse. In J. L. Mey, *The concise encyclopedia of pragmatics* (pp. 882-890). Oxford: Elsevier.

Reisigl, M., & Wodak, R. (2001). *Discourse and discrimination: rhetorics of racism and anti-semitism.* London: Routledge.

Renkama, J. (2004). *Introduction to discourse studies.* Amsterdam and Philadelphia: John Benjamins.

Richardson, J. E. (2004). *(Mis)-representing Islam: The racism and rhetoric of British broadsheet newspapers.* Amsterdam and Philadelphia: John Benjamins.

Sauer, C. (1997). 'Echoes from abroad - speeches for the domestic audience: Queen Beatrix's address to the Israeli parliament'. In C. Schäffner (Ed.), *Analysing political speeches* (pp. 33-67). Clevedon: Multilingual Matters.

Schiffrin, D. (1994). *Approaches to discourse.* Cambridge, MA and Oxford: Blackwell.

Searle, J. R. (1969). *Speech Acts: An Essay in the Philosophy of Language.* Cambridge: Cambridge University Press.

Segell, G. (2005). *Axis of Evil and Rogue States: The Bush Administration 2000-2004.* London: Glen Segell Publishing.

Seidman, S. A. (2008). *Posters, propaganda and persuasion in election campaigns around the world and through history.* New York: Peter Lang.

Shannon, F. (2007). A genre analysis of Martin Luther King's "I have a dream" and its use in the Asian EFL classroom. *Hwa Kang Journal of English Language and Literature, June* (13).

Statham, P., Koopmans, R., Tresch, A., & Firmstone, J. (2010). Political party contestation: emerging Euroscepticism or a normalization of Eurocriticism? In R. Koopmans, & P. Statham, *The making of a European public sphere: media discourse and political contention* (pp. 63-97). Cambridge: Cambridge University Press.

Taylor, C. R., Kozup, J. C., & McAndrew, J. (2006). *Matthew Outdoor.* Retrieved January 1, 2015, from http://www.matthewoutdoor.com/images/TheValueOfExposures.pdf

Teubert, W. (2001). A province of a federal superstate, ruled by an unelected bureaucracy: keywords of the Eurosceptic discourse in Britain. In A. Musolff, C. Good, P. Points, & R. Wittlinger, *Attitudes towards Europe: language in the unification process* (pp. 45-86). Aldershot: Ashgate.

Toulmin, S. (1958). *The uses of argument.* Cambridge: Cambridge University Press.

Trew, T. (1979). Theory and ideology at work(eds). In R. Fowler, R. Hodge, G. Kress, & T. Trew, *Language and control* (pp. 94-116). London: Routledge and Kegan Paul.

Turner, J. C., Hogg, M. A., Oakes, P. J., Reicher, S. D., & Wetherell, M. S. (1987). *Rediscovering the social group: a self-categorisation theory.* Oxford: Blackwell.

Van Dijk, T. (1991). *Racism and the press. Critical studies in racism and migration.* London and New York: Routledge.

Van Dijk, T. A. (1985). Handbook of discourse analysis: dimensions of discourse. In T. A. Van Dijk, *Introduction: levels and dimensions of discourse analysis* (Vol. 2, pp. 1-11). London: Academic Press.

Van Dijk, T. A. (1997). Discourse as interaction in society: Discourse as Structure and Process. In T. A. Van Dijk, *Discourse studies: a multi-disciplinary introduction* (Vol. 2, pp. 1-34). London: Sage.

Van Dijk, T. A. (1997). The study of discourse. In T. A. Van Dijk, *Discourse studies: a multi-disciplinary introduction. Vol. I. Discourse as Structure and Process*. London: Sage.

Van Dijk, T. (2009). *Society and discourse. How social contexts influence text and talk*. Cambridge: Cambridge University Press.

Van Dijk, T., & Wodak, R. (2000). *Racism at the top: parliamentary discourses on ethnic issues in six European states*. Klagenfurt: Drava Verlag.

Van Eemeren, F. H., & Grootendorst, R. (2004). *A systematic theory of argumentation: the pragma-dialectical approach*. Cambridge: Cambridge University Press.

Van Eemeren, F. H. (2009). The study of argumentation. In A. A. Lunsford, K. H. Wilson, & R. A. Eberly, *The Sage handbook of rhetorical studies* (pp. 109-124). London, Thousand Oaks and New Delhi: Sage.

Van Eemeren, F., & Grootendorst, R. (1984). *Speech-acts in argumentative discussions. A theoretical model for the analysis of discussions directed towards solving conflicts of opinion*. Berlin: Foris, Dordrech/Mounton de Gruyter.

Van Eemeren, F. H., & Houtlosser, P. (2009). Strategic maneuvering: Examining argumentation in context. In F. H. Van Eemeren, *Van Eemeren, Frans H. andExamining argumentation in context. Fifteen studies on strategic maneuvering* (pp. 1-24). Amsterdam and Philadelphia: John Benjamins.

Van Leeuwen, T. (1996). The representation of social actors. In C. R. Caldas-Coulthard, & M. Coulthard, *(eds) Texts and practises: readings in critical discourse analysis* (pp. 32-70). London and New York: Routledge.

Van Leeuwen, T. (1999). *Speech, Music, Sound*. Basingstoke and New York: Palgrave Macmillan.

Vasta, N. (2005). "Profits and Principles: Is There a Choice?" The Multimodal Construction of Shell's Commitment to Social Responsibility and the Environment in and across Advertising Texts. In G. Cortese, & A. Duszak (Eds.), *Identity, Community, Discourse. English in Intercultural Settings*. Berne: Peter Lang.

Verschueren, J. (2003). *Understanding pragmatics*. London and New York: Oxford University Press.

Wardhaugh, R. (2006). *An introduction to socio-linguistics*. Chichester and Malden: Blackwell-Wiley.

Weiss, G., & Wodak, R. (2003). *Critical discourse analysis: theory and interdisciplinarity*. Basingstoke and New York: Palgrave Macmillan.

Weiss, G., & Wodak, R. (2007). *Critical discourse analysis: theory and interdisciplinarity*. London, Basingstoke and New York: Palgrave Macmillan.

White, P. R. (2003). Beyond modality and hedging: a dialogic view of the language of intersubjective stance. *Text - special edition on appraisal*, 259-84.

Wilson, J. (1990). *Politically speaking*. Oxford and Cambridge, Massachusetts: Blackwell.

Wodak, R. (2000). Does sociolinguistics need social theory? New perspectives on critical discourse analysis. Keynote speech at SS 2000, Bristol, April 2000. *Discourse and Society, 2*(3), 123-147.

Wodak, R. (2001). The discourse-historical approach. In R. Wodak, & M. Meyer, *Methods of critical discourse analysis* (pp. 63–95). London: Sage.

Wodak, R. (2007). Critical discourse analysis. In C. Seale, G. Gobo, J. Gubrium, & D. Silverman, *Qualitative research practice* (pp. 185 – 201). London: Sage.

Wodak, R., & Meyer, M. (2001). *Methods of critical discourse analysis.* London: Sage.

X, M., & Haley, A. (2001). *The autobiography of Malcolm X.* London and New York: Penguin.

Zinken, J., & Musolf, A. (2009). A discourse-centred perspective on metaphorical meaning and understanding. In J. Zinken, & A. Musolf, *Metaphor and discourse* (pp. 1-10). Basingstoke and New York: Palgrave Macmillan.

Web References

2004. Wolves. *Political Advertising Resource Center*. N.p., 30 Jan. 2012. Web. 29 Aug. 2016. <http://parc.umd.edu/past-parc-projects-2/2004-wolves/>.

A Collection of English Corpora. N.p., n.d. Web. 29 Aug. 2016. <http://corpus.leeds.ac.uk/protected/query.html>.

Administrator, Mirror. A Century of Political Posters from the Provocative to the Downright Dishonest - Mirror Online. *Mirror*. N.p., 29 Jan. 2012. Web. 29 Aug. 2016. <http://www.mirror.co.uk/news/uk-news/a-century-of-political-posters-from-the-provocative-to-the-downright-658396>.

A Global Threat Needs a Global Response. *The Guardian*. Guardian News and Media, 05 Mar. 2004. Web. 24 Aug. 2016. <https://www.theguardian.com/world/2004/mar/06/iraq.iraq1>.

Avmorgado. Ronald Reagan TV Ad: The Bear *YouTube*. YouTube, 12 Nov. 2006. Web. 29 Aug. 2016. <https://www.youtube.com/watch?v=NpwdcmjBgNA>.

BBC News | UK | Northern Ireland | Text of Adams Speech in Full. *BBC News*. BBC, 06 Apr. 2005. Web. 24 Aug. 2016. <http://news.bbc.co.uk/1/hi/northern_ireland/4417575.stm>.

Blair, Tony. Full Text of Blair's Speech. *The Guardian*. Guardian News and Media, 11 Nov. 2002. Web. 24 Aug. 2016. <http://www.theguardian.com/politics/2002/nov/11/labour.iraq>.

Blair, Tony. Full Text: Tony Blair's Speech. *The Guardian*. Guardian News and Media, 18 Mar. 2003. Web. 24 Aug. 2016. <http://www.theguardian.com/politics/2003/mar/18/foreignpolicy.iraq1>.

Bloy, Marjorie, Dr. The Peel Web. *A Web of English History*. N.p., n.d. Web. 24 Aug. 2016. <http://www.historyhome.co.uk/peel/peelhome.htm>.

Book 9 - Chapter 1: Quintilian's Institutes of Oratory. N.p., n.d. Web. 29 Aug. 2016. <http://rhetoric.eserver.org/quintilian/9/chapter1.html>.British Political Speech | Speech Archive. British Political Speech, Speech Archive. N.p., n.d. Web. 24 Aug. 2016. <http://www.britishpoliticalspeech.org/speech-archive.htm?speech=284>.

Butler, Harold Edgeworth. Quintilian, Institutio Oratoria, Book 9. *Quintilian*. N.p., n.d. Web. 24 Aug. 2016. <http://www.perseus.tufts.edu/hopper/text?doc=Quint.%20Inst.%209.4&lang=original>.

Carlshamre, Staffan. Metaphors in Text Semantics. *Carlshamre: Metaphors*. N.p., n.d. Web. 24 Aug. 2016. <http://www2.philosophy.su.se/carlshamre/personlighemsida/staffanstexter/metaphors.htm>

Edmund Burke Speech on Conciliation with America March 22 1775. N.p., n.d. Web. 24 Aug. 2016. <http://www.let.rug.nl/usa/D/1751-1775/libertydebate/burk.htm>.

Eurobarometer 66: Public opinion in the European Union. (2006). Retrieved November 6, 2014, from http://ec.europa.eu/public_opinion/archives/eb/eb66/eb66_uk_exec.pdf

Farage, Nigel. (n.d.): n. pag. *The Andrew Marr Show Interview.* BBC. Web. 29 Aug. 2016. <http://news.bbc.co.uk/2/shared/bsp/hi/pdfs/0505132.pdf>.

Focus on Iraq. *BBC Today.* N.p., n.d. Web. 24 Aug. 2016. <http://www.bbc.co.uk/radio4/today/iraq/library_blairspeech.shtml>.

Full Text of Tony Blair's Statement to Parliament on Iraq. *The Guardian.* Guardian News and Media, 24 Sept. 2002. Web. 24 Aug. 2016. <http://www.theguardian.com/politics/2002/sep/24/foreignpolicy.houseof commons>.

Full Text of Tony Blair's TUC Address. *The Guardian.* Guardian News and Media, 10 Sept. 2002. Web. 29 Aug. 2016. <http://www.theguardian.com/politics/2002/sep/10/speeches.iraq>.

Full Text: Tony Blair's Speech. The Guardian. Guardian News and Media, 05 Mar. 2004. Web. 29 Aug. 2016. <http://www.theguardian.com/politics/2004/mar/05/iraq.iraq>.

Harris, Robert A. A Handbook of Rhetorical Devices. *A Handbook of Rhetorical Devices.* Virtual Salt, n.d. Web. 24 Aug. 2016. <http://www.virtualsalt.com/rhetoric.htm>.

Loughlin, Sean. Bush Tells Nation: 'A Mission Goes On' *CNN.* Cable News Network, n.d. Web. 24 Aug. 2016. <http://edition.cnn.com/2002/ALLPOLITICS/09/11/ar911.bush.speech/>.

McCarry, Charles. Star Wars and the Soviet Collapse. WSJ. N.p., n.d. Web. 29 Aug. 2016. <http://www.wsj.com/articles/star-wars-and-the-soviet-collapse-1446839909>.

MacDonald, Charles B. Thread: Fall of the Low Countries. Fall of the Low Countries. N.p., n.d. Web. 29 Aug. 2016. <http://www.war44.com/showthread.php?t=253>.

Malcolm X - Speeches God's Judgement of White America (the Chickens Come Home to Roost). *Malcolm X - Speeches God's Judgement of White America (the Chickens Come Home to Roost).* N.p., n.d. Web. 29 Aug. 2016. <http://www.malcolm-x.org/speeches/spc_120463.htm>.

Nigel Farage Quote. *BrainyQuote.* Xplore, n.d. Web. 29 Aug. 2016. <http://www.brainyquote.com/quotes/quotes/n/nigelfarag423531.html>.

Orwell, George. George Orwell: *Politics and the English Language.* N.p., n.d. Web. 24 Aug. 2016. <http://www.orwell.ru/library/essays/politics/english/e_polit/>.

Paine, Thomas. Introduction. Paine, Thomas. 1776. Common Sense. *Introduction. Paine, Thomas. 1776. Common Sense.* Great Books Online, n.d. Web. 24 Aug. 2016. <http://www.bartleby.com/133/0.html>.

Pope and Dryden From 'Lives Of The Poets' by Samuel Johnson. *Pope and Dryden, a Criticism by Samuel Johnson.* N.p., n.d. Web. 24 Aug. 2016. <http://www.ourcivilisation.com/smartboard/shop/johnsons/lives/popedr yd.htm>.

President Bush's Remarks on September 11, 2002. *CNN.* Cable News Network, n.d. Web. 24 Aug. 2016. <http://edition.cnn.com/2002/US/09/11/ar911.bush.speech.transcript/>.

Quick Takes: More Brexit Fallout. *Washington Monthly.* N.p., 27 June 2016. Web. 24 Aug. 2016. <http://washingtonmonthly.com/2016/06/27/quick-takes-more-brexit-fallout/>.

Resolution 1441. (2002): n. pag. *United Nations.* Web. 24 Aug. 2016. <http://www.un.org/Depts/unmovic/documents/1441.pdf>.

Ronald Reagan: Radio Address to the Nation on Terrorism. *Ronald Reagan: Radio Address to the Nation on Terrorism.* N.p., n.d. Web. 24 Aug. 2016. <http://www.presidency.ucsb.edu/ws/?pid=37376>.

Schuman Plan. *(Hansard, 27 June 1950).* N.p., n.d. Web. 29 Aug. 2016. <http://hansard.millbanksystems.com/commons/1950/jun/27/schuman-plan>.

Schuman Project. *Schuman Project.* N.p., n.d. Web. 29 Aug. 2016. <http://www.schuman.info/Strasbourg549.htm>.

Suez Canal Shares. *Suez Canal Shares.* N.p., n.d. Web. 29 Aug. 2016. <http://www.victorianweb.org/history/polspeech/suez.html>.

Thatcher, Margaret. Speech to the College of Europe (The Bruges Speech). *Margaret Thatcher Foundation.* N.p., n.d. Web. 29 Aug. 2016. <http://www.margaretthatcher.org/document/107332>.

Thatcher, Margaret. Speech to the College of Europe (The Bruges Speech). *Margaret Thatcher Foundation.* N.p., n.d. Web. 29 Aug. 2016. <http://www.margaretthatcher.org/document/107332>.

The Andrew Marr Show Interview. BBC. Web. 29 Aug. 2016. <http://news.bbc.co.uk/2/shared/bsp/hi/pdfs/0505132.pdf>.

The Iraq War. *The Churchill Society.* N.p., n.d. Web. 24 Aug. 2016. <www.churchill-society-london.org.ukIraqwar.html>.

Top 10 Memorable Debate Moments. *Time.* Time Inc., 26 Sept. 2008. Web. 24 Aug. 2016. <http://content.time.com/time/specials/packages/article/0,28804,1844704_1844706_1844612,00.html>.

Tropes and Schemes. *Tropes and Schemes.* N.p., n.d. Web. 24 Aug. 2016. <http://rhetorica.net/tropes.htm>.

UKIP Demands Apology from Cameron. *BBC News.* N.p., n.d. Web. 29 Aug. 2016. <http://news.bbc.co.uk/2/hi/4875026.stm>.

Welcome to the Definitive Record of the English Language. Home: Oxford English Dictionary. Oxford University Press, n.d. Web. 30 Aug. 2016. <http://www.oed.com/>.

White, Peter R. 2. Attitude/Judgement 12. 2. Attitude/Judgement 12. N.p., n.d. Web. 29 Aug. 2016. <http://www.languageofevaluation.info/appraisal/appraisalguide/framed/stage2-attitude-judgement-11.htm>.X, Malcolm.

Index

www.ingramcontent.com/pod-product-compliance
Lightning Source LLC
Chambersburg PA
CBHW072104020426
42334CB00017B/1622